The Many Lives of *It*

ALSO FROM RON RIEKKI

The Many Lives of The Evil Dead:
Essays on the Cult Film Franchise
(coedited with Jeff Sartain, 2019)

The Many Lives of *It*

Essays on the Stephen King Horror Franchise

Edited by RON RIEKKI

Foreword by Joe Mynhardt

McFarland & Company, Inc., Publishers
Jefferson, North Carolina

LIBRARY OF CONGRESS CATALOGUING-IN-PUBLICATION DATA

Names: Riekki, R. A., editor. | Mynhardt, Joe, other.
Title: The many lives of It : essays on the Stephen King horror franchise / edited by Ron Riekki ; foreword by Joe Mynhardt.
Description: Jefferson : McFarland & Company, Inc., Publishers, 2020. | Includes bibliographical references and index.
Identifiers: LCCN 2020010131 | ISBN 9781476680187 (paperback : acid free paper) ∞
ISBN 9781476640259 (ebook)
Subjects: LCSH: King, Stephen, 1947– It. | King, Stephen, 1947—Film adaptations. | It (Motion picture : 2017) | Stephen King's It (Television program : 1990) | Horror tales, American—Film adaptations.
Classification: LCC PS3561.I483 I83 2020 | DDC 813/.54—dc23
LC record available at https://lccn.loc.gov/2020010131

BRITISH LIBRARY CATALOGUING DATA ARE AVAILABLE

ISBN (print) 978-1-4766-8018-7
ISBN (ebook) 978-1-4766-4025-9

© 2020 Ron Riekki. All rights reserved

No part of this book may be reproduced or transmitted in any form or by any means, electronic or mechanical, including photocopying or recording, or by any information storage and retrieval system, without permission in writing from the publisher.

Front cover images © 2020 Shutterstock

Printed in the United States of America

McFarland & Company, Inc., Publishers
 Box 611, Jefferson, North Carolina 28640
  www.mcfarlandpub.com

Acknowledgments

Thank you to the following people who have been part of my involvement with the horror genre, whether in collaboration, inspiration, or encouragement: Kevin Atticks, Elizabeth Bagby, Dale Bailey, Betsy Baker, Tessa Baker, Steve Balderson, Alin Boeru, Cezar Botel, Octavian Botel, Matthew Bradford, Ayrton P. Bryan, Sally Brunk, Bruce Campbell, Sarah Cleary, Beth Cox, Josh Cox, Kevin Crispin, Horia Cucuta, T. Gene Davis, Codrut Dubat, Paul Dulski, Jared Duran, Steve Earles, A. Ebert, Emily D. Edwards, Deborah Eisenberg, L. Michael Elliott, Constantin Ene, Jr., Tim Frandy, Michelle Fuchs, Joy Gaines-Friedler, George ve Gänæaard, Vlad Ghinea, Erica Mary Gillheeney, Vince Gotera, Valerie L. Guyant, Stefan Hall, Kristal Hamby, Steve Hamilton, Lawrence Harbison, Erin Harrington, Matthew Humphrey, K.D. Hopkins, Del Howison, Sue Howison, Laura Iane, John Johnson, Amélie Jumel, Brandon Kempner, Jon Kitley, Sean Krumbholz, Eli Lester, Leon Lewis, Alex Liddell, Michael Locksmith, Annie Martin, Bogdan Mosorescu, Margaret Noodin, Anne-Marie Oomen, Stacy Overby, Valentin Paduraru, Charlie Perdue, Michael Phillips, Alex Pitofsky, Clayton J. Plake, Michelle Podsiedlik, Daniel Popa, Kyle Preston, Kirsten Ray, John Roseman, Rob Roznowski, Brian Ruby, Mihnea Teodor Rusu, Jeffrey A. Sartain, John Semley, Haerin Shin, Allison Shoemaker, Matthew Sorrento, Scott Sperber, Armen Taylor, Keith Taylor, Olga Tchepikova-Treon, "Fake Shemp" Bill Vincent, Carol Zombro, and all of the contributors to this collection.

Table of Contents

Acknowledgments   v

Foreword
    Joe Mynhardt   1

Introduction
    Ron Riekki   3

Part One: The Novel

"He hits his fists against the post": Stuttering Bill, Trauma and the Protective Power of the Imagination in Stephen King's *It*
    Hayley Mitchell Haugen   9

Seven Children and *It*: Stephen King's *It* as Children's Story
    Cory R. Goehring   18

Clowning Around: The Carnivalesque and Stephen King's Novel *It*
    Katherine A. Troyer   32

Doing *It*: Sex and the Monster
    Dominick Grace   44

"The turtle can't help us": Evil, Enchantment and the Magic of Faith in Stephen King's *It*
    Gregory Stevenson   56

Part Two: Television and Film

Changing Mike, Changing History: Erasing African-America in *It* (2017)
    Kevin J. Wetmore, Jr.   71

viii Table of Contents

"Best Not to Look Back": Monstrosity, Medium and Genre
in Tommy Lee Wallace's *It* (1990)
  JUNE PULLIAM   84

Stephen King, Endings and the Unburdening of *It*
  JASON V. BROCK   95

The Disturbing Appeal of Pennywise
  MICHELLE LEIGH GOMPF   109

Derry's Subterranean Carnival in Stephen King's *It*
  CONNY LIPPERT   120

Patriarchy and Abject Horror in Stephen King's *It*:
Young Beverly Marsh's Search for Subjectivity
  RALPH BELIVEAU *and* LAURA BOLF-BELIVEAU   134

From Page to Screen: Troubled Domestic Space
in the *It* Franchise
  REBECCA JANICKER   147

The Truth Inside the Lie: *It* and the Evolution
of the Serial Killer
  REBECCA FROST   159

Wuh-We Do It: The Losers' Club and Collaborative Leadership
in *It*
  ANDRÉ LOISELLE   169

The Clown Will Eat You Now
  BRIAN W. SMITH   181

Appendix: Interview with Erik Junnola
  RON RIEKKI   188

About the Contributors   193

Index   197

Foreword

Joe Mynhardt

Stephen King is a household name like few others. At least when it comes to us creative types. Walk into any conversation and you'll immediately get a response just by uttering his name—whether you're talking about his writing, the movies based on his work, or the man himself.

For a lot of us, Stephen King brings waves of emotions, memories, and opinions. There are plenty of non-horror fans who love some of his movies, even though they'd happily argue that there's no way it's based on a King novel. I am, of course, talking about *The Shawshank Redemption* and *The Green Mile*.

There's just something about King's work that makes you feel like you're sitting down with old friends you haven't seen in a while. Friends who'll always be a part of your life.

The book that best evokes that feeling is arguably King's *It*. It's just *so damn good*.

I was ten or eleven years old when I was first introduced to King's work. My sister's copy of *It* lay unguarded on her bed. Pennywise's eyes kept following me every time I walked past, peering out from the sewer as I kept looking into the room. I was already a fan of horror by then, having devoured *Dracula* and *Frankenstein*, but *It* elevated my love of horror and stories to a whole new level. I'd never seen such detail given to characters and setting, and I quickly fell in love with the characters. As for so many other readers, they became my friends, and I watched them grow up before my very eyes.

Needless to say, King's work really hooked me on reading, and eventually led me to writing. I was especially fond of King's short fiction, but *It* was truly special, and still is.

It taught me so much more than just the art and craft of writing. I learned about the ongoing battle between good and evil; to stand up for others; endearing friendship, especially the ones from childhood; the effects of bullying; love; confronting our fears; and, basically, just growing up. The list keeps going.

Once you dive into the collection you're grasping right now, you'll see just how deep King went with *It*—holding up a mirror to society regarding aspects such as race, sexism, parenting, and, as mentioned before, bullying. This book even covers topics about the different formats and versions of *It* that most of us have never even considered.

Now let's not forget about the man himself. Through reading about King's personal life and putting a face to the incredible imagination presented through his work, I saw that there were indeed others like me out there. There truly existed a Losers' Club to which I could belong. King also showed me a way to take what's inside us and actually do something with it—to create something physical from nothing but ideas.

King has an amazing passion and love for stories, and I truly believe he dreams about his characters, seeing them as living, breathing individuals. He probably misses them from time to time. Plus, he's connected his stories and books in so many unique ways that it elevates the man to a whole new level of genius.

King is an interesting man to research (most likely why you're reading this book right now). He's a huge inspiration to thousands of authors around the world, and in my opinion, an awesome role model, but also a genuinely all-around good guy. He is a great example of an author not giving up or giving in to the critics. Just look at the charity work he's already done.

In a way, *It* and Stephen King are a lot alike. They both focus on friendship, relationships, love, fighting evil and injustice, and facing our everyday fears. They both stand up to bullies and remind us to love each other, to never forget our childhood and where we came from. King and the characters in *It* remind us to focus on who we are deep down, beneath the layers we've added over the years—to keep confronting our fears until they are truly gone forever.

And he does it all without being preachy.

Just like the journey you're about to take, as we delve deep into the mind of King and the *It* phenomenon he created so many years ago, the many lives of *It* will continue the journey to inspire and enthrall new generations of readers, authors, and moviegoers.

Joe Mynhardt is a Bram Stoker Award–winning South-African publisher, editor, and mentor. Founder and owner of Crystal Lake Publishing, he has published and/or edited fiction and nonfiction by Clive Barker, Neil Gaiman, Stephen King, John Connolly, Jack Ketchum, Jonathan Maberry, Christopher Golden, Graham Masterton, Joe R. Lansdale, Wes Craven, John Carpenter, George A. Romero, and many more.

Introduction

Ron Riekki

Q: "What do you think of academics dissecting your work?"

A: "It's amusing, gratifying, disturbing."

The A here is Stephen King, as quoted from page 251 of Tim Underwood and Chuck Miller's fantastic *Bare Bones: Conversations on Terror with Stephen King*. Along those lines, I hope that *The Many Lives of It* will do those three things to you—amuse you at times, gratify you at others, and maybe hopefully disturb you a bit too.

A "Stephen King" and "academics" dichotomy is massively false. King, in many ways, is an academic; a writer who often writes about writers writing (or trying to write) is not someone disassociated from books and learning. Writing is, obviously, his life's work. Furthermore, a narrative that tries to separate King's fan base from those academics who read/view/analyze his work is not realizing how many of his fans are actually in academia. The simplicity of binaries that destroys so much of American (and global) conversation—by heightening arguments where there is actually a lot of agreement—needs to be let go of and replaced by a more fluid interweaving of fan and critic, because, obviously, they overlap. Any academic who spends the intensity of time and effort to write thoughtfully about King's work is, in large ways, a fan. You'll oftentimes get a sense of the love and admiration for King in these collected essays in *The Many Lives of It*. Contributors such as Joe Mynhardt and Cory R. Goehring analyze and reflect on how much King personally meant to them in their youth, providing them with understanding of bullies, sex, fear, and more.

For me, the attraction to King has always been how prolific he is. It's like Christmas when I discover and fall in love with a writer, then rush to the bookstore to see if there's anything else by them; I'm thrilled to be greeted (hopefully) by a whole shelf of their work—if it's a good bookstore—just waiting to be purchased. I've done it before, gobbling up everything I could from

4   Introduction

the likes of Jack Kerouac, Charles Bukowski, Tony Kushner, Kathy Acker, Sarah Kane, William Shakespeare, Samuel Beckett, David Mamet, Richard Brautigan, William S. Burroughs, Anna Deavere Smith, Lewis Carroll, Arthur Miller, Poppy Z. Brite/Billy Martin, George Orwell, Tom Bissell, James Joyce, Franz Kafka, Mark Leyner, Sylvia Plath, Edgar Allan Poe, Hunter S. Thompson, Irvine Welsh, Sherman Alexie, and so many more. (I even just like saying their names.) Ironically, I wish I could add King to the list, but he writes faster than I can read.

If you'll allow me a bad pun, I'm 6'6½", so I sometimes get into conversations about the tallest writers. Michael Crichton was reportedly 6'9". Thomas Wolfe, 6'6". Ta-Nehisi Coates, 6'4". My girlfriend asked me what size I think Stephen King is. My response: "Fantasize."

I apologize.

But it's true. King's imagination is epic. His mind reaches the highest heights of imagination. He offers such a massive array of discovery—sometimes falling flat, like *The Lawnmower Man*, and sometimes reaching and touching the stars, like *The Shawshank Redemption*. For myself, I despise *Gerald's Game* and *Secret Window*. But I'm a huge fan of *Creepshow* and *Danse Macabre* and "Survivor Type" and *The Shining* and *Misery* and "Mrs. Todd's Shortcut" and *Pet Sematary* and *Stand by Me*. These films create jagged memory markers for me, nostalgia for moments that are very specific where I can remember the theater where I saw, say, *Stand by Me* and how transformed I felt after the film.

It is more complicated.

For one thing, talking about *It* can morph from discussion of the novel to the miniseries to the films with such ease that it can become difficult to determine which is being talked about in casual conversation. Another thing is that my reaction to *It* is more complex than a simple *At the Movies* thumbs up or thumbs down. What do I think of *It*? I love it and hate it. I like it and dislike it. I find that my reading of the book changes, shifts, flip-flops—although my take on the 2017 film holds steady as one of the all-time great horror movies with much respect given to Chase Palmer's, Cary Joji Fukunaga's, and Gary Dauberman's screenplay, Chung-hoon Chung's cinematography, Bill Skarsgård's acting, and the huge team that did special and visual effects. But it is King who creates these opportunities that allow Andy Muschietti, Rob Reiner, George A. Romero, Frank Darabont, and Stanley Kubrick to shine. Overall, there's a whole hell of a lot more to love with King than to hate, but the great thing is there's such a variety, such a wealth of possibilities that if you dislike one book, just pick up another. It'll be different, hugely different. And monstrously imaginative.

(By the way, King's 6'4".)

It is, of course, part of King fandom to debate, criticize, and to judge his work. This collection is being completed during the release of *It: Chapter Two*. Upon sitting down in the theater to view the latest incarnation of Pennywise, my biggest revelation was just how diverse the audience was. I glanced around and saw such a variety of ages and ethnicities, an equal mix of men and women, all with this strong buzzing enthusiasm for what they were about to see. I sat in the very back row in part because I wanted to see the audience along with the film, to see the moments when they would be most invested in the film, and, funny enough, once the movie started, I forgot about that goal and fell solely into the movie (only being taken out of the experience during the low point of the film, for me, which was the indigenous cultural appropriation moments of the Ritual of Chüd). Otherwise, I was lost in story. I knew that fellow Finlander Erik Junnola was in the movie and I even forgot to look for him onscreen, instead just seeing his character, Erik having disappeared and been replaced by Scuzzah. Upon leaving the theater, a three-generation family followed me on my walk home, talking loudly, excitedly, and, above all else, debating with a passion. I eavesdropped the best I could and noticed the absence of Pennywise from the talk. This was a family talking about their love of another family. Ben and Mike and Richie and Eddie and Stanley and Beverly were their siblings. They loved them. Did they love the film? Yes and no. They complained and praised. They disputed. And, as a writer myself, that is the reaction you crave, that level of commitment and investment in your characters. The worst is to be met with neutrality, apathy. To be hated or loved is at least breaking through to another living being, to be heard and responded to.

I hope these pages allow you to eavesdrop intimately on the thoughts of some of the greatest horror scholars out there right now. As I was putting this collection together, I received abstracts from the contributors and would routinely yell into the other room where my girlfriend was working, saying, "Oh my God, I just received another great idea for a paper."

In Tim Underwood and Chuck Miller's *Bare Bones*, there is an infamous legend about Tony Magistrale's essay on *Children of the Corn* being read at a conference King was attending and how King's response to the essay was that the "thought of Vietnam never crossed my mind." Interestingly enough, essays about Stephen King are not only about Stephen King. They are also about the person writing the essay. Magistrale's essay gives insight into the imaginative, inventive, scholarly mind of Tony Magistrale, a mind given much respect in this collection. King scholars are a unique bunch, horror fanatics who realize how much Stephen King's macroverse/multiverse reveals about our own universe. Humbly, I'll admit that my own sexological analysis of Pennywise starts and ends with my noticing how the word "penis" is hidden in the name; then, I read Dominick Grace's "Doing *It*: Sex and the Monster" and I think, "Now there's a brilliant take on the significance of sex in the book." The same is true of my sitting in bed pondering how horror studies are really just theological studies, and then I read Gregory Stevenson's "'The turtle can't help us': Evil, Enchantment and the Magic of Faith in Stephen King's *It*," having wonderful revelations from viewing the book through the lens of the Book of Revelations, impressed at the theology of weakness perspective in which to view the Losers' Club. The writers in this book take us on their own filmic adaptations of King, having us see the images created via such different analytical directors as Magistrale, Mikhail Bakhtin, Heidi Strengell, and Linda Anderson.

The essays in *The Many Lives of It* reveal a rich understanding of Stephen King, as well as insight into the minds of Grace, Stevenson, Loyola Marymount University's Kevin J. Wetmore, Jr., Trinity University's Katherine A. Troyer, Concord University's Michelle Leigh Gompf, and other great analytical minds in these pages who all consider the *extraordinarily imaginative mind* of Stephen King.

PART ONE

The Novel

"He hits his fists against the post"

Stuttering Bill, Trauma and the Protective Power of the Imagination in Stephen King's It

HAYLEY MITCHELL HAUGEN

The hero of *It,* introduced as ten-year-old Stuttering Bill as the text opens, has nearly always had a stutter, but it is made worse after the violent death of his little brother George. As he grows up and becomes a writer, Bill loses the stutter, but it reemerges when he has to return to Derry and face the slowly remembered traumas of childhood to defeat It once again. In both instances—disabling It as a child and ultimately defeating It as an adult—imagination and creativity act as protective powers against past traumas and ongoing violence: the act of writing allows him to function, post-trauma, in society, and his powers of imagination literally save his life.

"In literary discourse, speech impediments open the door to a rich variety of possibilities," Patrick Müller writes in "'The impediment that cannot say its name'" (55). "Fictional representations of stammering can take the form of psychological probing into its causes and effects, [and] they can illustrate its consequences for the individual within society" (55). King probes the causes and consequences of stuttering and draws much attention to Bill's stutter in *It,* suggesting that it is not only a key component of his character, but that the stutter also serves thematic functions. Different forms of the word *stutter* (stuttering, stuttered, stutters) appear 117 times in the manuscript. Thirty of these uses are in reference to Bill as Stuttering Bill Denbrough. In addition to using the word in the context of Denbrough, King also uses *stutter* as a verb or adjective six times to describe the environment or the actions of other characters. For example, after she discovers he has committed suicide,

Stan Uris' wife's feet are "stuttering on the stair-levels" (King 73) as she goes to call an ambulance; when Beverly and Bill reunite and have sex as adults, Beverly's "body suddenly stuttered and seemed to leap upward" (1207); and during the climatic childhood scene in the sewers, the storm outside creates an environment of "darkness that screamed with wind and stuttered with electric fire" (1317). In short, readers are consistently reminded of Bill's stutter throughout the novel, whether the scenes directly involve him or not.

The origin of Bill's stutter is vague. His mother believes it to be the result of Bill being hit by a car when he was three (13). Müller argues that "one recurrent theme in all literature on stammering is that of the psychosocial issues involved" (56). Quoting Geoffrey Hartman's "Trauma within the Limits of Literature," Müller writes, "haunted by the 'idea that there was one irremediable event, or one discovery, which turned—overturned—the mind, many sufferers set the underlying psychological causes for their stammer in relation to their immediate social environment'" (56). Whatever its cause, Bill describes his early stutter as moderate (King 181), and it changes in severity, depending on the situation. He recalls that when he played with George, "his stutter was light" (12), but in school, "it could become so bad that talking became impossible for him. Communication would cease and Bill's schoolmates would look somewhere else while Bill clutched the sides of his desk, his face growing almost as red as his hair, his eyes squeezed into slits as he tried to winch some word out of his stubborn throat" (12–13). After the trauma of George's death, Bill's stutter is nearly constant in all of his interactions. As Richie Tozier recalls, Bill "could say nothing but '*Hi-yo, Silver!*' without stuttering so badly that it drove you almost dogshit" (89). As Bill faces additional horrors created by Pennywise, his stutter increases, such as when he describes to the Losers' Club the terror of seeing George's school picture winking at him: "It was a long, painful recital, and by the time he finished Bill was red-faced and sweating. Eddie had never heard him stutter so badly. / At last, though, the tale was told. Bill looked around at them, both defiant and afraid" (394).

Just as Bill's stutter is seemingly aggravated by the horrors he has faced, his stutter *itself* is a source of trauma for him. Müller writes, "trauma theorists generally distinguish between two basic types of mental wounds, individual and collective trauma. It seems that, in the case of speech defects, we are dealing with a special kind of individual trauma that blurs the distinction between these two basic types" (58):

> The traumatized person experiences the speaking block as a constant deviation from the "norm," and this excludes them from the community of those who are able to express themselves in a way society perceives as "normal." The stigma of being different from others, even "inferior" to them, is daily impressed on them anew. A speech defect is, then, what I would call a "perpetuated trauma" [59].

Following this logic, then, Bill experiences "perpetuated trauma" simply through the daily act of stuttering. His stutter, however, also begets additional difficulties in the form of bullying by Henry Bowers and his crew. As one might imagine, it is not unusual for children who stutter to be bullied, as confirmed by researchers Siobhan Hugh-Jones and Peter K. Smith (151). They note that stutterers may have difficulty making friends, and they hypothesize that those friends that stutterers do make "like themselves, tend to have rather low sociometric status in the class" (153). Readers see this dynamic of low sociometric status at work in the makeup of the Losers' Club, seven children, who for various reasons live at the fringes of their more popular peers. While the Losers ultimately find strength in numbers, initially, they are bullied as frequently as Bill. This dynamic fit Hugh-Jones and Smiths' conclusions about bullying and stuttering when they note that "although more severely dysfluent children may be more likely to be bullied, and although the bullying may often target the stammer, the more direct cause of the bullying is the friendship difficulties (lack of protection of high-status friends) resulting from the stammer" (153).

While Henry does not need much encouragement to bully anyone for any reason, Bill's stutter does make him a target for jibes, and Henry refers to him as a "stuttering little freak" (King 268). Additionally, Henry and his gang of bullies destroy Bill's damn (268) and squash his lunch (291), and after the epic rock fight with the Losers' Club, are "constantly on the prod for them" (617). As Tony Magistrale writes in *Stephen King: The Second Decade*, Bowers' gang is not a run-of-the-mill group of bullies. Rather, "Henry Bowers, Patrick Hockstetter, and Victor Criss are refinements of the vicious side of American youth" who "spend their days repeating grades in school and devising methods of spreading torture and destruction" (108). Not surprisingly, Bowers' torment increases Bill's level of anxiety after he's already suffering from the traumatic loss of his brother.

For Bill, suffering Bowers' torment is coupled with the additional trauma of his parents' emotional abandonment after George's murder. He lives within a realm of quiet coldness that "made suppers a kind of torture as his father leafed through electrical journals" and "his mother read one of her endless British mysteries" (King 867–868). Rather than tell his friends about his dismal situation at home, Bill, "a boy to whom invention came easily and naturally (sometimes more easily than telling the truth)" (868), describes his home life as much more cordial, an early example of his reliance on creativity to cope with life's hardships. Bill's behavior here is reflective of King's own attitude about writing. As King explains, "Sometimes for a writer the idea of explaining his own pain is harder than telling a story. So he turns to the act of storytelling, and this may touch on his pain and talk about it in a way that's more real to you and to me" (qtd. in Magistrale, *Stephen King: The Second Decade* 12).

Additionally, in *Writing Horror and the Body*, Linda Badley notes that many of King's writer characters

> discover their identities as writers first through telling stories to friends [...] The writer's role is a response to a community, and King's speaking narrators often act as the community storyteller performing on demand. [...] In *It,* Bill Denbrough, introspective stutterer-cum-successful professional writer, must perform as the Losers' spokesman.
>
> Wisdom may derive from the "inner child" but it can reveal itself only in the power of utterance [35].

The first character to remark on the creative skills which will later fuel Bill's success as a writer is George who thinks, "Bill was good at reading and writing," but "*Telling* was only part of it. Bill was good at *seeing*" (King 5–6). James Arthur Anderson responds to this quote in "*IT:* The Unnamable Horror," noting, "Writers aren't just good with words but are perceptive enough to see things that others might overlook, and this is what gives Bill his power, both as a child, and 27 years later as an adult when he returns to Derry to destroy It for good" (120). Bill taps into this ability to see and write when he begins to write stories "a bit more frequently since George's death," as "[t]he pretending seemed to ease his mind" (King 432). The pretending also leads to a career as a successful novelist whose books are "[f]ull of monsters chasing after little children" (51–52). Bill, however, does not initially connect the content of his work to his traumatic childhood. His first published story is "a tale about a small boy who discovers a monster in the cellar of his house. The little boy faces it, battles it, finally kills it" (165); the story, Bill recalls, simply flows "*through* him" (165) without him interrogating where he is getting his ideas. Müller maintains that "therapeutic strategies to overcome trauma are usually concerned with the verbalization of the traumatic experience," but for the stutterer, his "ability to give expression to his anxieties is limited, and so the wound is constantly reopened" (54). Fiction writing, Müller adds, can be a medium through which to "couch the traumata connected with stammering in words," to "place the impediment in the context of power relations—language appears as a means of exerting power over others" (54). Although he is consciously unaware of it, Bill exerts power over his stutter when he writes his stories about children conquering monsters. Furthermore, he "uses writing as a means of actively confronting the fear that represents the very heart of Derry's past and present," Magistrale attests (*Stephen King: The Second Decade* 122); "Denbrough writes tales that explore the unmentionable in Derry; in so doing, in retaining the courage to expose the lie, he gains a sense of strength and affirmation" (122).

King clearly encourages readers to connect Bill's writing with the horrors of his childhood when the narrator notes, "If someone had suggested to him that he was really writing about his brother, George, he would have been surprised. He has not thought about George in years—or so he honestly believes" (King 165–166). By age twenty-three, Bill sells his first novel to Viking and becomes a bestselling writer (167). It is not until Bill is recalled to Derry to face his past as an adult that he has an honest epiphany about the inspiration for his work: "All those stories I wrote, *he thinks with a stupid kind of amusement,*" on the plane. "All those novels. Derry is where they all came from; Derry was the wellspring. They came from what happened that summer, and from what happened to George the autumn before" (283–284).

Bill's writing life helps him, for a time anyway, to suppress the horrors of his childhood. He also takes measures to suppress his stutter, the symbol of all that childhood pain. He tells his wife Audra that when they met, "I didn't dare talk fast. It wasn't reflection. It wasn't deliberation. It wasn't wisdom. All reformed stutterers speak very slowly. It's one of the tricks you learn, like thinking of your middle name" (181). Later, he learns to "switch to French if I got badly stuck on a word" (182). Learning these little tricks of language play help Bill control his stutter, but it is not until he is able to forget the horrors of Derry that his stutter fades altogether: "all of that helped," he says, "but mostly it was just forgetting Derry and everything that happened there. Because that's when the forgetting happened. When we were living in Portland and I was going to Chevrus. […] My stutter and my memories faded out together" (182).

Not surprisingly, however, Bill's stutter returns when he is faced with the fact of needing to return to Derry after receiving Mike Hanlon's call. After not stuttering in "maybe twenty-one years" (182), he hears himself slipping into old patterns as he tells Audra of his impending trip. He explains, "On one level you're not even aware it's happening. But … it's also something you can hear in your mind. It's like part of your head is working an instant ahead of the rest" (182). In this case, his head is working ahead to both the remembered and new horrors that await him in Derry, soon confirmed by his feelings of "deep dismay" (617) as he rides in a cab down Main Street upon his return: "He remembered his childhood here as a fearful, nervous time […] that Derry was cold, that Derry was hard, that Derry didn't much give a shit if any of them lived or died, and certainly not if they triumphed over Pennywise the Clown" (617–618).

Later, Bill's highly symbolic rediscovery of his bike Silver at Secondhand Rose suggests his complete return to the physical and emotional trials of his childhood when he is unable to clearly communicate with the store clerk that he wishes to purchase the bike. Instead of allowing him to express himself, his mind stutters on a phrase from childhood meant to help him with his disfluency in an era when "most experts viewed stuttering as a learned behavior" (Logan et al. 616). It was "a single haunting sentence, words that drove away all other thought: *He thrusts his fists against the posts and still insists he sees the ghosts*" (780). The seemingly innocuous phrase serves as a great source of shame for the young Denbrough, for as Mike Hanlon later reminds him, "Your mother kept trying to get you to say it that summer. The summer of 1958. You used to go around mumbling it to yourself. [...] You must have wanted to please her very much. [...] You never made it" (King 790). Indeed, for Bill, the expression had once "taken on a talismanic cast in his mind: the day he could walk up to his mother and simply speak that phrase without tripping or stuttering, looking her right in the eye as he spoke it, the coldness would break apart; her eyes would light up and she would hug him and say, 'Wonderful, Billy! What a good boy! What a good boy!'" (867–868). Ultimately, Bill shakes off the memory of the saying in Secondhand Rose by relying on his old trick of translating tongue-tied situations into French in his head before speaking. Once he is able to creatively suppress the intrusion of the phrase, he is able to make his purchase of Silver, but the unsettling scene is a stark reminder of the combined traumas he once left behind: his encumbered speech and resulting bullying, the death of George, and the subsequent terrors generated by It.

While Stuttering Bill could never quite live up to his parents' expectations, he remains a hero in his friends' eyes. In writing Bill as a stuttering hero, King works against stereotypical cultural portrayals of stutterers that tend to be more negative in nature. Jeffrey K. Johnson examines the characterization of stutterers in his essay "The Visualization of the Twisted Tongue: Portrayals of Stuttering in Film, Television, and Comic Books." Although writers have begun to portray other disabilities more realistically, "one impediment that is still often typified by coarse caricatures is that of stuttering" (Johnson 245). Stuttering, Johnson says, is frequently used as "visual shorthand to communicate humor, nervousness, weakness, or unheroic/villainous characters" (245), developing "out of the popular misconception that stuttering is a sign of weakness" (248). As such, Johnson explains, characters who stutter are rarely cast as the hero, and they do not have the opportunity within their texts to become well-rounded (258). Instead, a character who stutters "commonly becomes a personification of his stuttering or a trait that is associated with it. This in turn serves to perpetuate a greater misunderstanding about people that stutter" (258).

That members of the Losers' Club are aware of these negative portrayals of stutterers is evident when Eddie Kaspbrak says, "I hate it when you stutter my name, Bill. You sound like Elmer Fudd" (King 306). Eddie then privately tells Ben Hanscom, "But his *brains* don't stutter—get what I mean?" (311). Despite Bill's stutter and their clear exasperation with it at times, the other club members view Bill not as weak but as their leader. They defer to him for decision-making and count on him to always come up with a plan of action. As Richie perceives:

> Bill was something else. Bill was their leader, the guy they all looked up to. No one said so out loud; no one needed to. But Bill was the idea man, the guy who could think of something to do on a boring day, the guy who remembered games the others had forgotten. And in some odd way they all sensed something comfortingly adult about Bill—perhaps it was a sense of accountability, a feeling that Bill would take the responsibility if responsibility needed to be taken [411].

Throughout the text, Bill is portrayed as quick-thinking, capable, and fully aware of, but rarely limited by, his speech impediment. When he rides Silver to the druggist to obtain a refill on Eddie's asthma inhaler, for instance, he wastes no time in relying on his faulty powers of speech and writes out his request instead (300).

Bill trusts the power of the written word, and he also trusts the voices of intuition that "sometimes seemed to speak in his head now, whispering to him (and surely they were not variations of his own voice, for these voices did not stutter—they were quiet, but they were sure), advising him to do certain things but not others" (303). Bill's biggest leap of the imagination occurs when he defeats the spider form of It as a child while performing the Ritual of Chüd. As he leads the Losers down to the sewers, with Henry Bowers in hot, angry pursuit with a knife, Bill already "felt his mind suddenly go up another notch, as if to a higher plane. There was no stuttering in his mind; he felt as if his thoughts had been borne away on a mad flow of intuition—as if everything were coming to him" (1261). This confident feeling continues when he faces It, and the ritual itself gives him a protective kind of power, enabling him to speak freely without stuttering, as Richie points out (1376), for the duration of the ritual. Above all else, during the ritual Bill must stay in uninterrupted mental communication with It, for "[t]o pass beyond communication was to pass beyond salvation; he understood that much from the way his parents had behaved toward him after George had died" (1369–1370). Bill gains the upper hand over It by "[d]ropping his voice a full register, making it not his own [...] he cried: 'HE THRUSTS HIS FISTS AGAINST THE POSTS AND STILL INSISTS HE SEES THE GHOSTS NOW LET ME GO!' He felt It scream in his mind, a scream of frustrated petulant rage ... but it was also a scream of fear" (1371). He maintains his power over It and ultimately forces It's retreat by invoking childhood beliefs. He thinks:

> believe that if you tell the policeman you're lost he'll see that you get home safely, that there is a Tooth Fairy who lives in a huge enamel castle, and Santa Claus below the North Pole, making toys with his trove of elves, and that Captain Midnight could be real [...] believe that your mother and father will love you again, that courage is possible and words will come smoothly every time; no more Losers, no more cowering in a hole in the ground and calling it a clubhouse, no more crying in Georgie's room because you couldn't save him and didn't know, believe in yourself, believe in the heat of that desire [1372].

The strength of Bill's childhood imagination is enough to overthrow It for the time being. Bill's stutter quickly returns, however, when he and Richie rejoin the other Losers in the sewer, suggesting that the brief relief of his stutter is symbolic of the temporary nature of It's defeat.

When the adult Losers return to the sewers to reenact the ritual, Bill taps into childhood's imaginative powers once again, for while "[t]*hey had grown up, and their imaginations had weakened,*" it was "*not as much as It had believed*" (1321). In fact, as Magistrale correctly argues, "Pennywise remains most frightened by Denbrough's powers. It appears to recognize that while Denbrough's stutter makes him the least articulate of all the children, his imaginative capacity, deepened and honed as a result of his occupation as a fiction writer, makes him the most dangerous" (*Stephen King: The Second Decade* 123). Thus, when the time for battle arrives, Bill is still able to make his voice "deeper, hardly his own at all" (King 1349), again shouting that once talismanic phrase: "*He thrusts his fists against the posts and still insists he sees the ghosts!*" (1349). Again, Bill thwarts It with the command of his words, and, significantly, he also experiences a psychological epiphany that helps heal him of his past traumas when he realizes that he is not to blame for the horrors of his childhood: "You're no ghost!" he exclaims to the ghost-image of his brother. "*George* knows I didn't mean for him to die! My folks were wrong! They took it out on me *and that was wrong! Do you hear me?*" (1349–1350). Erin Mercer writes in "The Difference Between World and Want" that this final confrontation with It results in catharsis for all of the remaining members of the Losers' Club. "By bringing the buried horrors of the past into the light," she writes, "through remembering trauma, facing psychological realities, or uncovering local history—the adult protagonists are able to exorcize their personal demons and those that haunt their hometown" (Mercer 325). Sara Martín Alegre agrees that each of the adult characters who survive the ordeal ultimately work through their childhood traumas. "Their final destruction of It as adults is, then, the culmination of psychological therapy for all," Alegre writes in "Nightmares of Childhood: The Child and the Monster in Four Novels by Stephen King" (110):

> This is similar therapy undergone by victims of child abuse: unearthing the memories of the confrontation with the monster in childhood means unearthing the memories of abuse that have conditioned their lives. The fantastic monster gives the children's grown-up selves a new sense of direction in their difficult lives and is also the excuse for a return to a time when intimate, personal problems could be discussed and solved in common. This is why, once they have solved their traumas, they may leave Derry and forget the monster forever [110].

Although Bill's stutter abates the first time he loses the memory of his childhood in Derry, he does not conquer his stutter until he entirely vanquishes It—the main cause of his childhood traumas—once and for all by tearing apart It's heart in his own hands. Magistrale interprets this scene in *Landscape of Fear*: "[a]s Bill Denbrough comes fully to understand at the conclusion of *It*, the imaginative faith of childhood was given to man to guide him through life. It can help him envision the moral constitution of the world; it can explain the nature of the human animal and its natural imperfections; it can even lead him to the threshold of recreating his personality and identity" (121).

Bill taps into this imaginative faith of childhood for a final time in the novel when he rides Silver to awaken his wife Audra from her catatonic state induced by the horror of It's lair. It is not until this final frantic ride through childhood that he is able to say with certainty, "My stutter is gone. […] I think this time it's gone for good" (King 1472). Bill takes comfort in the fact that he has regained his identity as someone who doesn't stutter, and as the book closes, "*he thinks that it is good to be a child, but it is also good to be grownup and able to consider the mystery of childhood … its beliefs and desires*" (1474), noting, "I will write about all of this one day" (1474): while his childhood traumas are now safely behind him, Bill makes it clear that his impulse to write is not.

WORKS CITED

Alegre, Sara Martín. "Nightmares of Childhood: The Child and the Monster in Four Novels by Stephen King." *Atlantis* vol. XXIII, no. 1, June 2001, pp. 105–114.

Anderson, James Arthur. *The Linguistics of Stephen King: Layered Language and Meaning in the Fiction*. McFarland, 2017.

Badley, Linda. *Writing Horror and the Body: The Fiction of Stephen King, Clive Barker, and Anne Rice*. Greenwood, 1996.

Hugh-Jones, Siobhan, and Peter K. Smith. "Self-reports of Short- and Long-Term Effects of Bullying on Children Who Stammer." *British Journal of Educational Psychology*, vol. 69, 1999, pp. 141–158.

Johnson, Jeffrey K. "The Visualization of the Twisted Tongue: Portrayals of Stuttering in Film, Television, and Comic Books." *The Journal of Popular Culture*, vol. 41, no. 2, 2008, pp. 245–261.

King, Stephen. *It*. Kindle ed., Scribner's, n.d.

Logan, Kenneth J., et al. "The Depiction of Stuttering in Contemporary Juvenile Fiction: Implications for Clinical Practice." *Psychology in the Schools*, vol. 45, no. 7, 2008, pp. 609–626.

Magistrale, Tony. *Landscape of Fear: Stephen King's American Gothic*, Bowling Green State University Popular Press, 1988.

_____. *Stephen King: The Second Decade, Danse Macabre to The Dark Half*. Twayne, 1992.

Mercer, Erin. "The Difference Between World and Want: Adulthood and the Horrors of History in Stephen King's *IT*." *Journal of Popular Culture*, vol. 52, no. 2, 2019, pp. 315–329.

Müller, Patrick. "'The Impediment That Cannot Say Its Name': Stammering and Trauma in Selected American and British Texts." *Anglia*, vol. 130, 2012, pp. 54–74.

Seven Children and *It*

Stephen King's It *as Children's Story*

Cory R. Goehring

I first read Stephen King's *It* when I was twelve years old.[1] The novel terrified me, inducing many sleepless nights, and it also taught me more about sex than my Sex Ed class. For these reasons, most people will believe that I was too young to read *It*, but I disagree. I fell in love with Stephen King as an author that spring because I fell in love with the characters he created. I wanted to be Ben; I wanted to marry Beverly; I wanted to chum with Stuttering Big Bill. I so completely identified with the Losers' Club that they felt absolutely real; they were about my own age, they thought pretty much the way I did, and they had many of the same desires and experiences that I had (minus the clown, of course).[2] In short, far from seeming too "big" for me, the novel seemed to be written for me.

Fast-forward just about twenty-seven years, and I recently returned to Derry with a whole new set of life experiences. I had graduated college and graduate school and had found employment as a college professor; I had moved away from my hometown; I had married and I had fathered five children. In short, I was a grownup; however, my experience of reading *It* remained surprisingly unchanged, if a bit deepened by my studies of children's literature. In fact, I became enamored with a rather bold and, on the surface at least, unsustainable argument: despite the fact that many consider Stephen King's *It* to be a masterpiece of horror, *It* is essentially a children's story.

Before making my argument, I need to begin by first offering a qualification: in suggesting that *It* is a children's story, I am not saying that it was written primarily for children, or even necessarily that children should read *It*. With that said, I would suggest that it is useful to consider *It* from the perspective of children's literature for three reasons: (1) *It* privileges a particular view of childhood that can be traced to the very roots of children's literature in the Romantic era; (2) *It* mirrors and sheds light on several issues within the field of children's literature; and (3) because *It* is self-conscious about its relationship to children's literature, considering it with that connection in mind complicates a reading of the novel and elevates our appreciation for King's mastery in the work.

I would like to begin with the last point—that King deliberately crafted his horror novel to take advantage of the conventions and allure of children's literature. Freddie Firestone remarks that "much of [Bill's writing] is about childhood" (634), and a similar observation could be said about King's early novels. King's writing tends to not only feature children, but also to represent childhood as a particularly potent time. King had been writing stories about children—and especially powerful children with fantastic abilities—since his first novel, *Carrie* (1974). His novels *The Shining* (1977) and *Firestarter* (1980) also feature powerful, special children, and so does *The Talisman* (1984), which King co-wrote with Peter Straub. But in the middle of the 1980s, when King was the father of three growing children (that is, independent readers), King seems to have become particularly concerned with his dual role as an author and father, noticeable in two ways.

First, when King's oldest child, his daughter Naomi, was thirteen years old, King wrote a story that he could share with her. The result, a novel King initially called *The Napkins* but re-christened *The Eyes of the Dragon* (1984), utilized the genre of the fairytale, and was published complete with illustrations, as any good children's story should be. Importantly, in the inside cover of the book King included a note on the text in which he explains that he wanted to write a story that his daughter would enjoy but that would still be authentic to himself as an artist.[3]

Secondly, as King was writing *Dragon*, he was also working on *It*. We know that King was still writing with his children in mind by the dedication that would accompany the novel:

> This book is gratefully dedicated to my children.
> My mother and my wife taught me how to be a man. My children taught me how to be free.
> NAOMI RACHEL KING, at fourteen; JOSEPH HILLSTROM KING, at twelve; OWEN PHILIP KING, at seven.
> Kids, fiction is the truth inside the lie, and the truth of this fiction is simple enough: *the magic exists* [v].

While *Dragon* deliberately adopted a conventional children's form, on the surface there may appear to be little to reveal that *It* had been written with his children in mind. And yet I suggest that that appearance is deceiving; evidence suggests that King borrowed heavily from the themes and conventions of children's stories.

First of all, *It* references many children's tales or texts. Near the beginning of the novel, when the unnamed narrator tells us that Georgie's boat sails out of the pages of the book (16), he is mirroring Robert Louis Stevenson's poem, "Where go the boats?" Interestingly, when It taunts the Losers through Mike Hanlon's album, the first way It defines Itself is through referencing a popular folktale turned into a nursery rhyme: *"You can't stop me! I'm the Gingerbread Man!"* (731). Consider as well Beverly's reenactment of "Hansel and Gretel" with Mrs. Kersh/the witch in Beverly's old apartment, along with many allusions to Peter Pan.

But perhaps the most enduring and compelling children's text that exists in the story is "The Three Billy Goats Gruff," which makes an appearance early in the novel when young Ben overhears story hour:

> When Ben came in today, story hour had just begun there. Miss Davies, the pretty young librarian, was reading "The Three Billy Goats Gruff."
> *"Who is that trip-trapping upon my bridge?"*
> Miss Davies spoke in the low, growling tones of the troll in the story. Some of the little ones covered their mouths and giggled, but most only watched her solemnly, accepting the voice of the troll as they accepted the voices of their dreams, and their grave eyes reflected the eternal fascination of the fairytale: would the monster be bested ... or would it feed? [178].

Although to say so is a gross oversimplification, it might be argued that *It* is essentially a modern retelling of the classic Norwegian folktale. Certainly, "Gruff" is an important touchstone in the story, reoccurring often,[4] including an almost identical repetition of the passage quoted above when Ben returns to the library as an adult and overhears the same part of the same story (539–40).[5]

But more than the plentiful allusions, King establishes other tropes quite recognizable in children's fantasy literature, including the decentralization of adults, the creation of a "magical" space (such as Wonderland, Neverland, Narnia, etc.), and the "quest" motif (e.g., to destroy the One Ring; to find the Horcruxes). In these ways, King's novel can be placed within a wider tradition, from Nesbitt's *Five Children and It* (1902) through Lewis's *The Lion, The Witch, and the Wardrobe* (1950) to Rowling's *Harry Potter* (1997–2007) series. One of the most visible tropes employed in *It* is the absent parent(s). To focus on children and their unique perceptions and preoccupations, children's stories often maneuver the parents out of the picture, either by having one or more parents killed (or simply unaccounted for), or by removing the children from their gaze. Mostly, this is accomplished by physically moving the children, but sometimes it happens by blurring the parent's focus. In Frances Hodgson Burnett's *The Secret Garden* (1911), for example, the grief and despair that Mr. Craven feels following the death of his wife causes him to both frequently leave his son, Colin, and to neglect him when he is there. Similarly, Bill feels like a ghost in his own house, feeling "no real concern" from his parents, who may make "fatherly gestures" (221) but take no notice of him (e.g., "*Neither of his parents noticed during that time that he was courting death by bicycle,*" 221–2).

Nevertheless, there is no question that *It* is a "horrorbook" (40), to quote Patty Uris, even if King makes use of themes and conventions more generally associated with a younger audience. Clearly, if King refused to be condescending in writing his modern fairytale for his daughter, he certainly pulled no punches in writing this other story for his kids.[6] But to answer the objection that *It* is too violent to be discussed as a children's story, I will point out that violence is not atypical of the genre. After all, Cinderella comes to us from Charles Perrault as a tale of dismemberment and self-mutilation, and while "Hansel and Gretel" and "The Three Billy Goats Gruff" may have escaped grisly fates, the stories gain their power through the implication that other children (and goats) had not been so lucky. And, of course, things do not end well for the Gingerbread Man. In other words, *It* might be different in degree, but not necessarily in kind, from children's literature broadly. Readers may recall being frightened for Alice as she is continually disoriented, abused, and eventually run out of Wonderland under threat of death—a death that might be all too real had she not escaped her dreamland, as the residents of a certain Elm Street might attest. Also, even if Disney chooses to ignore the fact, we can recall that Peter Pan had been in the habit of culling his own Lost Boys should they grow too large. These comparisons are perhaps all the more relevant because *Peter Pan* (1904) and *Alice's Adventures in Wonderland* (1865), like *It*, hinge upon the powerful imaginations of children to create or shape their realities.

This brings us to the second major point in considering *It* as a children's story: in this novel, King seems to embrace a distinction found in much Romantic era writing—a distinction that is crucial to the emergence of children's literature as a genre.[7] That distinction is between what can be called the faculties of "reason" and "imagination" (the terms were not consistently applied, even within Romantic philosophy, but they will suit our discussion here). Moreover, for the Romantics, and I argue for King here as well, there is an implied value-judgment in this distinction that is counter to the expectations of the culture at large: reason, often associated with logic, rationality, and calculation, is *less* valuable than imagination, or the associated intuition, instinct, and emotion. More to the point, reason is adult; whereas, imagination is childish.[8]

Of course, many critics have pointed out the importance of childhood and the imagination in *It* and in King's other works. Michael R. Collings (1987) has argued that, in *It*, King "resolves the long-standing conflict" in his works between "childhood and adulthood," a resolution that becomes possible when the adult Losers "recapture their innocence, their willingness to believe implicitly" (20, 22). In situating King's work in the context of Postmodern Gothicism, Jesse W. Nash (1997) discusses the "privileging of adolescent discourse over that of adults and rationalism" (154). Regina Hansen (2017) examines the way in which King's depiction of the "terror and wonder of childhood" is simultaneously a critical representation and an affirmation of masculinity (161). In her study of the relationship between magic, illusion, childhood, and fear, Lauren Christie (2017) suggests that *It* "explores illusion, deceit, and the power of imagination" (5). Indeed, Erin Mercer (2019) very recently has argued that perhaps too much attention has been paid to childhood and the imagination, suggesting that "the critical focus on youth and its imaginative capacities often overlooks the importance of adulthood in *IT*" (315).

Nevertheless, I would suggest that in spite of all of this attention to childhood and the imagination in *It*, critics have yet to acknowledge the important generic implications of the novel's marked preference for childhood imagination over adult reason. Children's literature and Gothic literature are cousins, offshoots of the same Romantic tree that sprung up out of a concern that the imagination was being undervalued in a Lockean, Newtonian universe. In placing a high value on imagination, *It* is underscoring this mostly implicit historical relationship between children's literature and Gothic literature.

To show that King clearly embraces the distinction between reason and imagination in *It*, consider a scene early in the novel that reveals the limits of rationality. The police detectives investigating the murder of Adrian Mellon are not interested in "fairytales" (35) of murderous clowns, even when those "fairytales" corroborate the facts of the case—for instance, the bite marks on Adrian's body do not match those of the suspects, but they do seem to support the eyewitness who saw Pennywise bite the victim under the armpit (35, 38). The larger narrative here, of course, is that rationality prevents adults from accessing the whole truth—just as our ability to vocalize all language sounds diminishes as we age (*Pet Sematary* 195),[9] so does our ability to comprehend the full spectrum of "reality," which includes the supernatural as well as the natural. By contrast, in discussing Richie, the narrator discloses: "The idea of ghosts gave his child's mind no trouble at all" (329).

The members of the Losers' Club possess "extraordinarily imaginative minds" (1017) that they use to help them navigate and interpret the world, which sets them apart from others. Bill, for instance, is able to accept that the scars on his hands returned only *after* Mike reminded him of his childhood vow, which is something that his wife, Audra, rationally suggests "isn't possible" (137).

Over and over the Losers' wholehearted faith in their imaginations distinguishes them from the adults—and even at times from other children in the novel. Eddie Corcoran, for example, despite being the same age as the Losers, cannot relinquish his rationality, his "need to see" and to "understand" the incomprehensible thing chasing him, an impulse that leads directly to him being caught. For Eddie Corcoran, this belief in "rationality" is so compelling that he is unable to stop insisting that It was "not … real" even as It choked the life out of him: "And yet some rationality remained, even until the end: as the Creature hooked its claws into the soft meat of his neck, as his carotid artery let go in a warm and painless gout that splashed the thing's reptilian plating, Eddie's hands groped at the Creature's back, feeling for a zipper" (264).

In direct contrast to Eddie Corcoran, Mike Hanlon allows himself to be guided by "dreams" and "impelled by nothing more than purest whim" (264–5), even when he does not understand the impulse, and even when it scares him to do so. In investigating the scene where Eddie Corcoran was murdered a few hours before, Mike rejects the rational explanation that the blood he finds is the result of a dog fight, and instead accepts as more "real" the "story" ("fairytale") that he imagines in his head. He never doubts the power of his imagination, the realness of it, and, therefore, flees from the danger it presents "without looking back" (286), allowing him to escape. Similarly, when fleeing from his encounter with It as a leprous hobo under the porch on Neibolt Street, Eddie Kaspbrak fights off an initial impulse to dismiss what happened as mere illusion or fantasy. He recognizes the temptation to do so as a "charm" that would be "fatal," (314), and he, too, flees "not looking back" (315).

This pattern is repeated in the novel with the Losers, whose refusal to "look back" indicates, as it does for Lot, their complete faith in the incomprehensible power behind them. And, the Losers demonstrate repeatedly how imaginative they are in other ways, too. For example, all are exceptionally and naturally creative: although only Bill and Mike write as adults, the other Losers demonstrate abilities to conjure stories as well: Richie imagines the life of the bachelor engineer who formerly lived at the "trim red Cape-Cod" on Neibolt Street (371), and Beverly easily summons up the experiences of the drowned boys in the Standpipe (416). All of the Losers, with the notable exception of Stan, also pursue careers or activities as adults that are essentially creative.[10]

King also consistently portrays the perception of children as being special or unique: when on the run for his life from Henry Bowers, Ben nevertheless notices and investigates the "low humming noise" that leads him to what they will call a "Morlock hole" (204). There are several points to notice here: firstly, we are told directly that "an adult … would have ignored it, or simply not heard it at all" (204), indicating not only the unique perceptiveness of children but also their ability to adapt and cope with life-threatening situations ("he was already getting over his fright"). Secondly, it reminds us that curiosity is an innate part of childhood, and one that we specifically undervalue in adults. Thirdly, considering the importance that the Morlock hole plays later in the novel, Ben's awareness seems prophetic.

At various times, the Losers do seem to exhibit something like precognition. For instance, an adult Stanley is able to predict with certainty where his wife would end up finding a job, even though he could not say why or how he knew (45). After the Losers build the dam, Eddie not only recognizes that Bill has something on his mind—which, of course, could be nothing more than simple empathy between good friends—but he also intuits that whatever it was would be "something terrible, something which would change everything" (303). Furthermore, his mind automatically makes a connection between what Bill has to say and Eddie's own first encounter with It: "In his mind a tenebrous, croaking voice whispered: *I'll do it for a dime*" (303). We are also told that "Although none of them would remember doing so later, all of them looked up at the exact moment Eddie Corcoran died ... as if hearing some distant cry" (256).

Likewise, examples of the Losers being guided by their instincts or intuitions—things more rational minds might dismiss—appear throughout the novel. Bill, in particular, seems to be guided by "voices that sometimes seemed to speak in his head now" (234). Beverly, too, obeys her instincts readily: "She was suddenly aware that her hair was now hanging over her shoulders in two thick sheaves, and that they dangled close—very close—to that drainhole. Some clear instinct made her straighten up quick and get her hair away from there" (393–4).

Of course, as Bastian learns in *The Neverending Story* (1979), a heightened capacity to believe brings an elevated sense of wonder—but also an increased risk and exposure to fear. It is true that this reliance on their imaginations makes the children vulnerable, or at least targets, for that which seeks to prey on them: "*Any of these seven alone would have been Its meat and drink, and if they had not happened to come together, It surely would have picked them off one by one, drawn by the quality of their minds just as a lion might be drawn to one particular waterhole by the scent of zebra*" (1017). Of course, Georgie himself is perhaps a great example of this. Georgie is marked as "special" by his intuited perception of the Turtle, triggered by his finding of a can of turtle wax (8–9), but while this special perception marks him as different from adults, it also leaves him exposed. He, after all, accepts the presence of Bob Gray, aka Pennywise the Dancing Clown, in the sewer when we are told that he would not have accepted what he had seen as real if he were sixteen instead of six (13).

Furthermore, the novel makes clear that It is not alone in preying upon the ripe young imaginations of Derry. Rather, the novel suggests that many adults can be vehicles for It as well, including the parents of the Losers. For some of the Losers, including Bill, Richie, and Stan, their parents are mostly absent or dismissive.[11] But for others, such as Ben, Eddie, and Beverly, their parents are more oppressive. For example, Ben is guided by instinctive emotions and even an unconscious yet powerful insight into his mother's smothering love for him to "distrust" his mother enough not to share his experiences with her (185–6).

Eddie and Beverly have parents who are more openly hostile: interestingly, in both cases, the parental aggression is discussed in terms of consumption. For example, in confronting his mother, Eddie sees that her "eyes were almost predatory" (789), and thinks, "*she's only eating me because she loves me*" (790). In the Hansel and Gretel reenactment with Mrs. Kersh, there comes a moment in which It drops the witch's guise in favor of that of her father in announcing that he/It wants to "eat" Beverly (572). The horror here is of course working on multiple levels, playing upon the pun of "eating" as both a culinary and sexual act, and the horror of the monster that devours children is multiplied by the horror of the father who harbors illicit desires for his own daughter. Moreover, the scene can represent all the various ways in which privileged adults take predatory advantage of weaker members of society, especially given the pervasiveness of the threat of being eaten within the novel: the giant/Paul Bunyan threatens to "eat … up" Richie (584); Eddie is certain that the goldfish/piranhas will "eat [him] alive" (683); and, of course, all of the victims of It have been "partially eaten" (702). Interestingly, Mr. Keene, the pharmacist, attempts to placate Eddie by offering him ice cream and insisting that he will not "bite" (769; 771), but Eddie knows instinctively not only that grownups sometimes *do* hurt you, but also that sometimes they enjoy it: "Grownups could be so hateful in their power sometimes. So hateful" (776). Eddie's revelation becomes our own: "And almost idly, in a kind of side-thought, Eddie discovered one of his childhood's great truths. *Grownups are the real monsters*" (772).

Bill sums it up nicely, stutter or no: "'*Duh-Duh-Derry* is It'" (972). He asserts that every adult in Derry is potentially under Its sway by their very decision to rest under Its domain. The reward for the townspeople's complicity is, perhaps, permission to partake in the bloodshed, as in the cases of the Black Hole and the Bradley Gang; the price is, like in *The Hunger Games*, the ritual murder of their children, the sporadic and periodic sacrifice of their own blood to the maw of an insatiable appetite, to an evil and hungry greed. Of course, the adults can claim ignorance, but they are not innocent; as Bill says, "*They let it happen, they always do*" (971). Some, like Herbert Ross, simply walk away and choose not to interfere (926); others, like Police Chief Rademacher, honestly believe that they are trying to fight evil while being its tools (1037).

However, if the Losers become targets because of their imaginations, they are at the same time made powerful by them. The children eventually learn, as Eddie puts it as an adult, to use Its power—their imaginations—against it: "That was always what was at the bottom of it. Just being scared. That was everything. But in the end I think we turned that around somehow. We used it" (288). It is fueled by their fear, but It is also limited by their conceptions of It, and consequently at the mercy of their imaginations. This is something that It comes to recognize, too:

> But together they had discovered an alarming secret that even It had not been aware of: that belief has a second edge. If there are ten thousand medieval peasants who create vampires by believing them real, there may be one—probably a child—who will imagine the stake necessary to kill it. But a stake is only stupid wood; the mind is the mallet which drives it home [1017].

Partly, the Losers' power comes from what the novel presents as the natural flexibility of a child's mind, the ability to roll with the punches, you might say. Consider, for example, Richie's reaction to watching a photograph in Georgie's scrapbook come to life: "And so, following an experience that might well have sent an adult running for the nearest headshrinker, Richie Tozier got up, ate a giant pancake breakfast, saw the ad for the two horror movies on the Amusements page of the paper" (341–2). In short, he incorporates his experiences, fantastical as they were, into his ordinary life. But more than this, the Losers demonstrate an extraordinary ability to respond to terror with pleasure—to laugh in the face of danger, if you will.

This phenomenon occurs throughout the novel,[12] and is reminiscent, perhaps, of the Burkean concept of the Sublime as Beauty + Terror. In any case, it seems to represent at least part of what King refers to in the Losers as "desire." To demonstrate this, consider these two quotes that bookend Richie's and Bill's first attempt to kill It on Neibolt Street. The first describes Richie's feelings as he and Bill are racing on Silver toward the confrontation: "'Ride it, Big Bill!' Richie screamed, so scared he was nearly creaming his jeans but laughing wildly all the same. '*Stand* on this baby!'" (370). The second comes from Bill's perspective as he is literally pedaling for his life, trying to outdistance the werewolf/clown in close pursuit: "And a crazy, ineluctable sense of exhilaration filled him—something that was wild and free and all his own. A desire" (381).

There is a second component to the power of imagination at work here, though, and that relates to the imagination's transformative or creative potential. As a child imagining the stake necessary to kill the vampire, the Losers have the power to hurt and even kill it with their minds. At times, the Losers use this power without volition, as when Richie channels a voice not his own to free Bill from the werewolf's clutches:

> Then, with no thought at all about what he was doing or why he was doing it, Richie heard the Voice of the Irish Cop coming out of his mouth, Mr. Nell's voice. But this

was not Richie Tozier doing a bad imitation; it wasn't even precisely Mr. Nell. It was the Voice of every Irish beat-cop that had ever lived and twirled a billy by its rawhide rope as he tried the doors of closed shops after midnight:

"*Let go of him, boyo, or I'll crack yer thick head! I swear to Jaysus! Leave go of him now or I'll serve ye yer own arse on a platter!*"

The creature in the cellar let out an ear-splitting roar of rage ... but it seemed to Richie that there was another note in that bellow as well. Perhaps fear. Or pain [377–8].

At other times, the Losers deliberately use their power to change their realities. Eddie's decision to continue using his aspirator—to pretend that he does not know that the medicine is not real—demonstrates the power of his imagination over knowledge (801). Later on, when the stakes are higher, Eddie once again uses this power to save his friends from the Crawling Eye/It. In an act of bravery and love, Eddie simply pretends that his aspirator is full of battery acid. Even though the pretense is a deliberate self-deception, he has complete faith in it working: "(*acid it's acid if I want it to be so eat it eat it eat*)" (1026). It's medicine if he wants it to be (out of love for his mom), and it is poison if he wants it to be (out of love for Bill).

Finally, it is this power that allows Bill and Richie to kill It, striking with the "mallet of the mind":

They struck together with their right fists, but Bill understood it was not really their fists they were striking with at all; it was their combined force, augmented by the force of that Other; it was the force of memory and desire; above all else, it was the force of love and unforgotten childhood like one big wheel [1092].

This leads to my last point concerning the magic of imagination: the greatest magic that the Losers possess, as Albus Dumbledore would attest, is the ability to love one another. In contemplating It's danger, It recognizes that the children are only powerful because "by coincidence" [as It tries to persuade Itself] the children had "bonded": "*if they had not happened to come together, It surely would have picked them off one by one*" (1017). But the very coming together of the children was no "coincidence"; the children were brought together by some "Other" force—namely, "the force of love," or more specifically the spontaneous and uncomplicated love of children. From the beginning, the Losers share a willingness to accept one another on impulse that is very clearly magical and beyond reason. Bill's and Eddie's twosome becomes a threesome that included Ben in an easy and amiable "silence" (236). When Richie and Stan join the threesome to build the dam, forming the core of the Losers, Eddie notices, and accepts, the rightness of the group's coming together: "They felt *right* together; they fitted neatly against each other's edges" (302). By the time that Mike is chased into the group (once again by Henry's gang), the Losers have been almost waiting for him (361; 408; 706–7), but the amount of precognition regarding his actual arrival is still impressive. Bill in particular was alert, "like a deer scenting fire in the air" (693). He is prescient enough to order the Losers to gather rocks as "ammo" before Mike bursts onto the scene. Richie, too, shares in the anticipation, taking off his glasses without knowing why he was doing it (694). After the apocalyptic rock fight, they accept Mike as one of them with the same kind of intuitive certainty: "*We're all together now*, he thought, and the idea was so strong, so *right*, that for a moment he thought he might have spoken it aloud" (700). Mike, too, demonstrates a sixth sense a few days later when he finds the Losers in the Barrens—he had known "*not just that they would be there, but* where *they would be*" (706).

Moreover, the Losers themselves acknowledge the depth of their natural attraction to one another, beginning with the spontaneous and unanimous confession of their mutual love for Beverly after her impassioned plea to be a part of the smokehouse ritual (747). As Mike, the most recent member of the group, sums it up: "'I don't know you well enough to love you,'" he said, "'but I love you anyway'" (748).

This power to love each other fully and innocently is ultimately demonstrated, of course, by Beverly's act of power sharing and bonding in the sewers. I use the word "innocently" only because from Beverly's perspective she *is* innocent, and not the "slutchild" that she is in her father's lecherous gaze (906). Indeed, Beverly's desperate and incredibly adult action could only make sense from the mind of an innocent child to whom sex can be seen as an appropriate act of connection and in which the voluntary surrender or exchange of power is completely without negative consequences. In other words, it only makes "sense" if Beverly is thinking with her heart and not her "rational" mind. As an adult in Eddie's hotel room, trying to decide if they should call the police to report Henry's attack on Eddie, Beverly recognizes the need to "think clearly again—not rationally but clearly. She was suddenly sure that rationality would kill them if they tried to use it now" (999). As a child in the sewers, Beverly is not thinking rationally, perhaps, but she is thinking clearly as she argues that having sex would be "[s]omething that will bring us together forever. Something that will show— [...] that I love you all" (1076). In other words, it demonstrates love and desire and power in a pure, childish way.

Of course, this begs the question: is the representation of an eleven-year-old girl having sex with six eleven-year-old boys sequentially in the sewers an appropriate or acceptable depiction of childhood innocence? This, of course, brings us to the third and final reason as to why it is worthwhile to consider *It* from the perspective of children's literature: *It* embodies several important questions of the genre.

The genre-specific questions at stake might be put this way: what is children's literature? What makes literature appropriate or unfit for children? Is children's literature even possible? The first question has been asked since the "inception" of the genre[13]; the last was raised initially by influential critic Jacqueline Rose in 1984, while King was in the midst of writing *It*. The root of both questions has to do with the obvious fact that children generally do not write the books that are published as "children's literature," a fact that led Rose to conclude that ultimately children's books are not for or about children, but rather are for and about an adult's "desire."[14] Rose's argument centers on *Peter Pan*, but the implications extend throughout the genre, and have inspired many critics to take up the issue in other texts. Although no one has claimed that Stephen King's *It* belongs in the genre, I am struck by how much it fits in this conversation. My argument has been that King attempted to represent in his fiction children having sex while remaining essentially innocent, but it certainly begs the question, what do adults get out of viewing children this way?

The final question that surrounds the academic discussion of children's literature is actually the same question that I started this essay with: when is literature too "dark" for children to read? That question came to the forefront after Meghan Cox Gurdon published her article, "Darkness Too Visible" (2011), making the claim that literature being published for teenagers has pushed the limits too far.[15] In this essay, I have presented *It* as a novel written in order to present children, who are often overlooked in our culture, as special and powerful, essentially the same empowering message that can be found in *Harry Potter* and *The Lord of the Rings* (1954). Should the scenes of explicit violence and sex prevent this message from reaching an audience that would benefit from hearing it?

While these are important questions, I do not claim to have the answers, only another question. As I write this, my eldest son is thirteen—would I let him read *It* if he wanted? Given how much the book has meant to me, it would be inconsistent and perhaps selfish for me to say no, but I must admit that the parent in me would be hesitant. Ultimately, it has not been my goal to argue that *It* was written for, or should be read by, children. I do suggest that reading *It* within the larger framework of children's literature enhances an appreciation for the book. It could even be argued that this perspective heightens the horror that the book is so well known for: after all, if two children involved means two turns of the screw, imagine what seven can do.

NOTES

1. King, Stephen. *It*. Viking, 1986. All in-text citations that follow will refer to this edition of the novel.
2. Harvey Roy Greenberg discusses King's ability to portray authentically "the vicissitudes, mores, and speech of pre-teenagers (particularly boys)" in his writing and in *It* specifically (28F). In his study on the depiction of friendship in the *Harry Potter* series, William M. Bukowski argues that such representations of childhood friendship in literature can be absolutely real and familiar to the children who are reading the stories. See Greenberg, Harvey

Roy. "IT: On the Unheimlich Maneuvers of Stephen King." *Psychiatric Times*, vol. 34, no. 11, Nov. 2017, p. 28E–28F and Bukowski, William M. "Friendship and the Worlds of Childhood." *New Directions for Child & Adolescent Development*, vol. 2001, no. 91, Spring 2001, pp. 93–106.

    3. King, Stephen. *The Eyes of the Dragon*. Viking, 1987.

    4. See for example 219–20; 740; 864; 894; 1031; and 1118, as well as a clever inversion with the "troll-like" Belch Huggins lurking above the underground hideout and Ben waiting below to "give him a surprise" (937).

    5. King wrote in a letter to Michael R. Collings that many of the central elements of It were inspired by his contemplation of the troll under the bridge in "The Three Billy Goats Gruff." See Collings, Michael R. *The Stephen King Phenomenon*. Starmont, 1987, 28–9.

    6. Critics have long noticed King's utilization of the conventions of the fairy tale to enhance the horror in his fiction. See, for example, Alexander, Alex E. "Stephen King's *Carrie*—A Universal Fairytale." *Journal of Popular Culture*, vol. 13, 1979, pp. 282–88, and Yarbro, Chelsea Quinn. "Cinderella's Revenge: Twists on Fairy Tale and Mythic Themes in the Work of Stephen King." *Fear Itself: The Horror Fiction of Stephen King*, edited by Tim Underwood and Chuck Miller. Signet, 1984: 63–73. Also, Greenberg praises King's ability to "newly mint fairy tales" (28F), and Heidi Strengell has argued that King uses the fairy tale as tool to revert the adult reader into a child (see Strengell, Heidi. *Dissecting Stephen King: From the Gothic to Literary Naturalism*, University of Wisconsin Press, 2005, especially "2. Myths and Fairy-tales in King's Works," pp. 108–178. But of course, the fairy tale in its origins was never intended for children alone.

    7. For an historical overview discussing the philosophical underpinnings of the emergence of children's literature and its connection to ideas of the imagination, see Manlove, Colin N. *From Alice to Harry Potter: Children's Fantasy in England*. Cybereditions, 2003. For a compelling examination of the way in which Lewis Carroll's *Alice's Adventures in Wonderland*, which launched the "Golden Age of Children's literature" in the 19th century, challenged prevailing medical opinions concerning the dangers of imagination in children, see Schatz, Stephanie L. "Lewis Carroll's Dream-child and Victorian Child Psychopathology." *Journal of the History of Ideas*, vol. 76, no. 1, Jan. 2015, pp. 93–114.

    8. For a fuller discussion of the emergence of the Romantic image of the child, see Coveney, Peter. *The Image of Childhood*. Penguin, 1967.

    9. King, Stephen. *Pet Sematary*. Doubleday, 1983.

    10. It is true that Eddie, a successful entrepreneur, has a career that is no more creative on the surface than Stan's accounting business; however, Eddie has also held on to his childish faith in medicine in general, and his aspirator in particular, which makes his daily life a form of "play." Additionally, in marrying a version of his mother, he has remained more essentially a child.

    11. While Zack Denbrough is merely cold and distant to Bill, Sharon Denbrough is actually "horrified" by and afraid of her own son (853). Maggie Tozier, the most "regular" of the parents, represents just how far afield adults can be from truly understanding the life of a child: "This failure to make his mother understand hurt much worse than being slammed into the gutter" (662). Even Mike, who otherwise has a good relationship with his father, cannot make him understand that Henry Bowers is crazy (669).

    12. For example: As Richie is re-entering Derry as an adult: "*There seems to be some mad part of him which actually looks forward to what may be coming*" (320); Beverly on the airplane: "We laughed a lot back then, *she thinks* […] We were afraid all the time, but we couldn't stop laughing" (384); when Beverly votes to try to kill It again, she does so looking "both tremendously excited and scared to death" (525); upon seeing a two-hundred-year-old picture of Pennywise, Bill "felt a crazy surge of terror, anger, and excitement rush through him" (727); on entering Neibolt Street, Ben "was becoming excited as well as afraid now" (857); Eddie, while Henry is breaking his arm: "in spite of the pain, in spite of the tears and the fear, he brayed a huge donkeylike hee-haw of laughter" (784); Richie, upon entering the Morlock hole, "was terrified of going into this concrete throat, but he still couldn't stop laughing" (980); an adult Richie, in It's lair: "although tears were running down his cheeks, Richie was grinning madly" (1051).

13. Holmes, Martha Stoddard. "Peter Pan and the Possibilities of Child Literature." *Second Star to the Right: Peter Pan in the Popular Imagination*, edited by Allison B. Kavey and Lester D. Friedman, Rutgers UP, 2009, pp. 132–150.
14. Rose, Jacqueline S. "The Case of Peter Pan: The Impossibility of Children's Fiction." *The Children's Culture Reader*, edited by Henry Jenkins, New York UP, 1998, pp. 58–66.
15. Gurdon, Meghan Cox. "Darkness Too Visible." *Wall Street Journal*—Eastern Edition, vol. 257, no. 129, 4 June 2011, p. C5.

WORKS CITED

Alegre, Sara Martín. "Nightmares of Childhood: The Child and The Monster in Four Novels by Stephen King." *Atlantis*, vol. 23, no. 1, 2001, pp. 105–114.
Alexander, Alex E. "Stephen King's *Carrie*—A Universal Fairytale." *Journal of Popular Culture*, vol. 13, 1979, pp. 282–88.
Bukowski, William M. "Friendship and the Worlds of Childhood." *New Directions for Child & Adolescent Development*, vol. 2001, no. 91, Spring 2001, pp. 93–106.
Christie, Lauren. "Stephen King and the Illusion of Childhood." *Pennywise Dreadful: The Journal of Stephen King Studies*, vol. 1, no. 1, 2017, pp. 3–15.
Collings, Michael R. *The Stephen King Phenomenon*. Starmont, 1987.
Coveney, Peter. *The Image of Childhood*. Penguin, 1967.
Greenberg, Harvey Roy. "IT: On the *Unheimlich* Maneuvers of Stephen King." *Psychiatric Times*, vol. 34, no. 11, Nov. 2017, pp. 28E–28F.
Gurdon, Meghan Cox. "Darkness Too Visible." *Wall Street Journal*—Eastern Edition, vol. 257, no. 129, 4 June 2011, p. C5.
Hansen, Regina. "Stephen King's *IT* and *Dreamcatcher* on Screen: Hegemonic White Masculinity and Nostalgia for Underdog Boyhood." *Science Fiction Film and Television*, vol. 10, no. 2, 2017, pp. 161–176.
Holmes, Martha Stoddard. "Peter Pan and the Possibilities of Child Literature." *Second Star to the Right: Peter Pan in the Popular Imagination*, edited by Allison B. Kavey and Lester D. Friedman, Rutgers UP, 2009, pp. 132–150.
King, Stephen. *Danse Macabre*. Everest, 1981.
_____. *The Eyes of the Dragon*. Viking, 1987.
_____. *It*. Viking, 1986.
_____. *Pet Sematary*. Doubleday, 1983.
Manlove, Colin N. *From Alice to Harry Potter: Children's Fantasy in England*. Cybereditions, 2003.
Mercer, Erin. "The Difference Between World and Want: Adulthood and the Horrors of History in Stephen King's *IT*." *Journal of Popular Culture*, vol. 52, no. 2, Apr. 2019, pp. 315–329.
Nash, Jesse W. "Postmodern Gothic: Stephen King's *Pet Sematary*." *The Journal of Popular Culture*, vol. 30, no. 4, 1997, pp. 151–160.
Rose, Jacqueline S. "The Case of Peter Pan: The Impossibility of Children's Fiction." *The Children's Culture Reader*, edited by Henry Jenkins, New York UP, 1998, pp. 58–66.
Schatz, Stephanie L. "Lewis Carroll's Dream-child and Victorian Child Psychopathology." *Journal of the History of Ideas*, vol. 76, no. 1, Jan. 2015, pp. 93–114.
Strengell, Heidi. *Dissecting Stephen King: From the Gothic to Literary Naturalism*. University of Wisconsin Press, 2005.
Yarbro, Chelsea Quinn. "Cinderella's Revenge: Twists on Fairy Tale and Mythic Themes in the Work of Stephen King." *Fear Itself: The Horror Fiction of Stephen King*, edited by Tim Underwood and Chuck Miller. Signet, 1984: 63–73.

Clowning Around

The Carnivalesque and Stephen King's Novel It

Katherine A. Troyer

Tim Curry's and Bill Skarsgård's respective performances have ensured that entire new generations will be terrified of clowns; however, it is Stephen King's original 1986 novel that first showed us why we should fear the "clown in the stormdrain" (*It* 13). It is a monster with many faces, capable of "*throwing back at the terrified viewer the worst thing in his or her own mind*" (King, *It* 1031), and yet Its most frequent face throughout the novel is that of Pennywise the Dancing Clown. And Pennywise can be a truly disturbing face, like the one that adult Ben Hanscom sees in the library, with its empty holes for eyes and killer smile (King, *It* 551). Yet while Pennywise is certainly a monster worthy of nightmares, this clownish form of It serves a greater purpose in the novel than just as the source of readers' newly discovered (or long suspected) coulrophobia.

Through Pennywise the Dancing Clown, the novel *It* invokes images not only of the circus but of the carnival—and more specifically, of the carnivalesque. With its homicidal clown, the novel might seem to be encouraging fear of the carnivalesque. And It (not to mention the rest of Derry, Maine) certainly does provoke unsettling feelings about liminality, the grotesque, and the profane that exist at the core of this concept. Lost in the tunnels beneath Derry, Beverly Marsh thinks: "*You laugh because what's fearful and unknown is also what's funny, you laugh the way a small child will sometimes laugh and cry at the same time when a capering circus clown approaches, knowing it is supposed to be funny ... but it is also unknown, full of the unknown's eternal power*" (King, *It* 1102–3). The novel, thus, exposes the ambivalent potential of the carnivalesque. The scariest and most treacherous summer of the Losers' lives is also one filled with joy and laughter, the power of unlikely companionship, the magic of ritual, and unrestricted freedom. By juxtaposing the horrors of Pennywise and the triumphs of the Losers, the novel suggests that it is not the carnivalesque we should fear but the monster who corrupts it. It, King's text reveals, can only be defeated by those brave enough to enter and—when needed—return once more to the liberating albeit precarious space of the carnivalesque at the heart of childhood.

The Festival Is Finished, but the Carnival Continues

It opens itself readily to being analyzed through the lens of the carnivalesque. The 1984 timeline of the novel begins with a chapter entitled "*After the Festival (1984)*." The weeklong event is seen as a success—both for the denizens of Derry excited about this boost to "morale, image … and pocketbook" (King, *It* 19) and for It, who snags the prize of Adrian Mellon. Perhaps a confrontation between the gay Adrian and the homophobic John Garton was inevitable in small-town 1980s America; however, as the novel carefully details, this particular deadly encounter happens in festival-time Derry when emotions are heightened and inhibitions are lowered even more than usual for this toxic place. Adrian's murder at the mouth of It might have been inevitable, but his death on that specific night could have been avoided if the carnival had not been in town.

The Russian theorist Mikhail Bakhtin argued that Western society could be understood through the patterns of behavior and thought produced by the regular presence and reoccurrence of the carnival. Tracing the existence of the carnival as far back as the early Greek and Roman cultures, Bakhtin saw the carnival as "a *syncretic pageant* form of a ritual nature. It is a very complex and diverse form, having many variations and nuances based on the general carnival principle and depending on various epochs, peoples, and individual festivals" (*Problems* 100). Yet even as individual carnivals adapted and transformed, there existed a symbolic language that spoke to a coherent carnival attitude that could be identified across periods and cultures.

In *Problems of Dostoevsky's Poetics*, Bakhtin provides sketches of this attitude at different points in history up through the Renaissance period, which he said marked a point of deviation. Starting in the 17th century, he argued, the practice of the carnival as a lived, regular experience waned. Bakhtin allowed that the carnival did not entirely die; however, too often it continued in mediated or demoted forms such as the circus or street performances (106–8). Today we might recognize this altered, new carnival form in the Rio de Janeiro Carnival or Mardi Gras, but Bakhtin seemed most interested in the carnival's new literary home. He coined the term carnivalesque to describe a trend he saw in modern literature, one that sought to subvert—within the pages of the text—dominant attitudes and beliefs. Within these texts, he claimed that the carnival's controlled and confined chaos was still recognizable, even in this new literary form.

There were several aspects of carnival that Bakhtin identified and he outlined them clearly in *Problems of Dostoevsky's Poetics*. "All *distance* between people is suspended and a special carnival category goes into effect—the *free, familiar contact among people*" (Bakhtin, *Problems* 101). This was, he claimed, a very important part of carnival as it ensured a freedom of interactions and words necessary for carnival performances and language to be shared. Because carnival allows for the suspension of hierarchically defined positions and roles, this free contact allows for social relationships to form amongst individuals who would, in non-carnival times, be restricted from interaction. Tied into this idea is the carnival attitude of eccentricity, which allows the aspects of humanity regularly undeveloped and concealed under society to emerge often in a sensuous way (Bakhtin, *Problems* 101). And it is not just people's interactions that become unfettered; carnivalistic mésalliances apply to "all values, thoughts, phenomena and things. All the things that were closed off, isolated, and separated from one another by the non-carnivalistic hierarchical attitude enter into carnivalistic contacts and combinations" (Bakhtin, *Problems* 101). The carnival's ability to unite the unexpected contributes to another carnivalistic category: profanation, "carnivalistic blasphemies" connected to bringing higher thoughts to earthly planes, "carnivalistic obscenities" attached to reproduction and the body, and "carnivalistic parodies" of religious and sacred texts (Bakhtin, *Problems* 101).

Bakhtin looked primarily at what we might today consider to be literature with a capital L. His study of writers such as Shakespeare, Rabelais, and Dostoevsky may seem far removed from a study of a popular writer like King. Yet as Linda Hutcheon points out in her own investigation of the carnivalesque, the folk culture that Bakhtin studied is what we would now refer to as pop culture (85). Furthermore, she says, Bakhtin understood that fear was instrumental to the continued power and solemnity of the official culture against which carnival provided temporary relief (85). Fears of formal rebuke and repercussions could be briefly mitigated through sanctioned and temporally limited opportunities to transgress against cultural, societal, and literary norms. During times of carnival, "the hierarchical system and all the connected forms of fear, awe, piety, etiquette, etc. are suspended" (Bakhtin, *Problems* 100). In this way, a popular horror novel about an unlikely group of hormonal adolescents that appropriate a sacred Himalayan ritual to defeat a monster in clown-skin seems a perfect text to explore the carnivalesque.

Where There Is a Clown, There Is Probably a Carnival

Laughter, bawdy and irreverent, reigned during the carnival as traditional forms of authority were subverted and the liberation of ideas and identities became momentarily possible. *It* is a novel with a remarkable amount of laughter. This seems both surprising and unsurprising when one remembers that the monster's primary form is a clown. Bakhtin wrote: "Civil and social ceremonies and rituals took on a comic aspect as clowns and fools, constant participants in these festivals, mimicked serious rituals" (*Rabelais* 5). All forms and sources of humor—from joyful celebration to ridicule—combine to form carnival laughter (Bakhtin, *Problems* 104). This carnival laughter emerges throughout the summer of 1958 for the Losers as they bond and clown around; however, their cathartic and pure laughter is constantly being threatened by Its presence as Pennywise. The first time we meet Pennywise, Georgie Denbrough tells him that he is "not supposed to take stuff from strangers" (King, *It* 14) and so Pennywise jovially introduces himself. Georgie giggles and then fatally forgets to uphold the practices of stranger danger as he moves to accept a balloon from Pennywise. Georgie dies, in part, because he is too young to understand that It, in its clown form, is mimicking and not keeping the societal rituals of caring for and protecting children.

As the novel unfolds, it becomes increasingly clear that Pennywise's presence exposes not the comic but the horrific aspects of the town's social and civil ceremonies. Clowns and fools became "the constant, accredited representatives of the carnival spirit in everyday life out of carnival season" (Bakhtin, *Rabelais* 8). In Derry, this carnival spirit is clearly corrupted. The carnivalesque moments in Derry—where hierarchies are suspended and the impossible becomes possible—involve murder, arson, savagery, hatred, and violence. The medieval clown, Bakhtin argued, was the voice, if not the harbinger, of the fundamental truths at the core of a society (*Rabelais* 92–94). And the truth of Derry is that it has gone bad or perhaps it was simply always rotten.

Mike Hanlon's father tells his son that it "seems that bad things, hurtful things, do right well in the soil of this town" (King, *It* 453). This is a truth that readers have known from the start of the novel as Derry is described early on as "a *bad* place" (King, *It* 28), one that "always felt like thirteen o'clock" (King, *It* 29). In her discussion of King's *The Shining*, Linda J. Holland-Toll asks what is to happen if "the carnival life becomes destructive, becomes a dark carnival instead of a site for working out or a safety valve" ("Bakhtin's" 134). The answer in *It* is a town caught in a monster's web; "Pennywise had been there, guiding them down the path toward another gaudy sacrifice—just one more in Derry's long history of gaudy sacrifices" (King, *It* 907). Every few decades, It forced Derry into a carnival period of hunting and devouring; "[c]arnival is not a spectacle seen by the people; they live in it, and everyone participates because its very idea embraces all the people. While carnival lasts, there is no other life outside it" (Bakhtin, *Rabelais* 7). During Its reign, there is no escaping the darkness; there is only immersion and varying degrees of willingness to acknowledge how completely one's life has been subsumed by this terror. Yet carnival is supposed to be a respite, a break that allows the inevitable return to the normal to be palatable. The carnival's power arrives, in part, from its temporally limited nature. But for the people of Derry, there is no escape from this topsy-turvy world of Its perverted and inescapable carnival where lives are literally liberated. Mike wonders: "Can an *entire city* be haunted?" (King, *It* 147). Bill Denbrough tells the Losers that the answer is yes because Derry is It (King, *It* 987). "*Derry was Its killing-pen, the people of Derry Its sheep*" (King, *It* 1023). Until that final showdown between the adult Losers and It, there is no escape from this carnival nightmare.

The Only Thing to Fear Is Fear ITself

Barbara Creed argues that it is unsurprising that the horror genre would be a perfect venue for the carnival as both center so fixedly on issues of grotesque humor, transgression, and the monstrous body. Bakhtin stated that the "essential principle of grotesque realism is degradation, that is, the lowering of all that is high, spiritual, ideal, abstract; it is a transfer to the material level, to the sphere of earth and body in their indissoluble unity" (*Rabelais* 19–20). Stan Uris is perhaps the first of the Losers to truly understand the grotesque nature of It. When he tries to later explain to the Losers his encounter with It in the Standpipe, he is unable or unwilling to explain to them that seeing the two drowned boys was more than frightening; it was offensive: "All the same, there were things that were not supposed to *be*. They offended any sane person's sense of order, they offended the central idea that God had given the earth a final tilt on its axis" (King, *It* 436). After adult Stan commits suicide, Bill reflects that Stan hated to be dirty more than he hated to be scared and suggests that maybe Stan thought the only way to stay clean was to not keep living (King, *It* 506). Perhaps Stan was correct, at least as far as Derry was concerned. Mike tells the other adult Losers that he believes It "leaves Its marks on people just by the nature of what It is" (King, *It* 521). They had all been undoubtedly marked as children by what Bakhtin would have described as the living carnival image, in which "death itself is pregnant and gives birth, and life-giving mother's loins become a grave" (*Problems* 137).

It is this very death begetting life that the adults cannot remember until their final showdown with It. Even after everything else comes back regarding the summer of 1958, this memory remains dormant until the very end. The adult Loser's rediscovery that "*It is female, It's pregnant with some unimaginable spawn*" (King, *It* 1065) is enough to nearly disrupt their sanity. Barbara Creed might have told them this should have been an unsurprising conclusion as she notes that, for Bakhtin, the grotesque body was linked frequently with the female body (135–36). Its "natural" form is not quite a spider, but Bill says that idea is as close an image as their minds can process. It is tall, "black as moonless night," thick-legged and muscular, with "jagged mandibles" that drip foam; It has a stinger that oozes poison and Its appearance is so horrific that the sight of it drives them all to the brink of madness (King, *It* 1064–65). This matches Creed's discussion of the grotesque body as being an obscene hybrid that moves beyond its boundaries in its inverted existence (135). The ultimate horror of the novel being the revelation of It as female fits into Creed's argument that in horror the female body is often depicted as grotesque precisely so that it can be made monstrous. She offers twelve categories that such a body should fall into, and the list reads much like a checklist for It, e.g., the metamorphosing, transforming body; the animal/insect/reptile body; the psychokinetic body; the female body; the body as living corpse, the maternal body; and the body of the archaic mother (127–59). Linda Anderson argues that the novel creates all mother figures as threats and monsters; It is just the symbolic version that must be destroyed. "The devouring BITch-mother can only be destroyed by masculine force, knowledge, and language in an exorcism of pre–Oedipal anxiety" (120). It is not just the grotesque manifested; It is the female grotesque in its most explicit form. And the only way to defeat It is through the Losers' experiences with the carnivalesque.

Good, Old Carnival Fun

Bakhtin's discussion of the carnivalesque remains rather consistent across his writings; however, there is a change of wording between two of his works that illuminates an intriguing aspect of the carnivalesque: ambivalence. In "Carnival and Carnivalesque," Bakhtin writes: "Because carnivalistic life is life drawn out of its *usual* rut, it is to some extent 'life turned inside out,' 'the reverse side of the world' ('*monde à l'envers*') (250–51). Yet in *Problems of Dostoevsky's Poetics,* this phrase '*monde à l'envers*' is translated not as 'the reverse side of the world' but rather as 'life the wrong way 'round'" (*Bakhtin*

101). Perhaps no more than a quirk of translation, this alteration nevertheless highlights the two sides that make up the carnivalesque. The carnival is freeing, but it also chaotic; it is subversive but also sanctioned. The carnivalesque can be dangerous and destabilizing. Yet, it also has the power to articulate that which was impossible to articulate before. The carnivalesque provides opportunities and experiences unavailable outside of that space and time. King's novel may create anxieties about this concept, but it also unequivocally celebrates that carnivalesque space of childhood where identities are formed, imagination is essential, and power and meaning are discovered.

A popular criticism about King's novel is the length, particularly as it pertains to the novel's set-up. And it is undeniably true that it takes hundreds of pages for the primary protagonists—Bill Denbrough, Richie Tozier, Ben Hanscom, Beverly Marsh, Mike Hanlon, Stanley Uris, and Eddie Kaspbrak—to form into the ragtag team of misfits known as the Losers. Yet this buildup is integral to the novel's acknowledgment that the carnivalesque is marked by unexpected and unlikely relationships. Until Mike joins them after the rock fight, there is an unspoken but deeply felt sensation that at six, they are "one shy of the magic number" (King, *It* 694). It is only as the group solidifies that their strength intensifies; this is a process that the novel depicts as being both organic and preordained. There is no reason why this group of children should have formed such an intimate friendship that summer. True, they were all victims … of Henry Bowers, of their parents, of It; however, that statement seemed true for most of the children of Derry. Instead, the novel suggests that the group formed due to both some unseen Other as well as the result of that magical formula for all childhood friendships: the right time, the right place, the right conditions. In this case, all of these are tied into the carnivalesque: the limited time of the summer, the carnivalistic space of the Barrens, the grotesque humor of a town's fate left to the misfits who are not entirely sure the town is worth saving. For the most part, the child-versions of the Losers just know that certain kids feel "somehow less important […] less *there*" than their fellow Losers (King, *It* 411), but the adult Losers often reflect on how it seemed that summer that something was "driving the seven of them together—tight, tighter, tightest" (King, *It* 487).

During that summer of 1958, anything and everything feels possible. With the formation of the Losers, Bakhtin's other characters of the carnivalesque fall into place: hierarchies are stripped away as seven individuals from different socio-economic backgrounds and life experiences bond a sensuous element emerges as a love-triangle of sorts forms between Ben, Beverly, and Bill; and all topics and experiences—from life-threatening attacks to hanging out in a clubhouse reading comic books—are treated with equal importance. The novel works hard to show how, in that carnivalesque space of a childhood summer, the big and small, profound and superficial, spiritual and physical conflate and merge into the same overall magic. Bill's belief in Silver, his trusted bike, is treated with the same gravitas as his interaction with the cosmic turtle that tries to help them. The monsters that terrify the children on the silver screen are just as deadly as Pennywise, as It assumes all of these forms with ease. As a group, the Losers face epic enemies from the knife-wielding Henry and ever-hungry It to the more mundane dangers of a smothering Mrs. Kaspbrak, a lecherous Mr. Marsh, and uninterested other parents. The group's development also allows for the crowning/discrowning of a leader that Bakhtin says appeared frequently in carnivals as a way to express "the inevitability, and simultaneously the creativity, of change and renewal" (*Problems* 102). Bill becomes the leader of his group despite his stutter and, as Eddie reflects, it is an awe-inspiring and perhaps terrifying power he has that his friends would die for him (King, *It* 980). At the same time that the Losers' power and Bill's authority grows, Henry Bowers is increasingly stripped of his power and his minions trust him less and less as he becomes increasingly unhinged.

There are many instances, like the waxing of the Losers and the waning of the bullies, where the novel illustrates what Bakhtin called the two-in-one images of the carnivalesque. Intended to allow for comparison and contrast, two-in-one images "unite within themselves both poles of change and crisis: birth and death [...], benediction and damnation [...], praise and condemnation, youth and age, top and bottom, face and backside, stupidity and wisdom" (103). *It* is filled with such images and most often they occur in relationship to the Losers. There is the image of a nearly adult Mike, not quite out of high school but in the prime of his life, sitting beside his father, who is withering away from cancer (King, *It* 458–60). There is the two-in-one images of Beverly's paramours, Bill and Ben—one thin and one fat, one the born leader and the other the inherent loner. There are the silver slugs, which even once molded still retain a shadow of their previous silver-dollar nature. There is the simultaneous image of a father Beverly loves and a father she hates. And there is the awkward and probably unnecessary scene of the group sex, where the boys have sex with Beverly to escape the tunnels after defeating It. The scene is both a moment of crisis and change, the death of the group as they know it and the birth of a girl becoming a woman. It is a scene that is both absurd and disturbing. Beverly thinks that there is power in this act though, even as she realizes that, for many girls, sex becomes the It that haunts their lives (King, *It* 1100–1). Even the more mundane moments of their summer experiences reflect this two-in-one sense of simultaneously juxtaposing what should be total opposite sensations. Richie rides behind on Bill's bicycle "so scared he was nearly creaming his jeans but laughing wildly all the same" (King, *It* 375). Ben and Mike spend an afternoon "actually screaming with laughter" (King, *It* 730); and Beverly appears in a dress looking "very adult but also somehow very childlike, like a girl playing dress-up" (King, *It* 816).

If the novel suggests that the young Losers experience the world in contrasting emotions, then it ensures that the readers will experience two-in-one imagery through its dual timelines between 1958 and 1985. After (temporarily) defeating It in 1958, the Losers no longer have the same impetus to be together as they did before until finally—as adults—they have completely forgotten one another. But the return of the past, with Mike's phone call in 1985, seems "marvellous ... but in an ominous way" (King, *It* 482). The descriptions of the adults' return to Derry, particularly those of Bill and Ben, are full of phrases like "a queer doubling sensation" (King, *It* 482) and "that queer feeling of time doubling back on itself that people call, for want of a better term, *déjà-vu*" (King, *It* 545). The longer they are in Derry, the more they feel a return of the power, the strength, the vitality of their youth. Richie reflects that he feels "*a mad, exhilarating kind of energy growing in the room*" that as an adult can only be gained through artificial stimulants, but as a child was present naturally every day (King, *It* 743). As the novel progresses, it is not just the characters that experience this conflation of past and present. It is also the readers of the novel. The two trips to Its lair weave together, bouncing back and forth with an ever-quickening tempo that requires diligence on the part of the reader as one timeline literally picks up in the same sentence as the other.

In this way, the novel links together the two timelines within the broader space of adolescence, lived first in 1958 and then experienced as an echo twenty-seven years later. Carnivalesque spaces are tied to both birth/procreation and to death, so the novel's portrayal of the carnivalesque in relationship to adolescence might seem out of place at first. Yet in truth, perhaps there is no better moment of carnival than that experienced by the adolescent. After all, it is a time filled with clear governing powers in the form of parents; generic adult authority; and school, which in Derry is a "typical confused educational carnival, a circus with so many rings that Pennywise himself might have gone unnoticed" (King, *It* 837). It is a time where everything—from rock fights to impromptu baseball games to Parcheesi tournaments—has clearly defined, almost ritualistic patterns of behavior. The power of religion often seems mystical in nature and, therefore, keenly felt (King, *It* 976–7). There is a tension between adults and children formed because, as Ben thinks, children "lived below the sight-lines, and hence the thought-lines, of most adults" (King, *It* 955). And yet that ghost-like state can shift overnight because adolescence is the liminal state between the death of childhood and the birth of adulthood. It is a time when it is possible to both think, like Eddie, that "*Grownups are the real monsters*" (King, *It* 782) and to think as Beverly does, standing before her mirror: "It was true; childhood would end; she would be a woman" (King, *It* 406).

Although the grown-up Losers cannot help but feel that their trip to

Derry is "*stapling past to present*" (King, *It* 711), they are also distinctly aware that coming back to the home of one's childhood is a near impossible trick to perform successfully (King, *It* 560). This truly temporary nature of their adolescence is what allows their actions in 1958 and 1985 to tap into the positive power and potential of the carnivalesque (as opposed to Its corrupted carnivalesque space). The Ritual of Chüd works the first time because Bill clings to the magic and belief only possible by someone on the brink of both childhood and adulthood. The ritual succeeds the second time only because, for a brief moment, they are allowed to return to that carnivalesque space of their childhood friendships and lives. But it is temporary. Not everyone survives and those who do begin to lose their memories—of what happened, of their childhoods, of each other.

In her discussion of *It*, Holland-Toll argues that there is something very problematic about the novel's suggestion that the sick community of Derry can only end at the cost of the treasured community of the Losers. To her, the novel's end is less bittersweet and more an uncomfortable look at how "the community defined in terms of love, courage, and generosity, is almost completely nullified" (*As American* 131). Yet through this carnivalesque lens, I think this conclusion becomes not only necessary, but healthy. While, as Mike reflects, the forgetting is scary (King, *It* 1141), it is also healing. Young Bill, leaving the Barrens after the Losers blood-swear to return if needed, thinks to himself that he never wants to play down in the Barrens again. What was once a sanctuary is no longer needed and the thought that he does not wish to return there "*is not terrible or distressing but tremendously liberating*" (King, *It* 1130). The dissolution of the adult Losers at the end of the novel seems to be equally liberating; "[a]t its core is an understanding that the price of temporary transgression is allegiance to the wider laws and codes of society" (Ravenscroft and Gilchrist 40–41). The Losers will now live free from Pennywise and while their friendship may seem the price, in reality this community, like their own childhoods, was never theirs to have forever. And so the novel ends with Bill Denbrough who sometimes finds himself thinking in the early morning after waking from dreams about the "mystery of childhood" (King, *It* 1152) and almost remembering his own childhood "*and the friends with whom he shared it*" (King, *It* 1153).

Returning Back to Derry

It offers a sprawling narrative that disregards conventions of length in favor of producing an inextricable relationship between the timelines of the 1950s and 1980s. At times, the novel seems to actively eschew coherence for a tale that combines the cosmic and the ordinary into strange orthodoxy and uncomfortably familiar ritual. But, in the process, the book offers something that perhaps cannot fully be contained in any adaptation that is not equally messy, irreverent, awkward, bloated, and disturbing even as it is triumphant, raw, honest, and beautiful. Stephen King's *It* offers us a uniquely crafted and distinctively carnivalesque space. Within the pages of *It*, Bahktin's carnivalesque and King's horror become their own two-in-one image.

"Carnival," Bakhtin wrote, "brings together, unites, weds and combines the sacred with the profane, the lofty with the lowly, the great with the insignificant, the wise with the stupid" (*Problems* 100). Perhaps no better description can be offered, not only for the carnivalesque but for the horror genre. King writes that horror has the ability to urge "us to put away our more civilized and adult penchant for analysis and to become children again" and, in doing so, these texts offer relief as such an "invitation to lapse into simplicity, and even outright madness is extended so rarely. We are told we may allow our emotions a free rein … or no rein at all" (*Danse* 185). Timothy Jones suggests that *It* uses its carnival space to direct readers "towards the fearful, horrible, and forbidden, but largely divested of their complicating politics. *It* engages with genuine discourses but retools them to its own carnivalesque ends" (171). The result is a carnival space where readers can immerse themselves in a story where domestic horrors are depicted with the same gravitas as a child-eating space spider. They can visit a world where the angst and confusion of crossing the border into adulthood occurs in tandem with the death of a cosmic turtle who vomited the universe into existence.

The novel allows its readers a temporary place where play and terror go hand-in-hand, where the dark is gleefully brought into the light, where the carnivalesque and the horror genres can be experienced in their truest intertwined forms. But *It* also promises a space that we can return to whenever we find ourselves in need of a break from the world around us. Stephen King's compelling narrative has ensured that, like Mike's father, Derry will never escape our minds. And like the Losers, we can return there to experience both a freedom and terror that is not present in our daily moments but which can nevertheless speak to our lives; "[b]y symbolically destroying and then rebuilding society, carnival both subverts and affirms the values of the community, providing a moment of contradiction within which change is imaginable" (Erisman 332). We can experience anew the horrors and magic of Derry, the final destruction of It and the town, and the promise that it might someday be better even if we won't remember how we got there. All we need to do is start reading again. After all, we are always welcome back to Derry, if we dare.

WORKS CITED

Anderson, Linda. "'OH DEAR JESUS IT IS FEMALE': Monster as Mother/Mother as Monster in Stephen King's It." *Imagining the Worst: Stephen King and the Representation of Women*, edited by Kathleen Margaret Lant and Theresa Thompson, Greenwood Press, 1998, pp. 111–25.
Bakhtin, Mikhail. "Carnival and the Carnivalesque." *Cultural Theory and Popular Culture: A Reader*, edited by John Storey, 2nd ed, Pearson, 1998, pp. 250–59.
_____. *Problems of Dostoevsky's Poetics*. Translated by R.W. Rotsel, Ardis, 1973.
_____. *Rabelais and His World*. Translated by Helene Iswolsky, The M.I.T. P, 1965.
Creed, Barbara. "Horror and the Carnivalesque: The Body-Monstrous." *Fields of Vision: Essays in Film Studies, Visual Anthropology, and Photography*, edited by Leslie Devereaux and Roger Hillman, U of California P, 1995, pp. 127–59.
Erisman, Wendy E. "Inverting the Ideal World: Carnival and the Carnivalesque in Contemporary Utopian Science Fiction." *Extrapolation*, vol. 36, no. 4, 1995, pp. 333–44.
Holland-Toll, Linda J. *As American as Mom, Baseball, and Apple Pie: Constructing Community in Contemporary America*. Bowling Green State U Popular P, 2001.
_____. "Bakhtin's Carnival Reversed: King's *The Shining* as Dark Carnival." *The Journal of Popular Culture*, vol. 33, no. 2, 1999, pp. 131–46.
Hutcheon, Linda. "The Carnivalesque and Contemporary Narrative: Popular Culture and the Erotic." *Revue De L'Universite D'Ottawa/University of Ottawa Quarterly*, vol. 53, no. 1, 1983, pp. 83–94.
Jones, Timothy. *The Gothic and the Carnivalesque in American Culture*. University of Wales P, 2015.
King, Stephen. *Danse Macabre*. 1981. Gallery Books, 2010.
_____. *It*. 1986. Scribner's, 2017.
Ravenscroft, Neil, and Paul Gilchrist. "Spaces of Transgression: Governance, Discipline, and Reworking the Carnivalesque." *Leisure Studies*, vol. 28, no. 1, 2009, pp. 35–49.

Doing *It*

Sex and the Monster

DOMINICK GRACE

When researching Stephen King's 1987 novel *It* one can encounter an instructive confusion. In its groupings by subject, the MLA database does not clearly distinguish between King's novel and the 1927 Clara Bow film "*It*," which itself plays on the implications of that most vague of pronouns. I do not mean to suggest that there is any connection between *It* (1987) and "*It*" (1927). King does not reference the film or its star in the novel, and there is no overlap in plot or structure. Nevertheless, there are interesting parallels, both in how "it" functions ambiguously as a pronoun and in how reading what "it" is can reveal the monstrous underpinnings of society, especially in its anxieties about sex. Evidently, "it" is a problematic concept; whoever is "it" can easily be othered and ostracized, read as transgressive and, therefore, cast out. The 1927 film is connected with Elinor Glyn's conception of "IT" as "animal magnetism": "The person who has IT suggests in his [*sic*] bearing, the flash of his eye, that it is impossible to control him" (qtd. in Desjardins 516). Clara Bow became known as the "it" girl due to her star turn in the 1927 "*It*" movie, and the clear "it" in question, despite Glyn's more complex conception, was sex, especially the sex appeal of women to men. As the "it" girl, Clara Bow came to be seen as the type of sexual excessiveness. As Mary Desjardins has documented, Bow was accused in an article in 1930 of various sexual transgressions, ranging from public sex through *ménage à trois*, venereal disease, and even bestiality (Desjardins 510). That she was not guilty of all these charges is probably evident; they reflect how easily the association with "it" can lead to hysteria and othering. Sexuality is easily scapegoated—and King's *It* uses this fact, just as it was used against Bow. Bow, Desjardins notes, was seen to demonstrate her "IT" quality "with the voraciousness of an animal" (516), and she was viewed for decades as the type not only of the sexually appealing but also of the dangerous (sexually) transgressive woman.

The pronoun "it," of course, has a long history as an ambiguous word. As a pronoun that stands in for a noun, "it" can often have a clear antecedent; however, "it" is also often used as a generic subject (e.g., "It is raining outside") in constructions in which what "it" is, exactly, is impossible to define. The ambiguity of "it" as a pronoun has often been exploited to suggest the terror of the unknown thing, notably in the horror and SF genres, as is evident in titles such as *It Came from Outer Space* (1953) (referenced in *It*, 581), *It Came from Beneath the Sea* (1955), and *It Conquered the World* (1956), all films the members of the Losers' Club may have seen. "It" is also, and notoriously, a stand-in for sex, an association King explicitly invokes late in the book, though readers have almost certainly already made the connection, given the various ways the novel has already invoked sex, and even the sex/horror connection. He does so in what is a climactic scene, in more ways than one.

A crucial scene in King's *It* depends precisely on the idea of the attractive female as object of male sexual desire, though conceived very differently from the idea of female sexual appeal as simultaneously irresistible and terrifying. The scene's problematic nature is evident in the fact that neither film adaptation of the novel chooses to include it, despite its crucial plot and thematic points. I refer, of course, to the scene in which eleven-year-old Beverly Marsh has sex with the six male members of the Losers' Club, all of a similar age to her, one after the other, to facilitate their escape from It's lair. During the scene, Bev has a revelation about the girls with whom she goes to school:

> she realizes that for many of them sex must be some unrealized undefined monster; they refer to the act as It. Would you do It, do your sister and her boyfriend do It, do your mom and dad still do It, and how they never intend to do It; oh yes, you would think that the whole girls' side of the fifth-grade class was made up of spinsters-to-be, and it is obvious to Beverly that none of them can suspect this ... this conclusion [King, *It* 1102].

In this scene, King attempts to reclaim sex from the horrific, as suggested by the correlation between the association of the pronoun "it" with both the monstrous and the sexual, not merely in his novel, but in Western culture. In doing so, he faces a challenge comparable to that of Milton in *Paradise Lost* (1667), when he chose to attempt to depict prelapsarian sex from a postlapsarian perspective. As C.S. Lewis famously noted in *A Preface to Paradise Lost* (1942), Milton "has dared to represent Paradisal sexuality. I cannot make up my mind whether he was wise" (117). King has dared to represent pubescent sexuality, and many have wondered whether he was wise.

Scholars have rarely addressed this scene at all, let alone in detail, though Anthony Magistrale does note it as one of the few instances in King in which sexual activity "appears in the form of a salvation; it forms a preventative bond against evil," he notes, before continuing on to articulate the more common critical view of King's representations of sex "in a more negative light," in which it is "most often a manipulative, enticing force that pushes characters toward greater levels of depravity" (*The Moral Voyages of Stephen King* 43). Indeed, King's treatment of sex generally (not only in *It*), and of female sexuality especially, has been much-criticized, even by King himself, for his propensity, again to cite Magistrale, to repeatedly invoke the image of "woman's role as modern Eve: an amoral seductress devoted to perverting men"[1] (51). Yet sex, and even the gendered stereotypes about sex, are more complex in *It* than such statements as this suggest.

Consider, for instance, King's invocations of homosexuality in *It*. King's depiction of homosexuality has been much discussed and often found to be problematic, even homophobic, as for instance by Michael Collings, who finds what he perceives as the homophobia in *It* to be "more openly vicious" (23) than anywhere else in King's fiction prior to the publication of that novel. Less tendentiously, Heidi Strengell suggests that "Although King seemingly defends the homosexual Adrian Mellon of *It* against his bullying attackers, he would appear to be taking pains to avoid expressing a sense of distrust" (41)—that is, King's ostensibly positive depiction is colored by (Strengell's sense of) King's own discomfort with homosexuality; however, King has noted that the homophobic murder in the novel is, in fact, based on a real incident that occurred in Bangor. It depicts a homophobia with undeniable real-world resonance. Furthermore, while one might object to the stereotypical depiction of homosexuality in *It* and elsewhere in King's work—and Collings, among others, do—it is perhaps worth noting that King's queer characters are arguably not significantly more stereotyped than any of his other characters.

More significantly, at least in *It*, non-heteronormative sexuality is clearly represented not as an inherently negative thing in itself (e.g., from a homophobic perspective on the level of the narrative), nor is one's sexuality even a necessary component in one being victimized by It. Rather, homophobia is itself one of the many manifestations in the novel of how fear of that which is other is explicitly the monstrous perspective. As Douglas Keesey has argued, "It [the monster] tries to project Its fear of Otherness onto specific others because others can be eliminated" (74), with homosexuals simply being one such group. And It does so by exploiting and arguably encouraging and enhancing the latent fears of any other already present in the townsfolk. The novel also associates the racist burning of the Black Spot club, and the targeting of African Americans in general with It, not to mention the massacre of the Bradley Gang (outlaws being by definition outsider/others) and the Losers' Club (notably, another club for outsiders, like the Black Spot, one of whose members is the son of one of the Black Spot soldiers) itself, made up as it is of social outcasts banded together and announcing their marginal status even in the name they assign themselves, as well as in the space they claim for themselves, the Barrens, literally the place where Derry casts off its waste product.

A homosexual filling the role of the ostracized Other, and being murdered as a result, is the first narrative fact of the novel, after its prologue detailing It's murder of Georgie. Juxtaposed are the inarguably horrific slaughter of a child with the ostensibly problematic depiction of Adrian Mellon's murder. Adrian's overt sexuality is explicitly the reason for which he is targeted and murdered—or, more precisely, John "Webby" Gardner's outrage at what he reads as Adrian's attack on his own sexuality: "'He called me a queer!'"[2] (King, *It* 23). Adrian, in fact, did no such thing, but "Webby" is so invested in his heteronormative identity that even an implied threat to it by an effeminized man is enough to push him to murder. Adrian's partner, Don, is viewed, even by the police, as ambiguously male at best: "This man—if you want to call him a man—was wearing lipstick and satin pants so tight you could almost read the wrinkles in his cock" (17), a description that blurs conventional gender markers; even the clearly perceptible penis has vaginal implications, given that it is defined by visible wrinkles.

Profoundly ironic is that Adrian loved Derry; whereas, his partner, Don Hagarty, is all too aware of Derry's hateful underbelly. Indeed, another club, albeit an unofficial one, Derry's gay bar, the Falcon, is important here, as well. The reality of the bar—a place "no different than thousands of workingmen's bars all across the country" (26–27), so much so that for several years its owner does not even twig to the fact that his clientele is gay—is perceived as a den of sexual depravity, where you could go in there any night and see men close-dancing, rubbing their cocks together right out on the dancefloor; men french-kissing at the bar; men getting blowjobs in the bathrooms. There was supposedly a room out back where you went if you wanted to spend

> a little time on the Tower of Power—there was a big old fellow in a Nazi uniform back there who kept his arm greased most of the way to the shoulder and who would be happy to take care of you [26].

One might recall the extravagant accusations leveled at Clara Bow. The real den of depravity, though, is Derry itself, which is evident to at least some of the Others, but not to the supposedly upstanding citizens. Don Hagarty, the homosexual man viewed even by the police out to nail the young men responsible for murdering Adrian with contempt, is the one who first articulates the truth about Derry, first figuratively—"'It's a lot like a dead strumpet with maggots squirming out of her cooze'" (28), a grotesque and horrific image of Derry as a place in which sex and death coalesce—and then more literally: "'It's a *bad* place,' Hagarty said. 'It's a sewer. You mean you two guys don't *know* that? You two guys have lived here all of your lives and you don't *know* that?'" (28). Hagarty is hereby allied with the other ostracized victims who can perceive more clearly than the general citizenry how It's presence has tainted the place. Even those ostensibly on the side of law and justice have been tainted; late in the novel we are told that Chief Rademacher "really believed he had tried his best to solve the new string of child-murders that had plagued Derry" (1053). It is insidious; It gets into It's victims and It's vessels, and It pushes their fears and desires (even the unacknowledged and unrecognized ones) to twist them to It's will. And sex and sexuality are frequently elements therein, as in It's exploitation of homophobia, presented so prominently by homophobia's importance early in the novel. It is perhaps unsurprising that King's cunning representation of homophobia as monstrous can be read as a depiction of homosexuality as monstrous.

Later in the novel (though chronologically earlier), Henry Bowers and his gang are similar to "Webby" as malign manifestations of male sexual aggression and anxiety. Though Henry has many reasons (from his point of view, anyway), to hate Ben Hanscom, part of why Ben is othered is that his fat body feminizes him. His excessive bulk has given him prominent breasts, prompting others to insult him by calling him "tits," first by Peter Gordon (176) but later and more significantly by Henry Bowers, multiple times immediately preceding and during his violent and phallic attack on Ben: "'Hi, Tits,' Henry said" (197). The capitalization here, in contrast to Peter Gordon's earlier use of the epithet, transforms the word into a proper noun. Henry is transforming Ben, linguistically, into a female form, defined by the most notably evident signals of the female form, breasts (significantly, Bev Marsh's breasts are a focus of attention not only to Tom Rogan but also when she is an adolescent, notably in the scene in which she literally loses her shirt, as markers of her incipient sexual maturity). The epithet is repeated several times, reinforcing that for Henry and the other bullies, Ben is not merely a victim but a feminized victim. Consequently, the attack has overtones of rape. For instance, "Henry stepped forward until his flat stomach almost touched Ben's belly" (198), at which point he pulls out from his pants his "long and wide" blade and the "tip glittered in the afternoon sunshine" (198). Shortly afterwards, we read, "They were close enough to kiss" (199), while Ben feels the point of Henry's weapon "dimpling his flesh" (199). Linda Anderson and Antony Magistrale have both argued that the climactic sex scene involving Bev and the six male Losers "comes to resemble a gang rape"[3] (*America's Storyteller* 131), an odd claim even on the face of it since it is clear that Beverly initiates the sex and the boys are reluctant, but even more surprising given the far more obvious analogue to attempted gang rape in this scene with Ben: two boys holding one victim while a third taunts the victim, promises to teach the victim a lesson, tears the victim's shirt open to expose the breasts, and threatens to penetrate that victim with an overtly phallic weapon. This far more clearly suggests gang rape, but that parallel has not been noted.

The association of masculinity with violent and especially sexually violent threat is, of course, no surprise in the work of Stephen King. As Magistrale has noted, "Violent sexual predators roam the landscapes of Stephen King's universe, and they are invariably male" (*America's Storyteller* 86). In *It*, this is complicated by the fact that It is gendered female. King's sexual predators may be male, but as many commentators have noted, women generally are often just as monstrous (some would argue more monstrous) in King; King himself has identified the *vagina dentata* as a personal terror, and "Monstrous and physically large women frequently people King's fiction" (Strengell 49). Eddie Kaspbrak's mother in *It* is a particularly relevant example here, as she is not only one of King's stereotypically fat women but is explicitly associated with It by Eddie. When he is hospitalized with his broken arm, he has a shocking revelation when looking at his mother: "a terrible thought came to him: those eyes were almost predatory, like the eyes of the leper that had crawled out of the basement at 29 Neibolt Street" (King, *It* 800). Shortly afterwards, he thinks, "*She's not the leper, please don't think that, she's only eating me because she loves me*" (801). The leper was the manifestation of It that Eddie experienced—Itself offering a threat of homosexual sexual consumption in It's offer to provide oral sex. Here Eddie does not want to face the reality of his mother's monstrosity; indeed, in a way, he never escapes his mother, as his wife, Myra, is a sort of doppelgänger of his mother. Before marrying Myra, Eddie places a picture of his mother (from her younger days, before her final years, when she "had become something nearly monstrous" [92] in her excessive bulk—a literalization of her moral monstrosity) beside one of Myra:

> He had made that comparison, he supposed, in a last-ditch effort to stop himself from committing psychological incest. He looked from Mother to Myra and back again to Mother.
> They could have been sisters. The resemblance was that close.
> Eddie looked at the two nearly identical pictures and promised himself he would not do this crazy thing. He knew that the boys at work were already making jokes about Jack Sprat and his wife, but they didn't know the half of it. The jokes and snide remarks he could take, but did he really want to be a clown in such a Freudian circus as this? [92].

That Eddie's involvement with his mother is complicated by a love tainted not only with possessiveness but incestuous undertones is evident. Eddie's thought of a clown here can't help but remind us of the connection to the horror in Derry, as Pennywise has already been established as the key manifestation of It. In a way, Eddie does not really escape the monster, still living with a version of his mother, one who manipulates Eddie much as his mother did, with the added benefit of being able to have a sexual relationship with him, a literalization of the corrupted possessiveness that lurks behind Eddie's mother's control over him, and his subservience to her.

But the femaleness of the monster is further complicated by the fact that the avatars It takes in the novel, whether mental projections (the various monster forms It takes to terrify the children) or actual humans It twists to It's will, notably Henry Bowers and Tom Rogan, but also Bev Marsh's father, are almost invariably male. It may be sexed female, but It is predominantly gendered male in the novel. The specifically sexual nature of the threat It represents, thereby, has already been noted, in relation to Henry Bowers, but Tom Rogan, the adult Beverly Marsh's husband, is also clearly akin to It, even before he becomes an agent of It. As Magistrale has argued, Bev is "the only member of the [Losers'] club whose childhood has continued to influence her adulthood to the point where she actually marries the monster" (*America's Storyteller*, 129). Though this assertion perhaps underrates Eddie's marriage to a version of his mother, Myra is less obviously horrific than is Tom and also disappears from the novel, so any associations she may have with It are less developed.

While Eddie's relationship with his mother has implicit sexual elements, Bev's with her father is more overtly sexually dangerous. Al Marsh's incestuous desire for his daughter is hinted at in several ways, notably in the "predatory concern" (King, *It* 401) he has about her emergent sexuality and whether she has been "doing something [she] shouldn't be doing, [...] something with some boy" (569), and his equation of his wife and his daughter in his comments at work: "*I got all the women* [note the plural] *I need at home*, he said on occasion, and when he said it a peculiar secretive smile would cross his face—it did not brighten it but did quite the opposite. Watching that smile was like watching the shadow of a cloud travel rapidly across a rocky field. *They take care of me, and when they need it, I take care of them*" (401). One might read into this statement, if taken in isolation, merely a hint at Marsh's physical abuse, rather than a hint of sexual abuse, but even here the representation of Bev as one of the women at home is disturbing. More explicit is Bev's mother's question, "'Bevvie, does he ever touch you?'" (409), a question that baffles Beverly, because, of course, "her father touched her every *day*" (409). Beverly's bafflement at the question tells us that however Al might touch his daughter he has not—yet—touched her in the ominous way hinted at by this question. Yet, assuming we can take It's word for it when It assumes the form of Al Marsh during the adult Bev's visit to her former home, Marsh's taboo concern for his daughter was in fact incestuous:

"'I beat you because I wanted to FUCK you, Bevvie, that's all I wanted to do, I wanted to FUCK you, I wanted to EAT you, I wanted to eat your PUSSY, I wanted to SUCK your CLIT up between my teeth, YUM-YUM, Bevvie, oooohhhhh, YUMMY IN MY TUMMY, I wanted to put you in the cage ... and get the oven hot ... and feel your CUNT ... your plump CUNT ... and when it was plump enough to eat ... to eat... EAT...'" [580].

Interestingly, the Al Marsh figure has morphed out of the elderly Mrs. Kersh, the only female avatar for It of any significance, and one that deliberately blurs questions of It's sexual identity. Though as Linda Anderson (among others) has noted, a "common element of nearly all of Its manifestations is that they are explicitly defined as male" (111), the climactic revelation about It is that it is biologically female, as reflected in Audra Denbrough's horrified thought "*OH DEAR JESUS IT IS FEMALE*" (King, *It* 1032). This revelation of sexual identity has led many to read It as an iteration of the female as monstrous Other and King's predilection for depicting female monstrosity does not discourage such a reading; however, I am not sure that such a reading is sensitive to the nuances of the novel. The scene in which Bev encounters It as her father explicitly creates a collision between It as male (Al Marsh) and female (Mrs. Kersh), and an inversion of clichés about invasion, when It announces, "'I have come to rob all the women ... rape all the men'" (King, *It* 581). More significantly, even biological reproduction becomes blurred (both in terms of parental sex and in terms of the orifice from which one is born). As Mrs. Kersh transforms herself into various iterations of It, she provides a sort of genealogy, first imaging herself as the child of the father, Pennywise the clown, also known as Bob Gray, who "'bore me rather than my mutter. He shat me from his asshole!'" (579). Shortly afterward, she redefines herself: "'my fadder and I are one'" (579). This equation of parent and child gets transformed later into "*my fadder was also my mudder*" (1012), as Beverly remembers Mrs. Kersh's transformation. Whether Bev is misremembering and creating the equation of father and mother (as the shift from "mutter" to "mudder" might suggest), or whether this passage extends the idea of It's sexuality to embrace both the masculine and feminine is perhaps subject to debate. Certainly, the predominant sense of the pregnant It we encounter in the final battle, and Thoens's argument that It's final defeat takes the form of a violent sexual act (tall thin bald Bill—short for William, which can also be abbreviated as Willy, a slang term for a penis—thrusting himself into the amorphous mass of the creature) seems impossible to resist (see Thoens 138). Nevertheless, the simple binary of male or female seems reductive.

It is not, I would argue, a simple version of the monstrous female Other. Similarly, though critics repeatedly read Bev as an equally simplistic idealized female symbol, there is more to her. Admittedly, King himself has suggested that she functions as a "symbolic conduit between adulthood and childhood for the boys" (qtd. in Thoens 136). Thoens has concluded from King's statement that Bev's function is conditioned by her relationship to males: "female sexuality functions as a male rite of passage" (136). Similarly, Magistrale has asserted that Bev's contribution to the defeat of It "is strictly sexual" (*America's Storyteller* 131). Anderson also argues that Bev's function is merely to be the "good mother" (118) while the male figures do all the work: "her part in both battles is limited to encouraging and comforting her male companion" (119). This is simply inaccurate. While Bev certainly does fall into many stereotypes, and while King disturbingly focuses far more frequently on her incipient maturation than one would expect in descriptions of an eleven-year-old girl (references to, and exposure of, her budding breasts, as well as her legs and panties, are uncomfortably frequent), and while one can lament (as many have) that she grows up into an adult who ends up in an abusive relationship, in effect reliving her childhood trauma with husband Tom Rogan a substitute both for her father and for It, she is more than a damsel in distress.

Key to the first (partial) defeat of It is Bev's facility with childhood toys that can assume symbolic weight or become weapons—or both (itself a recurrent King motif). She first impresses Richie with her facility with a yoyo—a circular object that functions by gliding out on a string only to be drawn back to its beginning point by the skillful manipulation of the person holding the yoyo. While this is not the only factor in her entrée into the Losers' Club, it is a significant element. More significant, though, is her facility with Bill's slingshot. Bev, not Bill, is the one able to use Bill's weapon against It. Henry's knife is an obvious phallic symbol. I would contend that a slingshot is even more so. A slingshot consists of a rigid shaft several inches long with a pocket attached by rubber thongs to a y-shaped prong at one end. One places projectiles into the pocket and fires the projectiles by placing tension on the rubber thongs and then releasing. The rigid shaft with a pocket holding projectiles (and in *It* these are explicitly described as balls) is irresistibly reminiscent of a tumescent penis.

Beverly uses this weapon twice, in the first confrontation with It, but also in an earlier encounter with one of It's lesser manifestations, in a scene that yet again emerges out of a complex sexual scenario. Bev happens upon Henry Bowers and some of his friends lighting their farts in the Barrens. She sees them with their pants down: "she could see their *things*. They were the first *things* she had ever seen" (King, *It* 826), which arouses complex and confusing desires in her, as she recognizes that Bill also has one of those things but also fears what might happen if Henry knows what she has seen: "Suppose he did something to her with his *thing?* Suppose he wanted her to put it in her somewhere?" (833). Note the shift here, as the thing becomes it, suggesting that Henry's penis can be linked with the monster. Like "it," "thing" is a word with a highly flexible function, as a substitute for objects (especially unknown and, therefore, possibly frightening ones: like "it," "thing" often represents the monster in horror titles, perhaps most famously in the 1951 film classic *The Thing from Another World*) and also as a euphemism, as is evident here. "It" is the euphemism for sex, "thing" genitals, more frequently male ones than female. The scene progresses to present a sexual encounter between Henry and Patrick Hockstetter, in which Patrick masturbates Henry, attention Henry initially enjoys until the realization that he is engaging in homosexual behavior sinks in. Henry is as horrified by the possibility as was "Webby," and Bev recognizes that the danger she is in may be mortal as a result of what she has seen.

However, she avoids being seen. Instead, she witnesses Patrick's death, when he is killed by vampiric insectile creatures with obvious phallic associations. The creature has a beaklike protuberance (reminiscent perhaps of the giant bird that earlier attacked Mike), "but this beak was not flat or pointed; it was tubular and blunt, like the proboscis of a mosquito" (845). It penetrates Patrick, draining his blood but also emitting another fluid when it withdraws from his flesh, "some yellowish-white liquid like pus" (845)—or, one cannot help but think, semen. The threatening "things" of the boys are transformed into the destructive penile proboscis of these vampiric creatures. One manages to attack Bev, but she is able to slay it with the slingshot. Beverly's agency, especially her ability to use a masculine tool against a masculine threat, is key here.

This agency is also key to the initial defeat of It. While the encounter in the sewers primarily involves Bill as the hero who grapples with It, the first encounter, which wounds It and drives It back underground, has as its key agent Bev. While she is unable to kill It in It's werewolf form, she is able to wound It, an achievement that weakens It and, therefore, contributes to the ultimate victory. Bev is also instrumental in the escape after the defeat of It, albeit, very differently, via the group sex scene. Reading Bev here merely as a passive agent whose function is simply to allow the transition into adulthood for the male characters (even if King himself has encouraged such a reading) seems reductive. We are reminded of the earlier "thing" scene, when Bev initiates the sequence by telling Eddie, "'*You have to put your thing in me*'" (1098), but, whereas, then the "thing" was a complex and problematic agent of destruction, it is here transformed into a bridge. The connection is not necessarily that of adult consummation—Stan evidently does not have an orgasm, Eddie apparently does, but without ejaculating, Bev does not achieve orgasm with each boy—but more importantly the intercourse is clearly not a connection associated with lust or domination, or any of the other monstrous ways that It has manipulated the emotions of It's victims. The act is love and desire, stripped of the complex burdens of adulthood. It is, in effect, an attempt at depicting sex as innocent, possessed of all the power and significance of sexuality but with none of its adult complications. This sex is literally sterile (and indeed, none of the Losers grow up to have children) but emotionally and morally rich. It confirms the purity of the child's love. And it does so through Bev's active agency. While seeing the power of the woman as sexual is indeed a cliché, and while Bev is unable to retain the agency she achieves here in her adult life, the scene is one in which Bev's active agency, not her passive victimhood, is crucial. Sex is not something done to her; it is something she does *with* those she loves, and she does it by choice. It opens possibilities, most immediately to escape from the underworld in which they are trapped.[4] That what it achieves cannot itself survive the transition to adulthood—not only the boys, but also Bev, forget the incident—it can restore what had been lost, temporarily closing the circle. That circle cannot be fully closed until It is completely destroyed, but it also could never be closed without the sexual intervention of Bev Marsh. Doing "it" is essential to doing It in.

Notes

1. For detailed discussions of the problematic depiction of women in King's work, see Burns and Kanner, as well as several essays in Lant and Thomson's *Imagining the Worst: Stephen King and the Representation of Women*, which includes two essays on sexuality in *It*. Heidi Strengell has noted that such readings can be reductive; for instance, she finds "it rather odd that [Linda] Anderson takes the domestic violence of the fathers for granted and accuses the mothers of their inability to protect their children" (176).

2. The nickname "Webby" signals John Gardner's link with *It*. "Webby" is the first human avatar for It that we meet. It manifests in It's most "real" form as a gigantic spider. Weaving was traditionally seen as a female occupation; spider monsters having female associations is common, with Shelob in Tolkien's *The Lord of the Rings* as perhaps the most obvious example.

3. Linda Anderson asserts that the group sex scene "is irresistibly reminiscent of gang-rape" (118), Tony Magistrale that it "comes to resemble a gang rape" (*America's Storyteller* 131). Such readings speak to the preconceptions of the readers, not to the reality of the scene. Indeed, Loren Rosson has argued that "what Beverly is doing in the sewer orgy amounts to rape" (1).

4. Bev's sexual acts with the boys echo her ability to send the yoyo out on the string and then bring it home, in the trick called Around the World (also a sexual slang term) that she taught Richie and that is recalled in his contribution to the killing of It when he metaphorically bites into It's tongue as "Richie the Human Yo-Yo, and Its tongue was the string" (1080). Richie is able to Yo-Yo back because of what Bev taught him. The connection becomes clearer when her sexual link with Ben is imaged as "*a strong circle*" (1102) and then the symbol for eternity that allows them to "*break through into the lifelight*" (1103), in contrast to It's deadlights, before returning to the underworld from which they are trying to escape ... and now can.

Works Cited

Anderson, Linda. "'OH DEAR JESUS IT IS FEMALE': Monster as Mother/Mother as Monster in Stephen King's *It*." Lant and Thompson, pp. 111–25.

Burns, Gail E., and Melinda Kanner. "Women, Danger, and Death: The Perversion of The Female Principle in Stephen King's Fiction." *Sexual Politics and Popular Culture*, edited by Diane Raymond, Bowling Green State University Press, 1990, pp. 158–82.

Collings, Michael R. *The Stephen King Phenomenon*. Starmont, 1987.
Desjardins, Mary. "The Perils of 'It': Clara Bow, Experience, Agency, and the Scandalous Life Story." *Celebrity Studies* vol. 8, no.4, 2017, pp. 510–26.
Keesey, Douglas. "'The Face of Mr. Flip': Homophobia in the Horror of Stephen King." *Stephen King*, edited by Harold Bloom, Infobase, 2006, pp. 67–82.
King, Stephen. *It*. 1986. Scribner's, 2016.
Lant, Kathleen Margaret, and Theresa Thompson, editors. *Imagining the Worst: Stephen King and the Representation of Women*. Greenwood Press, 1998.
Lewis, C.S. *A Preface to Paradise Lost*. 1942. Atlantic, 2005.
Magistrale, Anthony. *The Moral Voyages of Stephen King*. Starmont, 1989.
_____. *Stephen King: America's Storyteller*. ABC-CLIO, 2010.
Rosson, Lauren. "Stan Uris and the Sewer Orgy in Stephen King's *It*." *The Busybody*, 6 April 2017, rossonl.wordpress.com/2017/04/06/stan-uris-and-the-sewer-orgy-in-stephen-kings-it/comment-page-1/. Accessed 30 June 2019.
Strengell, Heidi. *Dissecting Stephen King: From the Gothic to Literary Naturalism*. University of Wisconsin Press, 2005.
Thoens, Karen. "*It*, A Sexual Fantasy." Lant and Thompson, pp. 127–40.

"The turtle can't help us"
Evil, Enchantment and the Magic of Faith in Stephen King's It

Gregory Stevenson

Religion and horror have a complicated relationship. Religion has long cast a suspicious eye towards the moral value of horror. The genre's frequent use of gratuitous sexuality, violence, the demonic, and borderline (if not outright) blasphemy has only lent fuel to the fire. For its part, horror is equally suspicious of the moral rectitude and efficacy of religion, frequently depicting religion as incompetent or ineffectual in the face of evil, or even as a source of evil itself. Yet horror and religion are far more closely related than is often acknowledged. Both typically deal in the same themes of redemption and judgment, despair and hope, good and evil, belief and unbelief. Perhaps more importantly, they share a similar worldview in that both religion and horror affirm that our mundane reality is not all there is. They both embrace the supernatural and the belief that there exist beings beyond our capacity to comprehend—and that some of them have sharp teeth.

This overlap between religion and horror explains an encounter that priest and novelist Andrew Greeley had with Stephen King at a cocktail party in New York, during which Greeley accused King of writing religious novels. Stephen King's reported response is instructive: "Of course I am," he said. "Most people don't believe me, but that's exactly what I'm doing" (Greeley 211). Could that be true? Is it possible that novels about vampires, rabid dogs, and haunted cars are actually religious novels? Could a novel about a demonic clown who enjoys eating little children really be a story about the value of faith?

Certainly, many Stephen King novels (*The Stand, Desperation, Revival*) incorporate religious themes and imagery or include characters with religious faith. But declaring something a "religious novel" requires more than the mere presence of religious elements. It's about perspective. Or, more accurately, it's about illumination. Does this work shine a light that allows us to see ourselves and our relation to the natural and, particularly, supernatural world around us with greater clarity? The biblical book of Revelation provides an example as its primary focus is to grant its audience a better understanding of themselves and their calling in light of both the social systems within which they live and the broader spiritual reality around them. In a nutshell, the book of Revelation situates its audience of seven churches within a supernatural conflict between good and evil in which evil has repeatedly manifested throughout history in various social institutions (the empires of Egypt, Babylon, and most notably Rome), leading to a final showdown. The story is heavily deterministic in that a divine force guides the action, an element that is reinforced by the symbolic importance of the number seven in the story. Ultimately evil is countered by an unlikely group of people who are powerless and weak according to the standards of worldly power but who combat evil by standing against it in faith (see Blount; Stevenson). Of course, everything I just stated about the book of Revelation is equally true of Stephen King's *It*. Although readers typically hail *The Stand* as King's most apocalyptic novel, a case can be made for *It* as equally representative of apocalyptic theology.

Apocalyptic theology presents evil in oppositional terms: good versus evil, light versus darkness, though with the assurance that good/God will win in the end. Such opposition is at the heart of *It* as well, yet the conflict exists to point us toward deeper truths rather than simply to depict the conquest of good over evil. Exploring those deeper truths involves examining the nature of evil and good in *It*, and, in particular, the way King guides his characters down the path towards victory and reveals the kind of "magic" required to defeat evil.

Evil Without, Evil Within

As a teenager, Stephen King reportedly collected scrapbooks full of newspaper clippings detailing the crimes of serial killers. When his mother became understandably concerned and asked him for an explanation, King replied, "I think there's evil out there. I want to know what it is, so when it comes, I can recognize it and get out of the way" (Blake). That is a notable insight for a teenager—the awareness that before one can combat (or, in this case, avoid) evil, one must first be able to recognize it. The recognition of evil, however, is a challenging task. For centuries, theologians, philosophers, and other great thinkers have wrestled with trying to define what counts as "evil." Is evil an external force with its own ontological existence (like the biblical figure of Satan) that actively seeks to corrupt and do harm, or is evil a more passive, internal privation—a sort of black hole of the soul? Is evil a spiritual reality or a fully human one? Is evil generated by social and environmental forces or is it genetic, ingrained in us from birth? This difficulty of generating a concrete definition for an abstract concept reveals that what we call "evil" resists easy categorization. King himself has long wrestled with this problem. In a 2014 interview with *Rolling Stone*, King stated, "I believe in evil, but all my life I've gone back and forth about whether or not there's an outside evil, whether or not there's a force in the world that really wants to destroy us, from the inside out, individually and collectively. Or whether it all comes from inside and that it's all part of genetics and environment" (Greene). Fortunately, when dealing with fiction, this difficulty is minimized as the depiction of evil need only make sense within the confines of that imagined world. At the same time, though, these fictional representations offer glimpses into an author's thinking on the role of evil in the non-fictional world. As such, part of the value of dark stories is their ability to provide recognition of evil in the real world by means of its fictional representation.

How is evil imagined in *It*? On one level, King presents his vision of evil in a way that fits comfortably within the apocalyptic conception of spiritual warfare between opposing entities: God vs. Satan or, in this case, It vs. the Turtle/the Other. The novel personifies evil as Pennywise the Dancing Clown, yet it is clear that this is an affectation masking a deeper reality, that of a being that is both primordial (as an alien entity having arrived in prehistoric times) and eternal (375, 723–728, 1008).[1] King draws some basic parallels between Pennywise and the Satan of Judeo-Christian theology, with Pennywise being referred to as "the devil" and once introducing itself as "Legion" in a nod to the demon Jesus encounters in Mark 5:9 (148, 190). Although Pennywise exists as a dualistic counterpart to some intangible force for good, that larger conflict is often muted, with Pennywise functioning independently (for the most part) in the world. Within Christian theology, the identity of Satan as some ethereal cosmic being locked in spiritual battle against God is of less significance than how that abstract conflict manifests concretely within human society. So also in *It*, the cosmic relationship between It and the Turtle/the Other serves as a backdrop to the more pressing issue of the interplay between good and evil within the flesh and blood characters. What matters most for King is not the metaphysical conceptions of evil on the cosmic stage, but how such evil plays out in the town of Derry, Maine.

Despite the cosmic and ancient origin of It, Stephen King focuses as much, if not more so, on the human and societal expressions of evil. People often unknowingly embrace what is called "the myth of pure evil," which involves accepting stereotypical conceptions of evil as obvious, unadulterated, and external to themselves, while viewing themselves as innocent and good

(Baumeister 72–73). Buying into this myth blinds us to the seductive, deceptive, and ordinary manifestations of evil. It becomes a means of absolving ourselves of our own complicity in evil. On one level, *It* might appear to justify the myth of pure evil in that evil appears as an external, demonic, and eternal entity, with the citizens of Derry its innocent victims; however, closer inspection reveals that though Pennywise may be the incarnation of evil in Derry—to the point that it can be claimed that the clown *is* Derry (34, 479)— this in no way absolves the citizens of responsibility for their complicity in its evil. In the novel, adults and adult institutions (police, courts, hospitals, etc.) are part of the problem. Adults don't see the clown and are blind to many of its tricks. They fail to believe those who report encounters with Pennywise, and when presented with evidence, find rational ways to explain it away. Even those adults who witness Pennywise in action, choose to stay silent. Bill acknowledges this truth when he declares that the adults "let it happen" (930). This depiction of adults and their institutions as ineffectual in the face of evil is part of a larger theme relating to the novel's contrast between adulthood and childhood (to be examined later), but one explanation is hinted at in the novel when Mike informs the others that despite all of the atrocities that occur in Derry, the town prospers (480–81), suggesting a sort of "deal with the devil." Trading blindness towards evil in favor of prosperity is one of the ways we engage in self-deception. When society turns a blind eye, for instance, towards its systemic racism in order to avoid rocking the boat and endangering continued prosperity, evil flourishes in that blind spot.

The novel presents It as an external, cosmic evil, but one that manifests within human social interaction and takes root in the human heart. Or, as Mike states, it "leaves Its marks on people," echoing the mark of the beast from Revelation (490). Though Pennywise's acts of destruction and gruesome murders of children are horrific, it is actually the *human* acts of violence that are most horrifying, from the hate-crime murder of Adrian Mellon to the racially-motivated burning of the Black Spot to child abuse. It is tempting to assign blame for such acts to the corrupting influence of It alone, essentially claiming "The Devil made me do it." But King won't let us off that easy. King's Derry may be a fictional town, but it is one that stands in for American society as a whole. Through Derry, King shines a reflective light on the human proclivity for evil, or, as Eddie reflects, "*Grownups are the real monsters*" (737). Though grownups may be the real monsters, Henry Bowers and the psychopathic Patrick Hockstetter, who murdered his baby brother, demonstrate that human monsters come in younger forms too.

This tension between an external evil and the internal impulse towards good or evil is in full force in *It*. Pennywise wields clear influence, yet the evil actions that occur cannot be ascribed solely to that influence. Pennywise works its will through the likes of Henry Bowers, Tom Rogan, or Bev's father only because they possess some innate quality or predilection that makes them fertile soil in which It's demonic seeds can grow. Evil flourishes in Derry because *people* are its willing co-conspirators. If the evil occurring in Derry was solely the result of Pennywise's domineering influence, then Pennywise should be able to work equally through Bill and his friends. That it cannot is a testimony to the nobility of their characters, as well as to an awareness that some other force is taking root in their lives.

The Turtle and the Other

Two significant features of apocalyptic theology are a dualistic conflict between opposing entities and a deterministic outlook in which some transcendent force guides the direction of certain events. For the Losers' Club (the band of seven who take their stand against Pennywise), there is a growing recognition that some outside force is guiding their steps, that at least in their lives, the balance between fate and freewill has tipped towards the former. References to themselves as "chosen" (347), to their path as "preordained" (515), to things that were "supposed" to happen (682, 709), or to events that "arranged themselves" (495, 581) reveal this growing awareness. But if they are not fully the masters of their own fate, who or what is guiding them?

Reflecting on events that facilitated his own involvement with the Losers' Club, Mike Hanlon writes, "If the wheels of the universe are in true, then good always compensates for evil" (428). The idea that good must balance evil in some fundamental way is a recurring theme in King's writings. The "good" in question here functions as a "counterforce" to the evil of Pennywise (709). In the cosmology of *It*, that counterforce remains somewhat undefined, represented simply as "the Turtle." Through vague foreshadowings and coincidental occurrences—Georgie finding an old can of Turtle Wax on the day he dies (8), Bill finding a discarded pair of Turtle sunglasses in a drawer (810), Ben thinking he sees the image of a turtle in a half-erased hopscotch grid (510)—the Turtle mostly remains a subtle presence, guiding without pushing. As Mike becomes increasingly aware of some invisible hand directing their lives, he begins referring to this divine guidance in terms of hearing "the voice of the Turtle," much as one might claim to hear the voice of God (141–42, 419, 877). Although at first glance the Turtle might be taken as a stand-in for God, particularly with it being described as "good," powerful, "kind," and the ancient creator of the world (1009–1010), it represents a kind of deistic conception of deity. The Turtle merely vomited the universe into existence and then retreated into its shell. The Turtle may be rooting for the Losers and may have created the world, but it is not the supreme power in King's cosmology. Witnessing to the Turtle's passive nature and ultimately ineffectual role is the repeated refrain uttered by Bill that "the Turtle can't help us" (143, 861). Perhaps the Turtle can't help, but might something else?

Rather than the Turtle, a closer approximation for God in King's cosmology is an all-powerful being referred to either as "Another" or "the Other." Contrasts with the Turtle highlight the supreme nature of the Other. The Turtle may have created the world, but the Other created the Turtle (1009). Though the Losers may have heard the "voice of the Turtle," it was the Other who invested the Turtle to speak (1048); whereas, It disdains the Turtle, It *fears* "Another" (972). While the Turtle took a passive role in the current conflict with Pennywise, telling Bill "I take no stand in these matters" (1009), the Other enlists the children as its "agents" (966), willing them to fight against evil and providing them the strength to conquer (1046).

The members of the Losers' Club are not mere pawns in some cosmic battle, but active participants in the fight against evil. Their role in this fight is one that fits well within the biblical theology of weakness. The theology of weakness is the notion that God typically chooses to work through individuals who are weak or insignificant by worldly standards (see Dawn; Ortlund). The self-proclaimed "Losers' Club," with their assortment of troubled home lives, handicaps (stuttering), physical and psychological (hypochondria) limitations, certainly fit the bill. When Mike compares the slugs they are making for their slingshot with the rock used by the child David in his battle against Goliath (814), he invokes a classic example of the theology of weakness. One reason for God relying upon the weak, upon the "losers" of the world, is that in their recognition of their own weakness, they see the need to be dependent on something greater than themselves, thus, allowing God to work through them.

The Losers exhibit dependence on an outside power in several ways. One is the use of prayer. Eddie prays for strength (89), while Mike prays for help (1002). Bev asks Mike to pray for her (101), while Bill prays for Audra (963). Even Stan's recitation of birds in his showdown with Pennywise functions as a sort of appeal to the divine, as evidenced by Eddie, Ben, and Bev comparing the action to saying the Lord's Prayer, reciting the 23rd Psalm, or holding up a cross (410). Faith is a form of magic all its own, not in the manipulative, ritualistic sense of spells and incantations, but in its connection to a transcendent power. Another way the novel emphasizes the Losers' connection to the divine is through its use of the Derry Theological Seminary. Two scenes in the novel take place on the grounds of this seminary and both represent moments when certain members of the Losers' Club find solace in religion. In the first, Bill and Richie have a conversation on the steps of the seminary about Bill's guilt over Georgie's death. Through this conversation, Bill finds a sort of forgiveness—a lessening of the burden of guilt he has been carrying (315–318). In the second scene, Bev is fleeing from her father after receiving a beating at his hands. Fearful that he will kill her, she runs to the grounds of the Derry Theological Seminary and hides behind a hedge, praying to God that her father will not locate her. She finds there the protection she seeks (873–74). By setting these scenes at the seminary, King, who is no great fan of organized religion, nonetheless, employs this setting as a means of highlighting the children's connection to and need for a higher power.

Despite their reliance on this higher power, the Losers are not mere empty vessels being used at the whim of the Divine. The tension between relying on God and relying on self is palpable in *It*. During the initial showdown with It, Bill pleads with the Turtle to help him. The Turtle replies that it cannot help, but that Bill must rely on himself and his friends (1010). The power of community, of friendship, in combatting evil is a prominent theme throughout the novel. Their hope for victory stems from their love for each other (669). Bill's mother recognizes power among the group (815). Mike reflects that they were able to defeat It the first time around because of their "group will" (492); furthermore, it is a power that transcends childhood. As adults they are able to stop the It-induced bleeding on their heads and later send their power to Mike in the hospital by holding hands in a circle (861–62, 1001).

The power of friendship and community is a form of magic in *It* as represented by the book's emphasis on the number seven. It is, in fact, only when Mike Hanlon joins their childhood group that they all view their community as complete because only then do they number seven (667). Within biblical literature, particularly the book of Revelation, the number seven holds great symbolic significance, especially as a representation of completeness and divine unity. In *It*, the grouping of *seven* individuals making up the Losers' Club signals that they are part of a larger plan, drawn together by some outside force to battle evil. Seven is "the magic number" (653, 711–12), and Richie notes that their grouping into this magic number was "supposed to be" (712). The creature It admits that it fears the *"mystical talismanic quality of seven"* (973) and so works to undo the group's *"bonding of seven"* (974). That this community of seven gains its power both from the love and faith that binds them and from the divine force that brought them together is evident when Eddie finally stands up to his domineering mother who, for the first time, is cowed by the power she sees in him, a power that she recognizes as coming both from his "friends" and from "something else" (763).

Mike Hanlon declares that "the source of power is faith" (855). This faith is forged by friendship and fueled by imagination. The combined power of these three forces (friendship, faith, and imagination), taken together, is what King, in this novel, calls "magic." In one self-reflective scene, Pennywise laments that it could have easily defeated the children one by one, but once they had bonded together, they learned that belief has "a second edge," the power of the imagination (974). Eddie expresses this connection between faith and power when he declares that all religions, which are based on faith, are "weird." Then, to himself, he thinks, "But *powerful* [...] almost *magical*" (921). If good and evil are in conflict in *It*, by what magic is victory achieved? What roles do faith and imagination play in achieving that victory? King's answer to these questions has repercussions not only for the world of *It*, but for our own world as well.

Adulthood and Enchantment

A common topic among theologians today is the re-enchantment of the world. This discussion revolves around the changing of worldviews and the significance of those changes for how people define reality and truth. In what's called the pre-modern world (prior to the Enlightenment of the 18th century), the world was an enchanted place. It was a world infused with belief in the supernatural, a world that was comfortable with mystery and the unknown. Magic, demons, miracles—though not ever-present—were at least *possible*. It was, in essence, a worldview characterized by *revelation*, by the belief that the divine reveals itself and reveals spiritual truth in this world in many ways.

As the dominant worldview in the west began to shift in the 1500s and 1600s, culminating with the Enlightenment, it brought about a fundamental change in how people viewed the nature of reality. Rationalism replaced revelation as the dominant mode governing the world. Rather than divine revelation providing access to truth, the human capacity to discern truth objectively and to solve the world's problems through the application of reason became the primary focus. Science, technology, and empirical data served as the basis for defining what is and is not possible. The acceptance of rationalism as the sole basis for defining reality led to a rejection of whatever might be deemed irrational. In this "modern" worldview, there remained no place for the supernatural, the miraculous, or a cosmology populated with spiritual beings, whether benevolent or demonic. This was not a wholesale transfer, as there continued to be segments of the population, particularly though not exclusively religious folk, who held onto aspects of a pre-modern outlook. But by and large, the modern worldview jettisoned the supernatural and the spiritual as irrational and instead confined reality to what can be measured, recorded, investigated, and calculated. Max Weber used the phrase "disenchantment of the world" (*Entzauberung der Welt*) to describe this shift, with "disenchantment," as a translation of the German word *Entzauberung*, meaning "losing its magic" (Weber, *Protestant Ethic* 53, 118, n. 22; Sherry 369).[2] For Weber, the modern world with its emphasis on human rationality had become a mundane place where there are "no mysterious incalculable forces" at work (Weber, "Science" 139).

Just as the rationalistic modern worldview rejected the pre-modern worldview of revelation and supernaturalism, the current trend (termed "postmodern" by some) involves a rejection of the modern worldview of rationalism and science as the sole basis of truth (Sherry 377). The human capacity for evil (genocide, terrorism, racism, etc.) exposed the flaw in "making the human references of scientism, rationalism and liberalism the ground for a just and humane world" (Baron 117). The recognition of rationalism's failure to solve the world's problems and to provide access to objective truth resulted in what many theologians and others call the re-enchantment of the world. This is an attempt to restore, in a sense, the "magic" to the world through an acceptance of spirituality, an awareness of the transcendent and supernatural as categories of reality, an embrace of mystery, and a return to imagination (Baron 116).

The manner in which Stephen King's *It* addresses childhood and adulthood bears striking similarities to this movement from enchantment to disenchantment to re-enchantment. For King the time of childhood corresponds closely with a pre-modern outlook on the world. Childhood is a time when one's ability to accept mystery and the unseen is most acute. The young are capable of squeezing much more into their worldview, as Ben Hanscom notes when he realizes that he can live with the horror that occurred in the house on Neibolt St. because "[t]he world was, after all, full of wonders" (839). A child's world is an enchanted one, full of magic, faith, and imagination. One reason Pennywise targets children is because, as Mike says, Pennywise feeds on faith and "who is more capable of a total act of faith than a child?" (855). For the seven Losers, it is their wide-open belief in the "magic" of the world, coupled with the untamable imagination of children, that gives them the power to stand against It. The reason why Richie is able to hurt It by doing voices (353), why Stan can defeat It by reciting birds (410), why Eddie could stop It by pretending his aspirator held acid (990), and why their silver slug worked on the werewolf form of It (837) was because they had invested these things with power through their imagination and faith. They defeated It as children because they *believed* (1012–1013).

Just as King paints childhood as a time of enchantment, he depicts adulthood as a time of disenchantment. In the movement from the premodern to the modern world, the Enlightenment represented a form of growing up and casting off of the naïve beliefs of childhood. King represents this transition from childhood to adulthood as a transition from magic to mundanity. The rationalistic mindset of adults blinds them to the magic in the world. In the novel, the adult Ben notes that children implicitly believe in the invisible and in miracles; whereas, adults become incapable of handling anything "beyond rational explanation" (510). Mike adds that when faced with something that defies "rational explanation," adults ignore it (681). It is this lack of imagination and the unwillingness to believe in mystery that keeps adults blind to the true face of evil in *It,* because evil is often mysterious and defies rational explanation. As a young Stephen King acknowledged, if you can't first recognize evil, you can't fight it.

Throughout *It*, a lack of belief and imagination characterizes adulthood and weakens their ability to confront evil. The Turtle had urged the child Bill, after his confrontation with Pennywise, to ensure that Pennywise was truly dead because *"what can be done when you're eleven can often never be done again"* (1013). The adult Bill later concludes that maybe this is why Stan killed himself, because he understood that the magic won't work for adults (492). Similarly, the adult Mike reflects back on their childhood showdown with Pennywise and concludes that when kids grow up, they either lose their capacity for faith or become "crippled by a sort of spiritual and imaginative arthritis" (855). He writes that it was the power of their belief that kept them alive and he is not sure that adults have that ability (892). This is why Pennywise was so eager to call them all back after twenty-seven years because it knew that, as adults, their worldview would have narrowed and their faith in the magic have worn off (855). Because adults believe only in mundane things, Pennywise felt assured of victory (975).

Due to this stark contrast, it's an easy move to characterize the novel as simply prioritizing the faith and imagination of childhood over the rationalism of adulthood. Such a move would miss the vital role that adults play in the novel (Mercer 315). I would argue that the novel is actually more about the adults than the children. After all, despite the novel's depiction of adults as blind and ineffectual in the face of evil and as devoid of faith and imagination due to an embrace of rationalism, it is, nonetheless, the *adult* Losers who ultimately defeat It. King's novel is about explaining how. What makes *these* adults different from the others? What gives them the power to defeat the monster? The answer lies in King's version of re-enchantment.

If adulthood is a time of disenchantment due to the embrace of a rationalistic mindset that forgoes imagination and mystery, for the adult Losers to defeat It, they must re-enchant their world. They must move from mundanity back to magic by reclaiming their childhood faith and imagination. According to Pennywise, Bill is the most powerful of the Losers because, as a writer, he had regularly trained his imagination, keeping those childhood muscles in shape (975). Yet, even then, the ravages of time and adulthood had taken its toll so that Bill himself realizes that to defeat Pennywise, he must become a child again and re-learn how to believe (1005). Likewise, the adult Eddie feels his childhood belief return when he once again pretends his inhaler is filled with acid (1023). Only by reclaiming the belief in things unseen, by regenerating their imagination, and by re-forging the bonds of friendship can the adult Losers defeat the monster. As Bill acknowledges, the force that empowers their adult versions to win is the "force of love and unforgotten childhood" (1046).

Stephen King's *It* is a reminder that the world needs faith, friendship, and imagination; that to face the evils in this world, we need *that* kind of magic. King essentially argues for a re-enchantment of the world through the reclamation of a sense of wonder and imagination that best characterizes childhood. In so doing, he challenges the modern embrace of rationality as the sole basis of truth by questioning which view of the world is in fact most rational: that of a mundane world devoid of mystery and spirituality or one that humbly acknowledges possibilities beyond our rational comprehension. At the end of the novel, King writes that life teaches us *"that there are so many happy endings that the man who believes there is no God needs his rationality called into serious question"* (1087).

Horror and fantasy are closely related genres, with horror lurking in the dark corners of fantasy; whereas, horror is often viewed as a genre best suited for adults, fantasy is frequently denigrated as being better suited for children. Two seminal writers of fantasy literature vehemently disagree with this assessment. Both J.R.R. Tolkien and C.S. Lewis argue that fantasy literature is more appropriate for adults than children (Tolkien 45–47; Lewis 59–60). Tolkien argues that "fairy-stories," the term he uses that approximates the fantasy genre, offer "these things: Fantasy, Recovery, Escape, Consolation, all things of which children have, as a rule, less need than older people" (46). Older people have become disenchanted, having lost the sense of wonder, faith, and mystery that children possess. Consequently, they need the magic more. For Tolkien, the function of Fantasy is "Enchantment" (53). Fantasy restores magic to the mundane world. It accomplishes this by providing, in particular, Recovery and Consolation. Recovery is the regaining of a clear view of things, which allows us to see the wonder in the world around us with fresh eyes (57), while Consolation provides us with a "glimpse of the underlying reality or truth," which, for Tolkien, included an echo of the Gospel story (71). Horror shares with fantasy this ability to provide glimpses of deeper truths, to open our eyes to the unseen, and to re-orient our perspective towards the potential for magic in the world. Apocalyptic literature (which shares many elements in common with both horror and fantasy) functions in a similar way by pushing its audience to view their social situation from a transcendent perspective and to face it with the power of faith.

Interestingly, many theologians and scholars who address the re-enchantment of the world argue that one of the primary means by which this occurs today is through popular culture and art (Baron 117; Sherry 382–84; Graham; Partridge 243). Artistic and aesthetic endeavors widen our eyes to greater possibilities in the world and foster belief and imagination. Stephen King's novel *It* is one such artistic endeavor. For all its nostalgic reminiscences of childhood, it is a book that is really for adults—to remind them not to lose sight of the magic in a sea of mundanity. The value of great horror is that it offers a reminder that the world is a mysterious, if fearful, place and that there are forces at work beyond our rational comprehension. Stephen King's *It* further reveals that though the unknown and unseen may be frightening, it can be comforting as well. *It* can adequately be termed a religious novel in this broader sense because the novel reveals that in the midst of the evil and horrors of the world, there is hope born of faith and imagination. When we re-learn to embrace those, the world once again becomes a magical place.

Notes

1. All references and quotations from the novel come from Stephen King, *It*. Signet, 1986.
2. Weber focused on the effects of rationalization for devaluing the role of religion.

Works Cited

Baron, Craig A. "Christian Theology and the Re-enchantment of the World." *Crosscurrents*, vol. 56, no. 4, 2007, pp. 112–123.
Baumeister, Roy F. *Evil: Inside Human Violence and Cruelty*. Henry Holt, 1997.
Blake, John. "The Gospel of Stephen King." *CNN Belief Blogs*, 2 June 2012, http://religion.blogs.cnn.com/2012/06/02/the-gospel-of-stephen-king/.
Blount, Brian K. *Can I Get a Witness? Reading Revelation through African American Culture*. Westminster John Knox, 2005.
Cowan, Douglas E. *America's Dark Theologian: The Religious Imagination of Stephen King*. NYU Press, 2018.
Dawn, Marva J. *Powers, Weakness, and the Tabernacling of God*. Eerdmans, 2001.
Friesen, Steven J. "Myth and Symbolic Resistance in Revelation 13. *Journal of Biblical Literature*, vol. 123, no. 2, 2004, pp. 281–313.
Graham, Gordon. *The Re-enchantment of the World: Art versus Religion*. Oxford University Press, 2007.
Greeley, Andrew M. *God in Popular Culture*. Thomas More Press, 1988.
Greene, Andy. "Stephen King: The Rolling Stone Interview." *Rolling Stone*, 31 October 2014, www.rollingstone.com/culture/culture-features/stephen-king-the-rolling-stone-interview-191529.
King, Stephen. *It*. Signet, 1986.
Kraybill, J. Nelson. *Apocalypse and Allegiance: Worship, Politics, and Devotion in the Book of Revelation*. Brazos, 2010.
Lewis, C.S. "Sometimes Fairy Stories May Say Best What's to Be Said." *Of Other Worlds: Essays and Stories*, Reissue edition, HarperOne, 2017, pp. 55–60.
Mercer, Erin. "The Difference Between World and Want: Adulthood and the Horrors of History in Stephen King's *IT*." *The Journal of Popular Culture*, vol. 52, no. 2, 2019, pp. 315–329.
Ortlund, Dane. "'Power is Made Perfect in Weakness' (2 Cor. 12:9): A Biblical Theology of Strength Through Weakness." *Presbyterion*, vol. 36, 2010, pp. 86–108.
Partridge, Christopher. "The Disenchantment and Re-enchantment of the West: The Religio-Cultural Context of Contemporary Western Christianity." *Evangelical Quarterly*, vol. 74, no. 3, 2002, pp. 235–256.
Sherry, Patrick. "Dis-Enchantment, Re-enchantment, and Enchantment." *Modern Theology*, vol. 25, no. 3, 2009, pp. 369–386.

Stevenson, Gregory. *A Slaughtered Lamb: Revelation and the Apocalyptic Response to Evil and Suffering*. Abilene Christian University Press, 2013.

Tolkien, J.R.R. "On Fairy-Stories." *Tree and Leaf*, edited by Richard Swedberg, Houghton Mifflin, 1965, pp. 3–84.

Weber, Max. *The Protestant Ethic and the Spirit of Capitalism*. Translated by Talcott Parsons, Norton & Company, 2009.

_____. "Science as a Vocation." *From Max Weber: Essays in Sociology,* edited by H.H. Gerth and C. Wright Mills, Oxford University Press, 1946, pp. 129–156.

PART TWO

Television and Film

Changing Mike, Changing History

Erasing African-America in It *(2017)*

Kevin J. Wetmore, Jr.

> "Americans can be notoriously selective in the exercise of historical memory."
> —Ralph Ellison, *Going to the Territory*

Stephen King's *It* reflects the lived reality of people of color in the United States. African American history and memory often offer a counternarrative to "Official" history—the civic narratives spoken of at official events, what is taught in public schools and how people generally remember the past, a counternarrative often more factually accurate and ugly than that official history. The official history erases people of color, idealizes, glorifies, and whitewashes a narrative that preserves the status quo, and erases the violence and oppression that has often been the lived reality of minorities in America.

Both Stephen King's novel and the 1990 miniseries based on it present Michael Hanlon as both the keeper of the secret history of Derry and not just the only member of the Losers' Club but indeed possibly the only person in the entire town who knows and remembers the actual violent, oppressive history of It and Derry. Mike Hanlon, the sole African American in the Losers' Club [indeed, according to the novel, the sole African American child in Derry (674)], is transformed in the 2017 film adaptation into a reluctant thug and one who is brought into the Losers' Club solely because of Henry Bower's bullying, and who adds little to the group in terms of personality or action (despite Chosen Jacob's competent and engaging performance—the script gives him little to do compared to the other characters). In doing so, the film erases not just the story of Mike Hanlon as a complete, round character, but also African American history as encoded within King's novel.

There exists a secret history of Derry, as there exists a different history of the United States. Instead of the official version that promotes (white) heroes and is full of words like "freedom" and the positive aspects of the community, the lived experience and memory of that by people of color is one of racial and class violence, one of oppression, cruelty and brutality, one that is full of words like "lynching" or "an all-white jury found the defendants not guilty." One that is more real and true than the official history of Derry or the United States. The entity known as It is, in some ways, the manifestation of the violence and oppression against the different and the marginalized, and ignorance of It by the adults of the town mirrors official histories that ignore that violence and oppression.

In his seminal book *Lies My Teacher Told Me*, James W. Loewen observes that African American and other minority students "view history with a special dislike" (12). The reason given for this is that the official history taught in school runs counter to their lived experiences, tends to focus on white achievement while ignoring white oppression of minorities, and disregarding the achievements of those minorities. Textbook authors go out of their way, argues Loewen, to erase the negative aspects of history, justify oppressive behavior, glorify violence towards minorities, and invert white responsibility—usually through the use of passive voice that something was done to someone without mentioning the doer, i.e., "Native Americans were resettled" or "The indigenous people were exterminated," as if it were something that simply happened to them (24–25; 64). The novel, of course, reflects this rejection of formal education by the Losers' Club as well—the kids find school oppressive both from the teachers and the bullies and they bond during the summer, when they can be more authentic versions of themselves.

In Derry, everyone forgets Pennywise, and the powers-that-be cover him up. Memory is selective—even the adult Losers' Club forgets until Mike calls them back. Mike remembers. As Robert O'Meally and Geneviève Fabre observe, memory "may become a form of counterhistory that challenges the false generalizations in exclusionary 'History'" (8). Mike Hanlon in the novel and miniseries serves as the living embodiment of counterhistory whose memory challenges the false generalizations of Derry's exclusionary official history that also ignores not only the realities of race but the realities of It.

Stephen King's Mike and African American History/Memory

The novel is set in 1957/58 and 1984/85. This overlap is appropriate. The 1950s was the age of the height of Jim Crow and the beginning of the Civil

Rights movement. In the 1980s, President Reagan while claiming a post-racial society and encouraging Americans to move beyond race continued to employ the "Southern Strategy" of Nixon and simultaneously stoked white resentment of blacks through stereotypes of urban violence, lazy Blacks, and "welfare queens," repeatedly misrepresenting a woman whom he claimed had "eighty names, thirty addresses, twelve social security cards" as emblematic of urban Blacks as "takers" (Maxwell). As Angie Maxwell observes, "In doing so, he portrayed racial minorities as undeserving 'takers,' while erasing the institutional racism at the heart of economic inequity" (Maxwell). King's novel taps into this dynamic of the "Official" version of history versus the actual lived experiences of minorities.

King crafted characters and a situation that fairly accurately reflect the racial reality of Maine in 1960 and 1990. Mike Hanlon's father served in the Army in a segregated unit with Dick Halloran, the cook from *The Shining* (in an example of classic King intertextuality). He was stationed in Derry during the Second World War and stayed to farm after being discharged. By remaining in Derry when the other members of his all–Black unit left Maine, Hanlon senior and his family were not merely a minority but a sole presence. According to the U.S. Census Bureau in 1960 (the census closest to the setting for King's novel), 3318 African Americans lived in Maine out of a population of 969,265, or .3 percent of the population (Gibson and Jung). By 1990, the census closest to the second era of *It* and the year in which the miniseries is set, the numbers rise to 5138 out of 1,227,928, or .4 percent of the population, the majority of whom live in urban areas (Gibson and Jung). Even in Maine, Derry is extremely white in population. The Hanlons are the sole non-white family that we know of, and thus uniquely situated to perceive Derry differently than the majority population.

Every member of the Losers' Club believes Henry Bowers hates him or her the most, and he does have his reasons to hate all of them, "but the boy in Derry who was number one on Henry's personal Hate Parade was not in the Losers' Club at all on that July 3rd; he was a black boy named Michael Hanlon" (672). Mike's father, Will, had Henry's father, Butch, thrown in jail for killing his chickens. Everything bad that happened subsequently to the Bowers family is traced back to that incident: "Everything was the nigger's fault" (673). Henry poisons Mike's dog in revenge, and his father's subsequent praise causes Henry to double down on his malevolent intent towards Mike.

His ethnic difference also makes Mike stand out to the other students in Derry. The kids know who Mike is, since "he was the only Negro child" in town (674); but he goes to a different school because the Hanlons are deeply religious. Mike attends a church school, so the other Losers do not know him personally. Mike is marked as different by his race, his faith and his school, all of which are minority and different from the majority.

As a result of his outsider status, Mike knows a very different history than the other children of Derry. After he joins the Losers' Club as a result of the rock fight in the Barrens, he brings his father's "Derry album" to the underground clubhouse. Mike's father "collects old pictures and clippings about the town" (728). The first image is from the early 18th century, a juggling clown (736). Pictures from 1856, 1891, 1933, and 1945 follow (737–739). It becomes obvious to the Losers' Club that It has been returning to the town regularly. Mike's father's album is an alternate history of Derry.

King directly invokes the idea of official histories versus the lived experience of the citizens repeatedly in the novel, especially the idea that minorities in Derry have an unofficial alternative history of the town. The adult Mike considers the Black Spot fire, "'A perfect example of how the Chamber of Commerce will try to rewrite history'" (446). The Black Spot was an African American nightclub on the outskirts of Derry. The "Legion of White Decency," a fictional citizens' organization dedicated to fighting civil rights and keeping minorities oppressed based on actual organizations from the time, set the fire. Sixty Black people were killed, including eighteen from Company E—soldiers who had literally fought for America in the Second World War. The Nazis did not kill them; white Americans did.

Mike directly states that history as written by historians hides the ugly reality of what actually happened: "Most of the history books talk more about the KKK than they do about the Legion of White Decency, and a lot of people don't even know there was such a thing. I think it might be because most of the histories have been written by Northerners and they're ashamed" (452). While all African Americans in Maine know what really happened at the Black Spot, official history and white Americans erased the actual event: "'And after the fire, they all just laid away their sheets and lied each other up and it was papered over.' [...] 'After all, who got killed? Eighteen army niggers, fourteen or fifteen town niggers, four members of a nigger jazz-band ... and a bunch of nigger-lovers'" (453). King reiterates what Loewen articulates: official history excludes events like this, and the (white) people "lie to each other." It is the Hanlon family that remembers what actually happened. Mike Hanlon in Derry, Maine, captures the history of the African American male: made invisible by slavery and segregation until made visible through Othering— Mike is the only African American in his entire school. Invisible, yet unable to not be seen as Other. He grows up to become the town librarian and thus becomes both part of the official history keepers of Derry while also serving as a counter to that history.

Interestingly, King was part of the curve here. To counter these official histories that erase the contributions of people of color as well as the violence done against them, new histories began to appear in the eighties, around the time Stephen King was writing *It*, most notably Howard Zinn's *A People's His-*

tory of the United States, first published in 1980, a few short years before *It*. King's novel shows the formation of African American history/memory in the face of official lies. Indeed, Susan Love Brown observes in her analysis of baby-boomer mythmaking in *It*:

> Mike Hanlon symbolizes the dilemma of African-Americans in the United States, who have always been aware of societal evil and its violent consequences, because they have been its victims. The civil rights movement of the fifties brought the realization of the foul presence of racism into every American home by television. Blacks were the first to protest over injustices in the post-war era, and it was their example and participation with them in the civil rights movement that spurred many young people on to protest the Vietnam war and the conditions of society in general. In this sense, blacks have always been the keepers of history and conscience for Americans. Since Mike Hanlon never left Derry, he never forgot the evil. Similarly, most blacks in the United States have never forgotten the past and have noted the continuing presence of racism, unlike their white counterparts who seem to have forgotten the past. Thus, the black experience is represented here accurately as one of continuity within American experience [Brown].

King's novel, in short, captures something of the experience of African Americans in Maine, and the United States, in the periods during which it is set. It is also important to note that young Mike (as depicted in the novel and miniseries) lives in a pre–Civil Rights Movement America; whereas, adult Mike functions in a world shaped by Dr. Martin Luther King, Jr., Rosa Parks, Malcolm X, and the Black Panther Party, all of which appeared on the cultural landscape between the two parts of *It*. Adult Mike can have a confidence and a place in Derry society that young Mike and his family would have found impossible. Yet, despite the improvement since Jim Crow, Mike's ethnicity still sets him apart in a predominantly white town.

Race is significantly underrepresented in scholarship on Stephen King's works and their adaptations, and often the focus is upon whiteness or the absence of people of color [see, for example, Regina Hansen's 2017 essay on *It*, which focuses on white masculinity and observes that "most of King's young social outsiders are white, straight, able-bodied males," and the only mention of Mike Hanlon is that he is "sidelined" in the novel; she also mentions King's use of "magical negro figures" such as John Coffey in *The Green Mile* (162; 165; 171)]. King does a better job than his critics in addressing the African American presence in Derry and its erasure by the white citizens and official history.

Miniseries Mike

The television miniseries adaptation was first broadcast in November 1990 and was subsequently released on home video. The four-hour adaptation is set in 1960 and 1990. Enacting its own alternative history, the miniseries removes the Black Spot Fire and Legion of White Decency. Nevertheless, the show still manages to construct Mike Hanlon as the keeper of the secret history of Derry and link to the African American experience of history. The period itself is close enough to the novel that it exists within the same social milieu: a time when George H.W. Bush as president continued Reagan's vision of America as both post-racial yet simultaneously under assault from Blacks as "takers" in a system in which the majority of people receiving so-called entitlements were actually rural whites. In 1990, "a full 135 years after the abolition of slavery, Black Americans still possessed only a meager 1 percent of national wealth" ("RACE–The Power of an Illusion"). That is the world in which the miniseries was broadcast.

We first encounter Mike (Tim Reid) in the miniseries in the opening scene as an adult. He is well-dressed and clearly middle class. He approaches a police line at the scene where a little girl has been taken and picks up a doll in a sewer grate. A cop comes over, friendly and respectful. "Chief is going to have a cow when he sees you nosing around, Mike," he states. "I won't tell him if you don't. What you got, Sam?" Mike responds. In this two-line exchange we can already surmise a few things. First, that Mike is a respected citizen of Derry, one who knows, is known by, and has a friendly relationship with the rank-and-file police. Second, that the town's power structure (i.e., the Chief of Police) believes Mike "noses around" and objects to his doing so. The chief is involved in ensuring the official history of Derry and the status quo are preserved; thus, Mike's questioning of them is not welcome. These surmises are confirmed when the chief approaches Mike after the cop tells him that "There's not much left, just like last time," this last statement demonstrating that there is a history of bad things happening that are again being covered up, yet Mike seems to know the truth. The chief interrupts, "I thought I told you to stay out of this, Hanlon." Unlike the beat cop, the chief is condescending and bullying.

> MIKE: I'm just a concerned citizen, chief, and I call six kids missing or dead a major cause for alarm.
> CHIEF: Maybe just a rash of runaways. Kids get itchy feet.
> MIKE: Right. A four-year-old in a day car just gets itchy feet. What—a seven-year-old trots down to Acapulco for a wild weekend?

Despite Mike pointing out the obvious, the chief claims nothing is wrong and the missing and dead children are not a cause for alarm.

Finally, Mike tells the chief point-blank, "Chief, there is something terribly wrong here in Derry. You know it." The chief's response is, "I'm the cop; you're the librarian," and he turns and walks away. Whereas, Mike sees the terrible truth of what is happening in Derry, the white police chief argues from his authority ("I'm the cop") while noting that Mike is just "the librarian," and, thus, not entitled to argue with him. Not only does this exchange establish Mike as the Derry librarian in the first few minutes of the miniseries, it also frames the story with the racial dynamic found in King's novel. The white authority figures turn a blind eye to crimes committed against those who "don't count" (children, African Americans), and write an official history devoid of the negative aspects of Derry. Mike, as librarian and as an African American knows not to believe official accounts or officials themselves, as their job is to protect the status quo, not the people.

In a flashback to 1960, the audience is shown Mike Hanlon (Marlon Taylor) transferring into the school that the rest of the Losers' Club already attend. He has been a resident of Derry but will now attend the public school. As part of his introduction to his new class, which contains both Henry Bowers (Jarred Blancard) and several Losers, he shows his dad's photo album, noting that his father was stationed in Derry during the Second World War and collected a history of the town. "Who'd want a history of this toilet?" snarks Henry, proving both his ignorance and his lack of use for history. Henry, a juvenile delinquent bully with white privilege, doesn't need to know the history of Derry, or at least doesn't see any value in histories, official or unofficial. This reason is one of many why he will ultimately be used by It to attack the Losers.

Mike shares with the class a history of Derry they could not have heard in school or through any civic Derry events: the explosion at the iron works during an Easter egg hunt that killed a number of people, mysterious deaths throughout the town, and, "maybe the biggest mystery is how 253 settlers could just disappear without a trace." In other words, from its very colonial origins Derry has been a place of violence, disappearances, and death, all of which are removed from the official history of Derry. But Mike Hanlon and his family, the only African Americans in town, know it. The Hanlons have always been outsiders, even the generation born in Derry (Mike), and as African Americans they experienced directly the violence that is removed from official accounts.

The teacher, a white authority figure, is dismissive of the account. "Thank you, Michael, for that illuminating if somewhat morbid history," she says as he heads to his chair. It is clear she neither approves of his presentation nor wants to follow up on it in any manner. The facts are to be forgotten or ignored, and the sooner the better.

In the miniseries, Mike is the reason for the full realization of the Losers' Club. Henry Bowers wants to put a cherry bomb in Mike's pants because Mike's family has caused problems for Henry's "Old Man," and while an adult distracts the bullies, Mike manages to grab his photo album from them and run. They pursue him. The rock fight is what cements the seven kids together and allows them to discover their collective power to fight both bullies and It. Indeed, it is possible to read into this moment a metaphor for the power of community action when a group of diverse individuals ignore their differences and work together for common cause. Henry claims he has bones to pick with all the Losers but will not bully them today if they hand over Mike. The other six will not. Even though they just met Mike that day, the fact that Henry wants to harm him is reason enough to protect Mike. "I think the six of us can put you in the hospital," says Bill (Jonathan Brandis). "Seven," amends Mike, cementing the group.

After Bowers leaves, the second thing to unite the Losers' Club is the secret history that Mike shares with them. He shows them the evidence that Derry has had a supernatural history of violence. A photo comes to life and Pennywise (Tim Curry) makes his presence known to the group. It is through defending Mike and learning about the reality of Pennywise that the seven agree first to fight to kill It and then promise to return should It ever also return.

When It returns twenty-seven years later, Mike is the one to call the other six now-adult Losers and remind them of their promise. Stan (Richard Masur) takes his own life rather than face It again. The others all return, although not entirely certain why. It is clear from the scenes of their phone call from Mike, always tied to a flashback of their individual encounters with It, that as adults they had not thought of or remembered It. When Bill (Richard Thomas) returns to Derry, he asks Mike, "Why do you remember?" "Because I never left," answers Mike.

This response is very telling. The others, all successful to some degree in their lives as writer, architect, comedian, businesspeople, and designer, all live privileged lives. They do not live in fear—they live in relative luxury with support networks of those who love them or work for them. It is Mike, the sole African American who stayed in the small town, who was never allowed to forget the violence and oppression, who kept the secret history of Derry, who remembers. It is literally Mike's birthright, both because of his father's photo album (he has been the keeper of a secret history since childhood), but also because he is a Black man in an almost entirely white town. There was never a question Mike would be the one to keep the memory alive, as he is never allowed to forget it.

The miniseries is able to subtly convey the same reality as the novel: that Mike Hanlon, as the only African American in Derry, has experienced the reality of violence and oppression and remembers it as a counterhistory to the official one. As an educated Black man, he is part of the town and yet always Othered by his ethnicity. As a result, he knows what others do not; he knows the history that the town would rather forget. Even in the absence of the Black Spot fire and even with Henry Bowers being the only character to make racist statements, it is clear that Derry is a place in which whites oppress minorities and the official history ignores that. But African American memory constitutes an alternative history that is more factually accurate than the official narrative. Mike, the librarian, is the one who keeps the truth, both in his building and in his head.

African American History Erased: Mike in It *(2017)*

With *It* (2017), the secret history of Derry and the African American role in preserving it are entirely erased. Set in 1989, created in the Post-Obama era of Black Lives Matter, the film is an odd step backwards. The first image of young Mike (Chosen Jacobs) is not with a photo album, as in the miniseries, nor fleeing racist bullies, but behind a weapon pointed directly at the camera.[1] His grandfather wants Mike to take up the family business of raising and slaughtering sheep. Mike must learn to use a bolt gun on a sheep, pressing it against its forehead and pulling the trigger, killing the sheep. He cannot.

"Pull it, Mike," demands Leroy (Steven Williams), speaking of the trigger of the bolt gun. "Go on, pull it!" Mike cannot, and Leroy kills the sheep in front of him with ease. "Your dad was younger than you when he killed his first sheep," Leroy tells him. "I'm not my dad, okay?" Mike begrudgingly responds, letting the viewer know that unlike the Mike of the novel or miniseries, this Mike does not have a father who was a soldier or who has a photo album of the secret history of Derry. This Mike is fatherless, being raised by his grandfather. This change from the novel flies directly in the face of King's African American characters (but is very much in keeping with American cinema's depiction of young Black men being fatherless). In the novel, Mike and his father are very close. Every other parental relationship is rather dysfunctional, yet, while not perfect, Mike and his father have a pure, loving, good relationship. This bond between generations of Black men is not present in this film. Entire generations of African Americans are removed from the narrative.

In the absence of a loving, supportive father, granddad Leroy turns the moment into a lesson on survival in the world if one is African American:

> There are two places you can be in the world. You can be out here like us, or you can be in there, like them [sheep]. You waste time hemming and hawing and someone else is going to make that choice for you. Except you won't know it until you feel that bolt between your eyes.

Leroy preaches a gospel of strong Black manhood. One is either a perpetrator or a victim. While his stance is justified by experience, it also leaves out more than two options. One does not have to be either a sheep or a killer of sheep. Mike wants to be something else.

On the one hand, the image is a positive one. Mike is non-violent and incapable of hurting something, even if necessary to maintain his family's livelihood or to avoid being victimized himself. He is physically big, larger than the other members of the Losers' Club, but there is a gentleness to him. He is a reluctant butcher, and a deliverer of meat. The next time the audience is shown Mike, he is riding his bike to deliver meat in the city and hides from Bowers and his gang. In the miniseries, Mike is a scholarly secret historian; however, the 2017 Mike is a reluctant thug. The shot of an out-of-focus Mike holding the gun pointed directly at the camera is one that audiences have seen many, many times in films with young African American men and weapons. Mike might be a reluctant thug, but he is visually identified from the beginning as a kind of African American "gangsta." There is something positive in his gentler side in this film, yet he has also been neutered. He is coded as safe because he is uncomfortable in the role of fighter. By taking away his secret historian role, the film demonstrates that his presence is welcome not because it adds something new to the group but rather because it doesn't offer anything threatening. He remains disconnected from the other friends but is welcome to join the fight against Pennywise.

This introduction to Mike Hanlon also carries visual and thematic echoes of Charles Burnett's 1978 film *Killer of Sheep*. Set in a slaughterhouse in Watts, the predominantly African American Los Angeles neighborhood best known for its riots in 1965 and folk-art towers, *Killer of Sheep* is an episodic narration of Stan (Henry Gayle Sanders), an African American slaughterhouse worker whose job, the monotonous carnage of the killing floor, corrodes his soul and begins to deteriorate his family life. Stan is what Mike Hanlon does not want to become. He rides his bike to deliver meat, but he does not want to be a killer of sheep. This tension, between killer and gentle, non-violent young man, is the 2017 Mike's burden and character arc.

Yet the film returns repeatedly to images and actions that paint Mike with the cinematic history of violent, young African American men ("you can either be out here with us or in there with them"). *It* continues to visually differentiate Mike from the others in the Losers' Club. Riding to the Pennywise house to do battle, everyone else has iron rods; Mike is strapping the sheep-killing gun, a bandolier over his shoulder with the cartridges at the ready, gun slung low on his thigh.

This Mike knows nothing of the secret history of Derry. Indeed, we know little about him as a person other than his family owns a slaughterhouse and he does not want to work there. The white kids in this film know about the Black Spot Nightclub (Mike never mentions it), but it is ultimately presented simply as a crazy conspiracy theory: Eddie Kaspbrak (Jack Dylan

Grazer) tells Stan (Wyatt Oleff) that "The Black Spot was a night club that was burned down years ago by that racist cult." He learned that fact by watching *Geraldo*. Immediately this locates the act of arson that burned the club into the realm of crackpot theories and removes the guilt of the citizens of Derry (who in the novel tacitly supported the work of the Legion of White Decency) and blame it on a "racist cult," absolving Derry and its white population of any responsibility for the fire or the deaths that followed, directly the opposite of what King has done. Mike does not know any secret history of Derry, but the white kids who watch crazy talk television do.

In this film, it is Ben Hanscom, the fat kid, who knows the secret history of Derry. He learns it from all the time he spends in the library reading since he has no friends since moving to Derry. This change feels unnecessary and arbitrary. While the reason for learning it all is plausible, the end result is that Ben takes over Mike's role as the secret historian and Mike is left with nothing to do within the group. Ben charts the events; Ben knows there is something happening in Derry. In the novel, Mike's history is hand-me-down; it's the stories he's collected and the pictures from his father's album. In this film, however, Ben's history is developed from "official" primary materials: newspapers, etc., and—unlike the Mike of the novel/miniseries—Ben is reluctant to share his findings at first; he hoards his knowledge in his room, only sharing when the group is threatened.

In 2017 Mike has no history, no stories, no knowledge handed down from his father. This Mike tells the other Losers "My grandfather thinks this town is cursed. He says that all the bad things that happen in this town are because of one thing—an evil thing that feeds on the people of Derry." The irony is that Leroy is right—there is an evil that feeds on the people of Derry. Yet this knowledge is not, as in King's novel, from his experience as an African American in a dominantly white society. Instead it is presented as superstition—a "curse," which has the effect of rendering him into a stereotype: the superstitious African American. The effect is not just felt by Mike and Leroy; the larger end result is the erasure of Derry's (and America's) African American history.

The problem with moving the real history of Derry from Mike to Ben is to foster a trend already growing in American culture: the erasure of Black history and suffering from the narrative. Writing in 2015 for *The Guardian*, Lindy West observed that the policeman who killed Michael Brown, an unarmed black teenager, "gets more sympathetic coverage than the dead teenager did":

> The victors (i.e., the beneficiaries of the status quo) are writing history, in front of our eyes, in real time—deciding what will endure and what will fade away. This isn't necessarily an overt, explicit or even conscious process—it's often just a series of seemingly innocuous choices that add up to a slow, grinding erasure. It's re-centering Michael Brown's story on Darren Wilson [West].

It re-centers Mike's story on Ben, and erases the novel's and miniseries' point that people of color often know the real history more than their white counterparts who get to choose "what will fade away." It is also worth noting that what It does to the children of Derry is a "slow, grinding erasure." Even the 2017 film demonstrates this aspect visually by showing one "missing child" flier stapled on top of others on telephone poles throughout town. As soon as a new child disappears, the old disappearance is already forgotten.

We see this process happening in textbooks right now. Leonard Pitts, Jr., a columnist for *Oregon Live* criticized the widely-used high school history textbook *World Geography* as it states that the Atlantic slave trade "brought millions of workers from Africa to the southern United States to work on agricultural plantations" (Pitts Jr.). In a word, slaves are transformed into "workers" who immigrated, rather than being seized, sold, tortured and forced to labor until their deaths. "We are witness to the vandalism of African-American memory, to acts of radical revision and wholesale theft that strikes at the core of black identity. Once your past is gone, who are you? What anchor holds you? [… a]ll the inconvenient pain, sting and challenge of African-American history, gone," writes Pitts Jr. This also applies to Mike.

The new *It* erases what makes Mike a significant and important character. Instead of the keeper of memory who fights the revision of history, he becomes a reluctant thug without much else to do. If he is not the one who knows the real history of Derry, why did he stay behind and become the librarian? Unlike the creative revision of the other characters in the story, the revision of Mike—as the sole African American in the Losers' Club and one of only three in the film (the other two being his relatives)—neither benefits the character nor the story and erases the African American history of Derry. Given the other erasures occurring in American culture right now, this seems a problematic choice.

Perhaps *It: Chapter 2* will offer new insights into adult Mike, why he stayed behind, and what role he plays in the Losers' Club. This does not erase the fact that Mike, in part one, has had his history erased and, in doing so, the film has removed a complicated historical reality that the novel and miniseries fully engaged, resulting in a more complex and significant character. As Lindy West notes, "these small choices accumulate […] It sandbags the tide of change […] And it changes the way we remember our own past, even just five, 10 years down the line" (West). The problem with the post–Obama *It* is that it has changed the way the past is remembered (and forgotten) in Derry, and erases Mike and African American history when it does so.[2]

NOTES

1. I am grateful to Deirdre Marie Flood who observed this and other images of Mike in her paper, "Who Is Allowed to Be a Hero? Gender and Race in *It* and *Stranger Things*,"

presented at the Ann Radcliffe Academic Conference, StokerCon 2019, Grand Rapids, Michigan, May 2019.

 2. I am also grateful to the anonymous reviewer who made suggestions for improving the essay and deeply grateful to Dr. Katherine A. Troyer for her insights and suggestions, which greatly improved the essay. Any mistakes are my own.

Works Cited

Brown, Susan Love. "Babyboomer Mythology and Stephen King's *It*: An American Cultural Analysis." *Americana: The Journal of American Popular Culture (1900-present)*, vol.7, no. 7, Spring 2008.
Flood, Deirdre Marie. "Who Is Allowed to Be a Hero? Gender and Race in *IT* and *Stranger Things*," conference presentation at the Ann Radcliffe Academic Conference, StokerCon 2019, Grand Rapids, Michigan, May 2019.
Gibson, Campbell, and Kay Jung. "Population Division: Historical Census Statistics on Population Totals by Race, 1790 to 1990, And By Hispanic Origin 1970 to 1990, for the United States, Regions, Divisions and States." Working Paper No 56. United States Census. Accessed May 17, 2019.
Hansen, Regina. "Stephen King's *IT* and *Dreamcatcher* on Screen: Hegemonic White Masculinity and Nostalgia for Underdog Boyhood." *Science Fiction Film and Television* vol. 10, no. 2, 2017: 161–76.
It. Directed by Andy Muschietti. New Line Cinema. 2017.
_____. Directed by Tommy Lee Wallace. Lorimar Television. 1990.
Killer of Sheep. Directed by Charles Burnett. Milestone Films. 1978.
King, Stephen. *It*. New York: Scribner's, 1986.
Loewen, James W. *Lies My Teacher Told Me*. New York: Simon & Schuster, 1995.
Maxwell, Angie. "What We Got Wrong about the Southern Strategy." *Washington Post* (July 25, 2019).
O'Meally, Robert, and Geneviève Fabre, "Introduction" in *History and Memory in African-American Culture*. Eds, Robert O'Meally and Geneviève Fabre. New York: Oxford University Press, 1994. 1–17.
Pitts, Leonard, Jr. "Erasing African-American History." *Oregon Live*. October 12, 2015. Accessed June 12, 2019.
"RACE—The Power of an Illusion." California Newsreel. 2003. Accessed August 9, 2019.
West, Lindy. "Black American Lives Are Being Erased. The Victors Still Write History." *The Guardian*. August 4, 2015. Accessed June 12, 2019.
Zinn, Howard. *A People's History of the United States*. New York: Harper & Row, 1980.

"Best Not to Look Back"

Monstrosity, Medium and Genre in Tommy Lee Wallace's It (1990)

June Pulliam

The 1990 adaptation of Stephen King's *It* is beloved by a generation of fans who were terrified by Tim Curry as Pennywise the clown. Laura Bradley's review in *Vanity Fair* of Andy Muschietti's *It* (2017) attributes fan affection for Wallace's *It* (1990) to its character development. Jump scares, gore, and CGI special effects are of no use in a horror film if its characters are so one-dimensional that the viewer does not care if they live or die. Even after the release of the first installment of Muschietti's *It* (2017), fan enthusiasm for Wallace's adaptation was so great that Chris Griffins was able to crowdfund his forthcoming documentary *Pennywise: The Story of It*, which interviews cast members and crew about making Wallace's miniseries. *It* (1990) was also a commercial success for ABC, the network that commissioned an adaptation of King's 1986 novel. ABC's original broadcast of *It* (1990), over two consecutive nights in November, put the network at the top of the Nielsen ratings for the first time that fall (Hastings), and composer Richard Bellis won an Emmy the following year for his original score of the miniseries (43rd Emmy). Wallace's *It* (1990), however, is so contorted by the conventions of the miniseries genre and the constraints of the medium for which it was created that the miniseries is about as frightening as an episode of *Scooby Doo*. It's (1990) happy and definitive conclusion is a radical departure from King's novel, which culminates in the destruction of Derry and the novel's narrator, horror novelist Bill Denbrough, hoping that they have actually killed the monster. Wallace's pat ending downgrades King's eternal meta-monster, which cannot be contained, let alone destroyed, by puny human logic, to a clown-cum-spider that five people without a flashlight, real weapons, or a clue can kill.

The monster at the heart of King's *It* (1986) is not a clown, or a spider; the creature just takes these forms, as well as many others, to terrify its victims, who taste better when they are afraid (King 1023). Unlike other monsters such as vampires or zombies, the shapeshifting It does not operate by a knowable set of rules. It is an eternal "Eater of Worlds" (1069) that has been sleeping below Derry "'since the beginning of time […] waiting for the ice to melt, waiting for the people to come'" (773). To defeat It, the adult survivors of the creature's 1958 feeding cycle must "*throw away the instruction manual*" (King 1071). King's final chapters, however, indicate that the surviving group of childhood friends might not have destroyed the creature who killed Bill Denbrough's little brother George in 1958 and Laurie Ann Winterbarger and Eddie Kaspbrak in the novel's present day, 1985. The adult Bill Denbrough, a professional expert on monsters, expresses doubt in the epilogue about the group's success: he confides in the reader that it is "best not to look back" on the now-ruined town of his childhood, but to instead "*believe there will be happily ever afters all the way around*" (1149). Bill's use of the conditional tense in this passage indicates his uncertainty about Its demise. *It* (1990) eliminates Bill's doubt about the final destruction of the chthonic shapeshifter, which makes the monster more ordinary and less frightening.

Bill's doubt that It is actually dead makes sense given the creature's constantly changing form and ability to paralyze victims with custom-made terrors plucked from their minds. It is a meta-monster who defies all binary categories and lays to waste all borders. In her genre-defining essay "Horror and the Monstrous-feminine," Barbara Creed explains that "the concept of a border is central to the construction of the monstrous," (Creed 71) which is frightening because its appearance threatens the stability of the entire symbolic order. The monster is the embodiment of the abject, bodily excretions such as urine, feces, and blood, which represent the imaginary maternal body that represents the lack of distinction between self and caretaker prior to the mirror stage and the subject's understanding of the symbolic order. In *The Powers of Horror*, Julia Kristeva explains how the abject must be expelled in its literal and symbolic forms to preserve the barriers between self and Other necessary to maintain the symbolic order. Most horror concludes after the monster is killed, which expels it from humanity. The monster's death constitutes a ritual purification of the abject that eliminates the threat to the symbolic order (Creed), at least for a while. As a horror novelist, Bill Denbrough understands that the ritual purification of the abject is not a one-and-done task. Instead, the symbolic order can only be maintained through repeated rituals such as those he describes in his novels because the borders undergirding the binary logic of the symbolic order that differentiate between self and other, male and female, white and non-white, child and adult, and good and evil, for example, are not solid distinctions, but permeable and often unreliable categories. King's shapeshifting meta-monster that is the center of *It*'s (1986) fictional universe cannot be so easily expelled from humanity. The binary-bound human mind has difficulty categorizing this creature, naming it as It, a pronoun used to describe both inanimate objects and anything that falls outside of these binaries.

Given *It*'s (1986) disturbing content, the big screen might seem to be the best vehicle for a filmic adaptation of King's novel given the success in the 1980s of the blood-soaked *A Nightmare on Elm Street*, *Halloween*, and *Friday the 13th* franchises. Yet the length of King's novel made the work difficult to adapt into a feature film in the late 1980s and early 1990s when most Hollywood movies were only ninety minutes long. At the time, the miniseries genre was better suited for bringing King's lengthy work to the screen because the genre lacked the time constraints of Hollywood films produced to attract audiences to first-run cinemas. For example, ABC's 1977 miniseries adaptation of Alex Haley's *Roots* was twelve hours long and shown over six consecutive nights of prime-time television. ABC only gave *It* (1990) a quarter of that screen time, but the final production was more than twice that of the average feature film in 1990. Unfortunately, the benefits of the miniseries-length format were outweighed by the constraints of the genre, as well as the medium of broadcast television.

First, miniseries generic conventions demand narrative closure. Unlike a continuous television series commissioned to run indefinitely, the television miniseries "has a fixed and limited number of episodes" that are "intended to reach some form of closure (however loose) in the final instalment" (Creeber 35). *It* (1990) follows this predictable pattern. The acting and plot conventions that characterize made-for-TV movies and miniseries are derived from the television melodrama genre, which enacts a "fantasy of reassurance" (Thoens 596) through happy or moralistic endings. *It* (1990) enacts this fantasy of reassurance in the conclusion, where the status quo is re-established after the threat to the symbolic order has been extinguished. Richie and Eddie's homoerotic friendship ends with Eddie's death, the only African-American member of the group (Mike) and one of its two authors is silenced, and two heterosexual couples reunite, putting everyone in their proper place within cis-het-white-patriarchy, which stabilizes the symbolic order. The semiology of the miniseries genre indicates that this conclusion constitutes a definitive ending.

One way that Wallace sets up *It*'s (1990) definitive conclusion is by coding the adult Eddie as gay so that his death indicates a return to normative gender roles. *It*'s (1990) adult Eddy is a sissy character, one of film's first stock characters dating back to the Hays Code, which censored "immoral content" in commercial films, such as the open representation of homosexuality. The effeminate and asexual sissy character circumvented the Hays Code because it represented homosexual men broadly through an absence of normative masculinity rather than by any homosexual behavior. The sissy as ersatz-homosexual was non-threatening because the character was either played for comic relief or as a villain who would be punished by the film's conclusion. Over two decades after the Hays Code's demise, the sissy character persisted in film and television. Wallace's Eddie, who is smaller and weaker than other men his age, emotional, easily frightened, enmeshed with his mother, and a virgin (Mislak), would be recognized as gay by 1990 audiences merely because he is not normatively masculine. It exploits the adult Eddie's insecurities about his masculinity when it appears to him in the form of the elderly pharmacist Mr. Keene and taunts him for being a "girly boy." Eddie's perceived sexuality in *It* (1990) gives a homoerotic subtext to his friendship with Richie in a coded way that would not be censored by ABC's standards-and-practices division, which, like other networks at the time, still prohibited open representations of homosexuality in its programming. Eddie's ambiguous sexuality in *It* (1990) taints his friendship with Richie in a way that sufficiently disrupts the cis-het status quo to require resolution. When Eddie cries and confesses to his fellow Losers that he is still a virgin because the only people he has ever loved are his six childhood friends, Richie's face momentarily registers disgust, as if he fears that being in Eddie's presence calls his own masculinity into question. Wallace's characterization of Eddie's and Richie's over the top revulsion have a basis in King's *It* (1986), which codes both boys as queer (Keaney). Young Richie consistently calls his friend "cute" (Burbatt), even pinching his cheeks in one scene as if Eddie were a little girl (King 288). Like the bully Butch Bowers, It harasses young Eddie for his perceived homosexuality, cornering him in the form of a leprous drifter who offers to "'do it for a dime'" to the scared boy and to "'blow [him] for free'" (King 291). This scene recalls the brutal murder of Andrew Mellon at the beginning of the novel by a teen homophobe. After Eddie's death, Richie can safely demonstrate the depth of his feelings for his childhood friend: the most distraught of the group, Richie openly weeps and kisses his dead friend on the cheek before the group must abandon his body in Derry's sewers (King 1054). *It Chapter Two* (2019) also references the homoerotic subtext to Eddie's and Richie's friendship in King's novel by making "Richie's perceived sexuality and potential attraction to his friend" (Keaney) a prominent element of the plot. After the adult Richie has a flashback about a childhood same-sex attraction and Henry Bowers bullying him for being "gay," Pennywise taunts him about his childhood "secret" (Keaney). Part of the status quo is restored in *It* (1990) after Eddie is killed protecting his friends from the monster. Eddie's selfless act removes the stigmatizing doubt about his normative masculinity. In *Its* (1990) conclusion, Richie also finds a "safe" way to express his love for his childhood friend. Richie returns to Hollywood and makes buddy comedy with a co-star "who bears more than a passing resemblance" to Eddie. Acting out his friendship with Eddie via a double of his deceased friend allows Richie a non-threatening way to maintain his deep emotional bond with another man because, in comedy, these bonds are perceived as funny rather than a threat to normative masculinity.

It (1990) also reestablishes the status quo by putting the one African-American character "in his place" within the cis-het-white status quo. Mike Hanlon, one of the two authors in King's novel, silences himself in *It*'s (1990) conclusion. *It*'s (1990) last image of Mike shows him alone in his hospital room, prematurely grey, and smiling as he writes the concluding chapter of his history-cum-diary as his memories of events fade, which is a stark visual contrast between the love-and-success-filled futures of his surviving childhood friends depicted in the finale. Mike is one of King's "magical negro" characters who sacrifice themselves for their white friends (Okorafor). Mike is the only of his childhood friends to remain in Derry after their traumatic summer of 1958, and he functions as the group's "lighthouse" whose job is to remain vigilant for Its return. Mike is the only one of the seven who has not repressed the memories of that summer, and the burden of this knowledge is acknowledged in *It: Chapter Two* (2019): he turns to heroin to cope with the burden of memory. In all versions of *It*, the adult Mike is the town librarian and amateur historian who writes an unofficial history of Derry, which serves an objective account of the creature's centuries-long predation on residents. The group uses Mike's history to retrieve their own repressed childhood memories about It and better understand how to kill the monster. Mike's role in *It* is similar to Mina Harker's role in *Dracula*—both are creators of objective accounts of a monster used as tools to fight the creature. But unlike Mina Harker, who has the first and last word in *Dracula* as the manuscript's editor, Mike opts to erase his voice from historical memory when he demotes his history to a diary, a document that is not meant to be shared with the world. Mike's decision effectively silences him, which confirms his "magical negro" role through erasing his voice. *It*'s (1990) conclusion is visually faithful to King's erasure of Mike after he has fulfilled his "magical negro" function. In *It* (1986), Bill is the frame tale's narrator who has the first and last word in the novel. In Mike's last scene, his expository voice-over narration of his surviving childhood friends' futures fades into *It*'s (1990) finale where Bill awakens Audra from her coma. *It*'s (1990) finale preserves Bill's role in King's *It* (1986) as the tale's narrator who is the keeper of the "official" version of events while erasing Mike's contribution to this narrative, which re-establishes the status quo by preserving racist hierarchies that silence minority voices.

It's (1990) conclusion most obviously reasserts the status quo through reuniting two heterosexual couples (Ben and Bev, and Bill and Audra) who perform their normative gender roles through their marriages. Ben and Bev are reunited and able to act on their unacknowledged childhood attraction to each other. Young Bev secretly reciprocated Ben's crush in *It* (1990): a flashback scene where Ben and Bev go their separate ways after their childhood confrontation with It, Bev reveals to the audience her feelings for Ben when she mouths "my heart burns there, too" to Ben's retreating form. These words reveal that she always knew the identity of the poem's author. As children, neither acted on their feelings because of Bev's overly protective father and Ben's fear of rejection; he fears his size prevented him from being normatively masculine and, therefore, worthy of Bev's affection. As adults, Ben and Bev are finally free to consummate their love after the monster is destroyed because Ben is now normatively masculine—he has lost weight and become sufficiently handsome and successful to bed a string of beautiful women before he reunited with Beverly. The couple leaves Derry in a red convertible to be married within the week, fulfilling their gender expectations after Beverly becomes pregnant. Bill and Audra are reunited after Bill rescues his wife from It and they leave Derry to begin a domestic life in earnest. Before Bill returns to Derry, he lives with Audra in the trappings of domesticity, but is unable to be an involved husband. In the scene where we first see the adult Bill, Audra is fulfilling her gender expectations as his wife: she has laid the table for dinner. Bill refuses to leave his writing to come to the table for this family meal, which emphasizes his inability to fulfill the expectations of his "proper" gender role. When Bill finally emerges from his study, it is only to leave for Derry without explaining his sudden absence to his hurt and confused wife. Bill's actions further demonstrate his failure to live up to his gendered expectations: although Bill's lack of information is meant to protect his wife from danger, it indirectly puts her in danger because her wifely concern prompts her to follow her husband to Derry, where she is promptly kidnapped by It. Bill fulfills his gendered expectations when he rescues Audra, then awakens her with a kiss in *It*'s (1990) finale as if she were a fairy-tale princess (after a harrowing downhill ride through traffic on his childhood bicycle). *It*'s (1990) conclusion is also a cliché of the miniseries genre's fantasy of reassurance. Bill and Audra kiss in the middle of an intersection while annoyed motorists honk their horns, the camera pans back into a wide-angle shot of them from above, and the happy-ending music is cued. The patriarchal family unit symbolically destroyed by Georgie's death at the beginning of *It* (1990), has been restored in the conclusion by the reunion of two heterosexual couples who are now performing their appropriate gender roles. After *It*'s (1990) characters are put in theirs place within gender and racial hierarchies, the threats to the symbolic order have been removed, which creates the miniseries' fantasy of reassurance via a definitive sense of closure not present in *It* (1986).

The miniseries genres' casting practices also undercut the horrific effect of *It* (1990). When the American miniseries/television movie industry became regular fare on the networks in the 1970s, it "developed its own star system" to fit within the genre's limited budgets. As a result, "a wholly new cadre of 'home grown' actors, some borrowed from prime-time series television, began to populate the TV movie [... guaranteeing] solid ratings by their presence in a telefilm" (Edgerton 168). *It*'s (1990) casting is typical of the industry's star system. The actors who played the adult Losers were all well-known from their roles on television. Dennis Christopher, who played the adult Eddie Kaspbrak, had previously made guest appearances on network television shows and starred as the disturbed young stalker in the 1980 horror film *Fade to Black*. Richard Maseur (Stan Uris) and Annette O'Toole (Beverly Marsh) were also television regulars for over a decade before they were cast in *It* (1990). *It*'s (1990) best-known stars John Ritter (Ben Hanscomb), Tim Reid (Mike Hanlon), Harry Anderson (Richie Tozier), and Richard Thomas (Bill Denbrough) were synonymous with their characters on their respective long-running television series that made them famous. It was difficult to believe that Jack Tripper (John Ritter) from *Three's Company* (1976–1984), Venus Flytrap (Tim Reid) from *WKRP in Cincinnati* (1978–1982), Judge Harry T. Stone (Harry Anderson) from *Night Court* (1984–1992), or "John-Boy" Walton (Richard Thomas) of *The Waltons* (1971–1978) could be harmed by It, which contributed to *It*'s (1990) fantasy of reassurance.

FCC Rules and ABC's standards-and-practices division also contributed to downgrading the terror threat of King's monster in the 1990 miniseries adaptation. Federal Communication Commission guidelines in the 1990s prohibited most cursing and frank representations of sexuality in prime-time. But ABC's standards-and-practices division was the real force that prevented the show's producers from representing critical parts of the novel onscreen. Larry Cohen, who co-wrote the script for *It* (1990) with Tommy Lee Wallace, described the difficulty of adapting King's novel under the constraints of Standards and Practices, whose "cardinal rule" was to "not show kids in jeopardy" when "the very basis of *It*" (1986) (Bradley) is the mortal danger to all the children of Derry. This limitation forced the show's producers to imply rather than explicitly depict violence directed towards children. *It* (1990) works around many of these prohibitions with scenes that are still disturbing. Georgie Dembrough's and Laurie Ann Winterbarger's deaths occur off-screen when It as Pennywise lures both children to their deaths with his Dancing Clown persona. Laurie Ann's murder is implied via reaction shots. In a close-up of Laurie Ann from Pennywise's point of view, the camera zooms in to focus on the child's terrified face just before the clown attacks her. Laurie Ann's death is implied in the next scene, a reaction shot of Laurie Ann's mother, who looks off screen and screams while she is presumably viewing her daughter's mangled body. Georgie Dembrough's dismemberment is similarly implied through his own reaction shot after he reaches into the sewer to take his lost boat that Pennywise offers to him. George screams, and the camera fades to black and into a wide-angle scene from above of a child's coffin surrounded by mourners. These two scenes are impressive for how they obliquely communicate Its stranger-danger. Veteran character actor Tim Curry who plays Pennywise also does a masterful job of scaring viewers with little prosthetic makeup and no CGI.

Other scenes that were toned-down to prevent showing children in danger were not handled so well; for example, in the scene where Henry Bowers and his gang have cornered Ben and Henry is about to use his knife to carve his name into the boy's stomach, Ben kicks his would-be assailant in the crotch and escapes by throwing himself down the hill behind him and into the Barrens. This scene would have still been effective had it not been for the production's ridiculous costuming of Henry's gang. Jen Cheney describes Henry and his gang's costuming as making them look like "mini-Squiggys and little Lennys than believably real kids," which diminishes their credibility as scary bullies. Muschietti's *It* (2017), on the other hand, represents Henry as a kid who is so dangerous that even his friends are afraid of him when he carves one of the letters of his name into Ben before he is interrupted.

ABC's standards and practices also removed from *It* (1990) references to what were considered immoral sexual behavior at the time. Some of these changes were unimportant, such as Bill's adulterous sex with Beverly before he realizes that his wife Audra has followed him to Derry and been captured by It. Other omissions more radically change King's characters. Standards and practices' imperative to not show children in danger eliminated Al Marsh's incestuous desire for his daughter and changed him from an abusive father to a strict one. Al hits Bev only once, in the scene where he accuses her of having "done something she shouldn't" with a boy after he finds Ben's poem to her. Al backhands his daughter once before she escapes the house. *It*'s (1990) rare scene of an adult harming a child was mitigated as a once culturally—if extreme—acceptable way of disciplining children in 1960. *It* (2017) picks up on King's characterization of Al as his daughter's future rapist: every time Beverly is alone with her father, she is visibly uncomfortable under his gaze. When Beverly comes home with a paper bag of sanitary pads, Al ominously informs his daughter that she "is a woman now" and looks at her in a predatory way that prompts her to lock herself in the bathroom and cut off her hair. When Al sees Beverly's home haircut, he complains that she now looks "like a boy." Beverly's intention was not to pass as male, but to help her escape the menace of her father's gaze. Later, after Al discovers Ben's poem to his daughter hidden in her underwear drawer, he locks her in the house, accuses her of doing "womanly things" with her male friends, and tries to rape her; Beverly uses lethal force to defend herself. Because *It* (2017) is set in the 1990s and made in the #metoo era, Beverly leaves Derry to live with her aunt instead of being punished for defending herself against a rapist.

ABC's standards and practices also minimized the gore and other bodily fluids shown throughout *It* (1990). Network programming in the 1990s did not show gore to prevent alienating viewers who wanted to protect their children from disturbing media. This reluctance diminishes the efficacy of Stan Uris' suicide scene in *It* (1990). When Stan's wife discovers her husband is dead in the bath and the word "It" is scrawled on the tile next to the tub in blood, how he died is not apparent until the camera pans to a close-up of a razor blade on the side of the tub with just three drops of blood beside it. Although Stan died by cutting his wrists, the water where his cooling body rests is impossibly clear, and the trickle of blood running down his arm that dangles outside of the tub is not enough to permanently stain the grout in the pristine white bathroom. Tamed-for-television scenes such as these undercut *It* (1990) as a horror film and make it difficult for the viewer to suspend disbelief.

Other scenes from King's novel are sanitized in *It* (1990) to avoid visual references to menstrual blood and feces. Television networks' standards-and-practices divisions have been reluctant historically to even hint at menstruation or menstrual blood, urine, and feces in their programming. The scene where It covers the walls, window, and ceiling of Beverly's bathroom in *It* (1986) is tamed in *It* (1990) because of its implied connection to Beverly's impending menarche (Thoens 136). Instead, It sends a blood-filled red balloon up Beverly's bathroom sink, which explodes in her face. The scene becomes comic when Al responds to his daughter's resulting screams: Al cannot see the blood and so does not know as he peers down the drain for the phantom spider that his hands are covered in the invisible substance. Al unintentionally smears the invisible blood on Beverly's face when he grabs her chin in a fatherly gesture of reassurance. In *It* (2017), Beverly and her fellow Losers spend hours squeezing and scrubbing the thick gout of blood coating her bathroom that only they can see. The monster's connection to other bodily fluids such as feces and urine are avoided in *It* (1990): the production's set of Derry's sewers is so clean and well-lit that they could be like a subterranean water park rather than a conduit for the city's bodily wastes. On both occasions when the Losers emerge from these sewers, they are impossibly clean and dry: only a few smudges of dirt on their faces and hands indicate that they have been crawling around somewhere dirty. Even Eddie's body, which is retrieved from underground in *It* (1990), shows no signs of trauma or being dragged through a sewer. One of the reasons that King's *It* (1986) is an effective work of horror is due to the monster's ability to break down the symbolic borders between self and other by dragging its victims through a stew of bodily wastes that are the fluids of abjection. *It's* (1990) failure to adequately represent these bodily wastes on the screen diminishes the monster's ability to be a credible existential threat.

It's (1990) special effects that are "less than 'special,'" (Magistrale 169, *Hollywood's*) also defang King's monster by making "the viewer conscious of their contrivances and intrusions into the narrative" (Magistrale 169, *Hollywood's*). *It*'s (1990) poor special effects are due to the small "operational budgets for made-for-television films," which were approximately "five times smaller than the average Hollywood feature film" (Edgerton 169) in the miniseries' and made-for-television film's heyday. The scenes where the Losers confront the creature in its Pennywise and spider forms are so obviously contrived that they are laughable. When the Losers best It-as-Pennywise, the monster shrinks and disappears into an approximately three-inch diameter drain hole. This effect was achieved with a Pennywise puppet twisted through and down the drain, but the film's transition from actor to puppet is so clumsy that the effect detracts from the terror of the moment. Its spider form is even less persuasive. The giant spider puppet operated by someone inside of the costume is so rigid that It, the creature, is about as threatening as a child's toy. B-movies like Jack Arnold's 1957 *The Incredible Shrinking Man* offer better models of how to create a credible giant spider on a tight budget. The most effective part of *It*'s (1990) spider-dismantling scene occurs when there is no faux spider in the shot: Bill hoists the It-spider's bloody heart as the camera pans to focus on the shadows behind the group that reflect their actions in pantomime. Horror film does not have to be gory, or even explicit, to be effective, and both clumsily executed special effects diminish the monster's ability to frighten, which supports the ending's closure in unintended ways.

Finally, King's non-linear narration, which suggests that the monster is indestructible, cannot be easily translated in a visual medium. As he does in many of his novels, King blurs past and present in *It* (1986). Magistrale describes how King's narrative techniques forgo "linear plot development and chronological character growth" in favor of highlighting "the internal workings of the mind" via "recollections, reflections, and remembrances" (Magistrale 114, *Landscape*). King's non-linear plot development in *It* (1986) makes the narrative resistant to closure because it suggests that the creature is a cyclical force of nature instead of a finite entity with a definitive beginning and end. As well, King's non-linear narrative in *It* (1986) makes "making memory and reality synonymous." (Magistrale 114–15, *Landscape*), which forecloses the possibility of anyone turning memory into an objective, documented reality that could be used by future generations to stop the monster's cycle of violence. Non-linear narration, however, is more difficult in television created before the pre-streaming era because content was created for viewers who would only have one opportunity to watch a story written to be interrupted by commercial breaks. If viewers who didn't have the opportunity to rewind and re-watch a segment became lost in the plot, they were more likely to stop watching. *It* (1990) was structured in eight acts to be shown over two nights with lengthy commercial breaks in between each act, so the writers replaced King's non-linear narrative with a story told in chronological order that is occasionally interrupted by individual characters' flashbacks to their childhood. This narrative structure also changes King's chthonic shapeshifter into a finite creature that can be ended by a group of adults who are only armed with a slingshot loaded with silver slugs.

The lengthy format of the miniseries genre allowed *It* (1990) to preserve most of the essential elements of King's novel. The constraints of genre and medium, however, had the unintended effect of domesticating King's meta-monster by imposing narrative closure on King's story, and even Tim Curry's performance as Pennywise was insufficient to make the miniseries frightening.

Works Cited

Bradley, Laura. "How the Original *It* Miniseries Traumatized a Generation of Kids." *Vanity Fair*. 31 August 2017.
Burbatt, Jamie. "Stephen King and the Ambiguously Gay Trope." *Geeks*. November, 2018.
Cheney, Jen. "The 1990 *It* Mini-series Is Not as Scary as You Remember." *Vulture*. 7 September 2017.
Creeber, Glen. "The Mini-series." *The Television Genre Book*. London: British Film Institute, 2001. 35–36, 38.
Creed, Barbara. "Horror and the Monstrous-feminine: An Imaginary Abjection." *Horror: The Film Reader*. Mark Jancovich, ed. Routledge, 2001. 67–76.
Edgerton, Gary. "The American Made-for-TV Movie." *TV Genres: A Handbook and Reference Guide*. Brian G. Rose, ed. Westport, CT: Greenwood, 1985. 151–80.
"43rd Emmy Award Nominees and Winners." *Emmys*. Television Academy.
Hastings, Deborah. "ABC Posts First Ratings Win of the Season." Associated Press. 26 November 1990.
It. Andy Muschetti, Dir. 2017.
_____. Tommy Lee Wallace, Dir. 1990.
It: Chapter Two. Andy Muschetti, Dir. 2019.
Keaney, Quinn. "Let's Discuss Richie's 'Secret' in *It Chapter Two* for a Sec." *Popsugar*. 7 September 2019.
King, Stephen. *It*. New York: Scribner's, 2016. Kindle edition.
Magistrale, Tony. *Hollywood's Stephen King*. New York: Palgrave, 2003.
_____. *Landscape of Fear: Stephen King's American Gothic*. Bowling Green, OH: Popular Press, 1988.
Mislak, Mikayla. "From Sissies to Secrecy: The Evolution of the Hays Code Queer." *Filmic*. April 2015.
Okorafor, Nnedi. "Stephen King's Super-Duper Magical Negroes." *Strange Horizons*, Archive. 25 October 2004.
Pennywise: The Story of It. Chris Griffins, Dir. 2019.
Thoens, Karen. "*It*: A Sexual Fantasy." *Imagining the Worst: Stephen King and the Representation of Women*. Kathleen Margaret Lant and Theresa Thompson, eds. Westport, CT: Greenwood, 1998. 127–40.
Thornburn, David. "Television Melodrama." *Television: The Critical View*. 6th ed. Horace Newcomb, ed. New York: Oxford University Press, 2000. 595–608.

Stephen King, Endings and the Unburdening of *It*

Jason V. Brock

> "There is no real ending. It's just the place where you stop the story."
>
> —Frank Herbert

Beginnings—The Search for Meaning

Humans are natural storytellers.

Whether via metaphor or direct appeal, from prehistory to the present, they have developed and utilized a wide variety of expressive means to convey their understanding of the world, their place in the universe, the very machinations of the cosmos itself. Some individuals are more adept communicators than their peers, of course. Indeed, there are many who remain relatively obscure despite the fact that they have been gifted at imparting hard-earned insights about the human condition; perhaps they simply failed to connect with, or never tried very hard to reach, a receptive audience for differing reasons. Possibly a lack of self-confidence, or because they were too far ahead of their time. Still others may eventually find their audience but years later, or after they have passed on.

Yet, something drives all of them. Cognizant of it or not, they are struggling to reach the same interpersonal connection, the same intimate understanding, others across time have pursued: a search for purpose, fulfillment, and warmth in an indifferent universe of ultimately incomprehensible isolation and bleakness. They seek the only thing dreamers intuitively understand as true immortality: *to be remembered.* Because to be remembered is to have existed; humans *are* their memories, after all. Without memories there is no sense of self, no cohesive reality in which to ground the actions, the words, the deeds, of existence. To remember and to be remembered is to be fully human, to have truly lived. This is what is so devastating about a diagnosis like Alzheimer's Disease—it erases our memories, robs us of our self, and replaces it with a non-entity, a thing that exists but does not live outside an endless, agonizing "now" devoid of temporal context.

Nevertheless, even if these creators consciously understand the cold truth—that they are most likely toiling in obscurity … that they will probably be consigned to the same yawning void as many who have come before them … that they will, very likely, never achieve anything more than a few modest ambitions—they persist. Their final comfort is unspoken: At least they will *be remembered* for something. Even if it means they are destined to be the stuff of future recollection after they have died—that possibility alone gives life meaning aside from simply being a mindless, unremembered, genetic replication method. After all, precious few are able to resonate in their own time, on their own terms, even in this age of instant communication and widespread multimedia awareness … it seems an almost impossible task, frankly.

And yet, someone in the modern era who *has* been able to transcend such oblivion is wildly bestselling author Stephen Edwin King, a man of humble origins—and an implausible candidate for such unbridled success.

*Interlude One—*It, *Pennywise and Remembrance*

The story of King's 1986 epic novel *It*—about a malevolent, shapeshifting entity that reappears periodically to harvest the children of a small Maine town—is well-known, so overly detailing it here is unnecessary, but there are certain aspects which deserve to be considered, as this is a touchstone book in the long career of its creator, and is significant in a number of ways that are not readily apparent to the casual reader. A novel four years in the writing according to King (Stephen King, *It* 1473), this was, at the time, one of his most complex and variegated works, and, despite some issues, stands as a towering achievement in his output.

Without getting into too many plot points, the final result is a curious mélange of influences, styles, approaches, and ideas, and seems at once determined to play with the reader's intellectual perceptions of linearity, as well as emotionally payoff sprawling and intricate tableaux—to include a Dantesque descent into a subterranean *Inferno* of sorts by way of the Derry sewer system-cum-dark carnival, the various configurations of "It," and a mysteriously metaphysical "Turtle" figure. *It* nearly succeeds as a novel, and is quite compelling in places as well as being conceptually outstanding; but in execution, the book is hampered due to a lack of focus about what the author is trying to express. While not on the level of William Faulkner with respect to intricacy, for a popular novel rooted in the gothic horror tradition, with a sneaky aside to literary fiction construction-wise, It demonstrates a reach beyond its grasp, though the effort is heroic in scope. In the end, the book is mired by too many needless digressions, thus, bogging down in places as it struggles for unity as a novel. King's personal fixations about his childhood—and perhaps why as a successful creator these issues still haunted him—are on full display by way of the various techniques he deploys within the narrative structure.

To that end, the myriad themes range from customary King fascinations—the adult forged by the crucible of childhood experience/trauma, particularly at the hands of neglectful, absent, or abusive parents; the redemptive power of love, especially in relation to friendships and what constitutes a family unit; the lasting scars of youth, whether from bullying, class, or other mechanisms—to more atypical concerns for the author, the latter to include defining the nature of "absolute" evil, sexual/emotional bonding as ceremonial antidote to noted evil, the changing nature of threats to people over time, specifically as filtered through their vulnerabilities, and finally confronting the terrifying forces of the cosmos, the apparently random nature of the destruction and loss of self, or even the shades and intentions of a supernatural deity.

Central to some of these subjects were King's apparent personal pain around being "othered" as a youth. An awkward, bookish type, he has noted in interviews how out of place he felt as a youngster (Norden 33–35). In the novel, the so-called "Losers' Club" is a collective of "outsiders" who bond over their unique attributes: being black, or female, or overweight, or Jewish, or having a disability, etc. Related is King's unorthodox handling of sex within the context of the Losers' Club, who are going through puberty in this part of the book. Their actions, meant to provide an unbreakable group bond in the physical realm, seem also to be an effort to dispel the "shame" of sexuality through an act of symbolic absolution within the story, and, by extension, with positive attributes of the cosmic—a counter to the negativity of Pennywise/"It." Certainly, this act contributed later to a form of "communal amnesia" for these characters, similar to the effect Pennywise has on them, and, rather than being a true positive as intended, seems to become a type of collective repression. The fact this whole ritual is instigated by the sole female member of the group, Beverly Marsh, could also be read on her part as an act of personal defiance against her abusive father ... a way of proving both her agency and "self" (subjectivity) against one of the "real" monsters in It. That "It" is later revealed to be female, and "gives birth" to fear and horror in a literal sense in the book is worth noting in this light, and seems to point toward a particular ambivalence King had with respect to the power of women, as mothers, as lovers, and over men.

Other layers of complexity are addressed within the novel, also: the ravages of childhood bullying and neglect, financial deprivation, prejudice, even the pall of "survivor's guilt"—as an adult, one of the Losers' Club members commits suicide prior to the group regathering in 1985, unable to confront "It" again. The combined melancholia of the survivors is redeemed by their reckoning with "It" to finally vanquish this malignant force, something they failed to do as youths. The many perils of the adult world—drug abuse, the dangers of success, alcoholism, financial anxiety/providing for offspring, and so on—are background concerns as well; this is a book that dimly reflects King's dawning awareness of his own problems surrounding sobriety, and full-on "adult maturity," projected as violations or confirmations of his personal rules through the actions of malignant clowns, creatures of darkness, and so on (Stephen King, *Bare Bones* 12–13).

Curiously, *It* was greeted with tepid to negative reviews upon release. By this point, perhaps, there was some King backlash; possibly it was due to the length of the book, and there is an argument to be made that it could have been more tightly edited. Maybe it was felt that King was just plainly "too successful." Overexposed. Regardless, it was still a bestseller, would go on to have a large following, and the image of the primary "It" manifestation, Pennywise the Dancing Clown, a Thomas Ligotti–esque being informed by King's own fear of the dark and coulrophobia, was to become a frightening and enduring favorite at Halloween and in the nightmares of people around the world.

The critical and popular reception duly noted, the novel has a noteworthy construction. Throughout, there are a series of historical asides about the fictional setting of Derry, Maine, told through a Lovecraftian frame-of-remove technique, cited as "Interludes" in the context of the book: A fake manuscript written in the manner of diary-like fragments by one of the characters. These "Interludes" are woven into the narrative, within the body of the story pertaining to the seven major characters comprising the Losers' Club and break up the book's structure, which alternates between the events of 1957/1958 (when they were children), and approximately twenty-seven years, roughly a generation, later (1985), when they are adults. Along the way, King touches upon a panoply of other characters (*Jaws*, the Mummy, Frankenstein's Monster, et al), situations, and pop culture references as he builds the story backboning the novel, namely that the "It" of the book's title is an "absolute" evil capable of feeding on the fears and weaknesses of its victims, and is something otherworldly, simultaneously of the moment, yet beyond human conceptions of space/time. These elements are rooted in King's youth, chiefly things inherited from his father, such as his first horror anthology, featuring an H.P. Lovecraft tale, discovered in his family's belongings along with home movies of his father and other personal artifacts from a man the author really never knew, and does not actually *remember*, interestingly (Norden 34–37).

Memory and remembrance, of course, are prominent components throughout the novel; the remembrances of the characters, of the documented history of the town of Derry, and also with respect to the striking *loss* of recall by the characters after their confrontations with "It." Pennywise/"It" acts as both a siphon of memory and as an intruder into the conscious world for unwanted thoughts or recollections. King exploits this power by way of the shapeshifting aspects of "It" on the personal level—it manipulates feelings and appears to read minds and emotional states—as well as the way the thing controls the fate of Derry over time, a more collective concern, suggestive of the way myths and legends operate throughout history. The insightful use of memory is fascinating and appears to speak to King's thoughts about the existential importance of such a phenomenon to both individuals and with respect to communal identity.

Additionally, in King's efforts to understand himself and his relationships to his *actual* children as they matured—since age is closely associated with memory, and contrasts with knowledge, intellect, or wisdom—this set-up reveals something about his admitted parental anxieties early on due to the failings of his father and his impoverished upbringing (34–35). He appears to be expressing his unspoken hope that he will be remembered fondly, especially by his offspring, in contrast to his own recollections about his father, which was nothing. At pending midlife when the novel was published, King's place in the world, unsurprisingly, is an undercurrent in the various characterizations and scenarios he presents during the course of the book.

In the final analysis, *It* offers quite a lot to unload and decipher, and even more to carry around in one's psyche; no doubt confronting, examining, and documenting all this was a huge unburdening for King, a catharsis.

Middles—The Personal Foundations of It

While tempting to think that creators, especially writers, imbue a great deal of themselves into their work, the reality is more complicated.

King himself has observed in the past that he draws ideas and inferences from his physical surroundings, but his characters are mostly fictitious products of his mind, noting: "It's not enough to have imagination. […] You have to be able to tap into it" (Hanlon 220). Obviously, based on his output, he has a fertile and active imagination, and has done quite well tapping into it. Combining this ability with a drive to write and a disciplined work ethic, he has instilled his vision into the bedrock of the American, even global, subconscious. Who has not felt the sting of being an "outsider," as his creation Carrie White (1974's *Carrie*) so painfully embodies? And who has not wanted to change events to forestall a possible negative outcome, as Johnny Smith tries to do in *The Dead Zone* (1979)? King's ideas and characters often appeal to deep levels of our unconscious dreams and desires, although they frequently shock and surprise us with unexpected results when played out on the page. This is likely another key aspect to his appeal: an uncanny ability to communicate near-universal insecurities and compassion within the confines of sheaves of paper and ink.

A "lark" (early-riser), King has stated that he usually writes in the morning: [after personal chores] "I get back at 9:30 and write to 11:30. Every day I write 1,500 words" (Hanlon 218). He writes and revises into the evening. This is his schedule even on the weekends. If this seems to be the work of a desperate man, there is some truth to that notion. After all, he has not always been a successful and well-known author, with riches in the bank, awards overflowing in the trophy room, and an assured place in collective memory.

Early on, there was no sign that he would succeed as a writer. Born in Portland, Maine, even a cursory review of his troubled upbringing and young adulthood shows this. Growing up in poverty in rural Maine, King, his mother Ruth, and his adopted older brother David were abandoned by his father, Donald. As a result, his mother was forced to take odd jobs to make ends meet, frequently relocating the family to the Midwest and other places for work (Norden 33–34). No doubt this history of relocation and the ritual of making and losing friends played a part in his understanding of people and his affinity for the troubled children who have frequently populated his work. Nowhere is this on display more tellingly than in *It*, whose child protagonists are well-realized and deeply developed over the course of the story, to extend into their adult incarnations later.

Eventually, as an adolescent returning to Maine with his family, he discovered the work of Lovecraft in an old anthology, as noted, and became determined to be a professional writer—thankfully he appeared not to have read about Lovecraft's own career obstacles. Still, nothing was certain, and the family struggled. All this adversity would later become fodder for his works, including *It*.

As an adult working menial jobs to provide for his own young family—he married his wife Tabitha in 1971; Naomi, their only daughter had come along in 1970, ahead of marriage; eldest son Joe, later known in his own right as the author Joe Hill (2010's *Horns*), was born in 1972—things appeared grim, suffocating, although he was able to put his English degree to some use teaching at a local high school. Of course, the economy was challenging in the early 1970s, so nothing was a given. He kept writing, however. And, more problematically for a time, drinking. Publications in men's magazines helped pay the bills in the interim. Desperation fed his ambition, as tough times were always only a missed paycheck away. Slowly, he was making his mark, chipping away. Eventually he had a few unpublished novels under his belt, and his confidence grew (32–33).

In retrospect, it is an astounding story of overcoming long odds, yet he never gave up. He kept writing, even when it appeared that a breakthrough was not in the offing, even though he had children to feed. He was striving for something more, it appears. Sadly, just before his debut novel *Carrie* was published, his mother died, so she did not live to see his impending triumphs. He was twenty-seven at the time—and possibly the significance of the number twenty-seven in *It* is a nod to this. After *Carrie*, of course, his fortunes undeniably improved, and he became a remarkably successful author, both popularly, with reviewers, and financially. This positive upward trend was to continue for around a decade, right up to 1986's *It*. Revealingly, he noted during some interviews when the novel was first released, that as his kids were growing up (his youngest child, Owen, was nine by the time the book was out), his enthusiasm for writing stories about children waned as a result (Schaefer 199). This looks to be confirmed by the dedication to the novel itself.

To further illuminate this, an informal survey of the author's work reveals that this marked a change, in broad terms, regarding his story-focus— a general shift away from books centered on the lives and experiences of children to more "adult-oriented" efforts, such as *Misery* (1987), *Gerald's Game* (1992), and others in this "post-childhood" phase. According to King's online bibliography of novels oldest to newest, *It* was his thirteenth published novel under his own name; the book appears to signify, for a variety of reasons, not only the end of childhood as the foundation/inspiration for his anxieties about many things, but also as a final goodbye to his father—consciously unrecalled, yet looming in his subconscious like some ghastly apparition. Concurrently, the book seems to be a love offering to his children.

Interlude Two—Disruption, Cultural Shapeshifting and Social Memory

Today mass media is in a state of flux; commonly this is referred to as the Internet Age, which presents both challenges and opportunities.

Although King has been a reliable literary and cinematic staple for over forty years, of late there has been a resurgence in many of his properties, to encompass re-conceptualizations of earlier films, as well as adaptations of new and older works or ideas in his catalog, such as content provider Hulu's

2018 original *Castle Rock*, and the Shudder *Creepshow* anthology series in 2019, based on King's 1982 collaboration with director George A. Romero. His influence is so vast, even "Stephen King–adjacent" products—books and films reminiscent or inspired by King and his creative output—are popular as a grounding for others. This "Stephen King Aesthetic" generally comprises "special" children in peril, with certain stock characters or tropes as part of the overall dynamic (e.g., religious fanatics, corrupt authority figures, dangerous or tragic animals, mysterious or shadow institutions, conspiracies, rustic people and their value systems, as well as frequent supernatural elements). Characters in King's universe are often plainspoken; the written stylistics are not flashy but have a "cinematic" quality. The people feel "lived-in," real, and the scenarios ring true, if at times far-fetched. "Twist" endings are rarely employed; good almost always triumphs over evil; there is a general ambiance of hope or positivity about the future in many of his works, as well as the idea of the basic decency of most people, even in extreme situations. As a consequence, King's typically character-driven stories are often comforting in their resolutions, which may explain his continued popularity.

Recently, perhaps the most obvious example of the "Stephen King Aesthetic" in popular culture comes from streaming giant Netflix. *Stranger Things* (2016–present), rides high on a wave of pure nostalgia for the late 1970s/1980s, fomented by the series' creators and visionary force, the North Carolina–born identical twins known collectively as The Duffer Brothers. This duo has unabashedly paid homage to a host of iconic creatives and images from this era, to include filmmakers John Carpenter, Steven Spielberg, innumerable movies and shows of the period, and, most obviously, Stephen King himself as they mentioned in an interview with *The Hollywood Reporter*, all generally cloaked within the aura of the times—the music, fashions, and other trappings. Even the most recent reimagining of *It*—retroactively dubbed *It: Chapter One*—is rooted in their attempts to remake it prior to their success with the Netflix series, and was a catalyst in getting the 2017 hit produced.

Since these transmedia ventures have been quite successful, anticipation has been high for the second installment, and presumed finale, *It: Chapter Two* (2019). Indeed, just as the 2017 reworking was a worldwide blockbuster according to website BoxOfficeMojo.com, the site likewise reports that the sequel has set box office records of its own. With modern film and CGI techniques guaranteeing virtually anything conceived can be rendered with stunning visual detail and realism, the appetite for King and the era he is so strongly associated with, the 1970s and '80s, has likely never been greater.

This seems especially true for the *It* franchise. While the first attempt at adaptation—the films, taken as a duology, are updates of the two-part 1990 ABC television miniseries—is a reasonable effort, time has not been kind to it. Though performances are strong overall, and the direction is solid, the medium of network television—and the attendant censorship endemic to early 1990s broadcast TV—conspired to undermine the final product. During this time, although he was already an immensely popular author with several successful film adaptations of his work, lengthy books such as King's over 1,100-page opus were somewhat disadvantaged, mainly due to a generally unstated lack of respect for genre works rather than anything related to King or his writing specifically.

Undeniably, "the times were different." These offerings, whether TV or film, were treated as mere "popcorn" fare, not "serious" art, and were not as critically fashionable as "gritty" dramas or "witty" comedies. Since 1990, however, things have progressed; one positive development has been a shift in acceptance for what was once deemed "transgressive" material, particularly during the more religiously conservative 1980s. King himself could be seen to have had a major hand in this due to his prolific, influential output and bankable cinematic impact.

Positive as this has been content-wise, a negative unintended effect of change, principally in technological terms, is that the media-scape vying for the public's attention has splintered; for a novelist, this has meant, in practical terms, that the number of potential readers has dropped. It is simply not enough to have books, movies, and TV anymore. What once passed as must-see entertainment even a scant few years ago has been rendered practically quaint with the overwhelming ascendency of the Internet and related digital media—video games, podcasts, YouTube, social networking sites, online shopping, audio books—and the subsequent collapse or outright loss of physical spaces in which to congregate. It is noteworthy the way all this has played out since 1986, the year *It* was published. Given the collective geopolitical and social churn, particularly 9/11 and after, dynamics surrounding group-experiences—live performances, concerts, workplaces—have changed greatly, and shared monocultural moments have become increasingly rare.

As a result of this accelerated fracturing of time and attention, society seems to have graduated to a stage of vicarious yet immersive spectacle, with shorter and shorter memory and attention spans. Brandishing ever more powerful wearable devices and mobile gear, the public is now continually inundated by huge science fiction extravaganzas (the ongoing *Star Wars* franchise), sweeping works of high fantasy [*The Lord of the Rings* cycle (2001–2003)], anime and manga, numberless comic book movies from Marvel and DC, and even horror revivals in the guise of remakes and re-imaginings of older stories [*The Shape of Water* (2017)]. In other words, audiences have become accustomed to *more*—their expectations heightened, their sensibilities jaded, by interactivity and technological innovation. Over this same interval, fandom itself has exploded and split into innumerable niches. This is how the 2011 sensation *Fifty Shades of Grey* and its sequels by E.L. James began, for example—as a work of so-called "online fanfic" by a devotee of author Stephenie Meyer's *Twilight* books (2005–2015); both series were later filmed, to great financial success (BusinessInsider.com).

Thus, has the creative aspiration morphed; remembrance and fortune may be attained simply by "being (in)famous": self-published web-comics, blogs, digital music, viral video clips, Twitter activism, and so on. The old gatekeepers and even the notion of permanent libraries have diminished in importance and cultural value. While traditional fiction and publishing still has a place, increasingly the world seems to be moving toward an ephemeral, post-literate, visually based multimedia ecosystem—memes, streaming, Internet distribution channels—to capture the hearts and minds of the multitudes. Due to greatly lowered technological barriers to entry into enterprises such as publishing, music, and filmmaking—fused with new channels for promotion and monetization and a sort of shared cultural amnesia/nostalgia about efforts and conventions from and of the past—the ability of new and unknown voices to be heard has blurred the edges of commerce, art, and what it means to be a professional brand. Like anything, this all has good and bad aspects. Could a mainly literary phenomenon such as Stephen King happen today? Would the masses have the patience to follow his introspections and realizations in books like 1978's *The Stand* or, later, *It*? Or has the appetite for such non-media-driven printed epics permanently dwindled in favor of e-books, streaming, and other digital manifestations?

Not even one hundred years ago, there was another disruptive cycle similar to the one happening now: the dawn of the television epoch.

At first the nascent medium struggled due to lean budgets and lack of original content, even relying for a while on film as a conduit to fill airtime. This early period of network TV, from roughly the early 1940s, was defined by the Big Three major broadcasters in the beginning: CBS, NBC, and ABC. By the mid–20th century, this time would eventually be recognized by institutions such as the *Los Angeles Times* and others as the Golden Age of Television, and was generally symbolized, perhaps unexpectedly, by a pantheon of highly influential directors and, especially, writers, to include Sidney Lumet and Paddy Chayefsky [*Network* (1976)], Horton Foote [*To Kill a Mockingbird* (1962)], Rod Serling [*The Twilight Zone* (1959–1964)], Reginald Rose [*Twelve Angry Men* (1957)], and a few others who would also come to define cinema in the coming decades. These were the inheritors, as it were, of the fading radio traditions of such luminaries as Orson Welles (Halloween 1938's *War of the Worlds* panic broadcast), Arch Oboler (*Lights Out!*), and Norman Corwin [*On a Note of Triumph* (1945)]. Once this live-TV era itself passed into history, and multi-camera filmic dramas, sitcoms, and other "cinematic"-style productions ("special presentations" and, later, "Movies of the Week") rose to the fore, television truly fulfilled its role as *the* major entertainment and informational source for several decades. This situation was not to last.

By the late 1980s, network TV had the cachet and budgets to accomplish sophisticated, "serious," large-scale productions. Dan Curtis, creator of *Dark Shadows* (1966–1971), mounted immense adaptations of Herman Wouk's classic World War II novel *The Winds of War* (aired in 1983) and its sequel *War and Remembrance* (aired in 1988; both distributed by ABC). Predating the ABC *It* effort, this was nonetheless a time well before the contemporary "Platinum Age of Television" (Gross) ushered in by current offerings—replete with graphic content, realistic writing, and "method acting" performances—generated via pay television companies such as HBO, AMC, Starz, and others. Prior to this "content revolution" there were, of course, significant efforts at so-called "must-see" network television based on respected and challenging literary properties [Alex Haley's family-slave miniseries *Roots* (1977)] as well as one-off dramatic presentations, sometimes based on current news or literary works. It was during this late 1980s/early 1990s period that the *It* miniseries appeared, and while a credible effort, as noted, it fell into an abyss—too early for the technological innovations needed to pull it off, too soon for the respect the source material deserved by the television powers of the day. In 1990, *It* had simply been too vast for broadcast television, or even the movie theater, due to its challenging content, breadth of vision, and state-of-the-art requirements. Technology and attitudes would finally catch up in 2017—twenty-seven years later, ironically.

In retrospect, is deep content—and the ability to access it physically—still imperative in the search for personal meaning, social memory, and cultural relevance? That has yet to be determined in this restructured and changing environment. Current scenarios promise a strange mixture of trepidation and wonder at what lies ahead.

Endings—A Bid for Remembrance

Ultimately, *It* and its adaptations are about *endings*: of innocence, childhood, memory, fear. As such, it inevitably becomes a tale about new beginnings and how they are birthed, even if unobserved: of accomplishment through adversity, of attaining adulthood, of moving on from tragedy, and of overcoming immense obstacles.

That said, endings are its primary fuel, the source of power for its narrative engine. Unfortunately, King has long had a weakness when it comes to satisfying conclusions to his books—logically, not emotionally—and *It* is no exception in this regard. Once again, the actual ending is supplanted by the *deus ex machina* of the final scene, which presents a sort of "false closure" to the reader. The last chapter, depicting triumph by way of the protagonist and his wife finding happiness after the apparent banishment of "It," comes close to being anti-climactic without *quite* tipping the novel into later Bradbury mawkishness [though at times *It* feels like a modern answer, update, and/or counter to *Something Wicked This Way Comes* (1962)]—luckily for King. It is perilously close, however. Many have found the ending—especially for *this* book—to be unfulfilling; the ABC miniseries followed this arc to the same predictable, and disappointing, conclusion.

Regardless, some of the successful "endings" addressed by *It* include character archetypes, plot devices, authorial interests, and other elements, which, as a result, freed King to explore deeper themes, characterizations, and ideas in later efforts. In essence, *It* can be viewed as a transitional work by the author, one where he attempts to remedy his own dependencies on techniques, storylines, and characterizations he had made somewhat "expected" and cliché in his literary universe. *It*, in many ways, was an exploding of these tropes and personal mythologies, and an exploration of not only his triumphs—via wildly successful characters in the book and the trappings of fame/wealth—but also as a requiem ode to those foundational aspects of his upbringing and youth that he held the most nostalgic longings for, be they films, comic books, or even the rougher, simpler life he endured as a child and adolescent.

It functions as a personal "childhood's end" work. A way for the author to unburden himself from the bitter or sad elements of past experiences, such as his absent (unremembered, thus, dead) father, the loss of his mother before achieving success, and the bittersweet final separation of his children from himself. In doing so, he establishes a new way ahead; cathartically divesting negative elements by way of "accelerated emotional distancing," represented in the novel via rapid "forgetting" of the troubling circumstances in the story by the main characters. *It* also, intended or not, closes the author's own "childishness," as he throws in all the monsters and interests from his youth to feed the fire of the narrative.

Another King trope largely purged with the closing of the covers of *It* is his apparent fascination that children somehow possess "special gifts" and are able to tap into an intrinsic and unique understanding of the adult world, including how to fix the problems therein. This is an idea he has explored in multiple volumes, and with this book, he puts the innocence of children as the chief remedy for adult anxieties mostly to rest, though he would revisit this notion in less overt terms in later works. Likewise, there is the concomitant notion of the adult duty to "put away childish things" inherent in the concept of the Losers' finally overcoming "It"—and returning to their present-day lives, full of wistful hope, though gradually losing memory of the events that transpired—a display of unease about the creeping senescence that seems to await us all ... haunted still, despite their best efforts to exorcize the cursed history of Derry, Maine, a place rife with the residue of past evils.

This is all enough to bundle into several novels, much less a single volume, yet, as noted, this seems to be a kind of swansong for many things for King. Afterward, he looks to have divested himself of this emotional and psychological detritus and moved on to other, more adult, preoccupations. Despite the book's complexity—its sprawling timeframe, large ensemble of characters, and sometimes vexing aspects—*It* still surprises and shocks the reader. Although not his best-realized novel—King attributes that to be *The Dead Zone* due to its plot-driven narrative (Stephen King, *Bare Bones* 13–14), though *Pet Sematary* (1983) is a strong contender—it is undoubtedly a powerful work for which he will be long remembered, which is the best outcome any artist can hope for. While the original TV series was acceptable for what it was given the constraints of the time, the remakes are much better able to fully explore the potential of this complicated tome; only time will tell where Pennywise takes future readers and viewers. Wherever that may be, *It* is sure to be fascinating.

WORKS CITED

Business Insider. "'Fifty Shades of Grey' Started Out as 'Twilight' Fan Fiction Before Becoming an International Phenomenon." *Business Insider*, 17 Feb. 2015, www.businessinsider.com/fifty-shades-of-grey-started-out-as-twilight-fan-fiction-2015-2.

Fienberg, Daniel. "The Duffer Brothers Talk 'Stranger Things' Influences, 'It' Dreams and Netflix Phase 2." *The Hollywood Reporter*, 1 Aug. 2016, www.hollywoodreporter.com/fien-print/duffer-brothers-talk-stranger-things-916180.

Gross, Terry. "'The Greatest Hits of the 'Platinum Age of Television.'" *Fresh Air*, NPR, 10 Nov. 2016, www.npr.org/2016/11/10/501556982/the-greatest-hits-of-the-platinum-age-of-television.

Hanlon, Michael. "Horror Writer Stephen King Is Afraid There's Something Awful Under His Bed." *Toronto Star*, Oct. 1983. Rpt. in *Feast of Fear: Conversations with Stephen King*. By Tim Underwood and Chuck Miller. 1st ed. New York: Carroll & Graf Publishers, 1992, pp. 218, 220. Print.

"It (2017)." *Box Office Mojo*, www.boxofficemojo.com/movies/?id=it.htm.

"It: Chapter Two (2019)." *Box Office Mojo*, www.boxofficemojo.com/movies/?id=it2.htm.

King, Stephen. "An Evening with Stephen King at the Billerica, Massachusetts Public Library." Colony Communications, Inc. 1983. Rpt. in *Bare Bones Conversations on Terror with Stephen King*. By Tim Underwood and Chuck Miller. Warner Books, 1989, pp. 1–24. Print.

_____. *It*. Pocket Books, Paperback Edition, Dec. 2016.

_____. *StephenKing.com—Novels—Oldest to Newest*, www.stephenking.com/library/novel/index_old-new.html.

King, Susan. "'The Golden Age of Television.'" *Los Angeles Times*, 28 Nov. 2009, www.latimes.com/archives/la-xpm-2009-nov-28-la-et-classic-tv28-2009nov28-story.html.

McNelly, Willis E. "Interview with Frank and Beverly Herbert." *Interview with Frank Herbert and Beverly Herbert by Willis E. McNelly*, www.sinanvural.com/seksek/inien/tvd/tvd2.htm.

Norden, Eric. "Playboy Interview: Stephen King." *Playboy*, Jun. 1983. Rpt. in *Bare Bones Conversations on Terror with Stephen King*. By Tim Underwood and Chuck Miller. Warner Books, 1989, pp. 24–56. Print.

Schaefer, Stephen. "Interview with Stephen King." Portions published in *Boston Herald* Jul. 1986 and in *Men's Guide to Fashion (MGF)* VOLUME TWO, NUMBER NINE Oct. 1986. Rpt. in *Feast of Fear: Conversations with Stephen King*. By Tim Underwood and Chuck Miller. 1st ed. New York: Carroll & Graf Publishers, 1992, pp. 198–199. Print.

The Disturbing Appeal of Pennywise

Michelle Leigh Gompf

Since the release of early promotional materials for the film *It* (2017) a cursory internet search for Pennywise reveals that, at least some, viewers are attracted to Pennywise. This attraction may be due in large part to people being aware of the actor and being attracted to him, seeing him through the clown makeup and, therefore, not fully getting into the spirit of the horror, or not suspending disbelief and entering the world of the film in the first place. Another reason for attraction to Pennywise may be related to an attraction to anti-heroes and even villains, being similar to an attraction to Loki or Hannibal Lecter; however, other possible explanations can be explored. Shifting the focus to his appeal as opposed to attraction allows consideration of not only the explicitly stated attractions to Pennywise, but also those who in addition, or instead, focus on the aesthetic appeal of the character. Even before the film was released, when photos of the 2017 Pennywise costume were released as promotions, reaction focused on the aesthetics of the costume and their effect, wondering if it was scary enough or too silly or weird, or if it looked too scary and wouldn't be able to trick children. The 229 comments on Barkan's article are typical of these varied reactions and Breznican subtitled his article on the costume "Go ahead laugh. It'll be easier for him to find you in the dark." All of the reactions agreed that it was not a typical clown costume of the kind one sees contemporary circus or birthday clowns wearing, or finds in costume shops, lacking big baggy pants and a colorful shirt for example. The aesthetics of Pennywise are central to viewers' reactions to him, as well as to the reactions of the kids in the film, placing *It* (2017) in the company of other recent works of horror that use aesthetics to guide and create emotions and reactions. It is the visual aesthetic of the character, including his uncanny aspect, and his facial expressions and posture, that lead the Losers' Club and others, including viewers, to be curious about him, even if they are scared. His appearance is a way for Pennywise to get closer to his victims and ultimately be more terrifying.

Instead of getting articles about the aesthetics of Pennywise that discuss artistic aspects of the character and the filming—the costume design and makeup, for example—one gets many results in which "aesthetic" is used as a noun, meaning an artistic production. Search results are filled with links to various Pinterest and Tumblr accounts where people have posted their Pennywise or *It* (2017) "aesthetics": collages of images from the film or original artistic images based on the film. The collages are clearly arranged with an eye to color and design and the original works make clear artistic design decisions, often involving a bright splash of red, often red balloons, against a darker background. While some of these "aesthetics" indicate a sexual/physical attraction to Pennywise, many do not and seem instead to enjoy playing with various artistic elements of the character and, in particular, the color contrast. The use of color and design to make the film—but also Pennywise himself—appealing should not be surprising given that other films and TV shows have made the violent or disturbing appealing through color and design, particularly the TV shows *Hannibal* and *The Handmaid's Tale*. While the clown costume is meant to seem otherworldly and not quite human, the colors and design are beautiful, leading to a visceral attraction, in the same way that *Hannibal* used a visual aesthetic to make murder scenes works of art and *The Handmaid's Tale* makes the vision of the handmaids in their dystopia beautiful. These two shows are vivid examples of the power of aesthetics to create a desired reaction in the viewer: both appeal and fear; fear, in part, because of the viewers' realization of finding the disturbing beautiful. In both of these shows, the aesthetic appeal is predominantly created through stark color contrasts, close-ups, and lighting; in *It* (2017) the appeal is created in a similar way. Before Pennywise is examined, let's take a brief detour through these two other works to see further examples of how this type of aesthetic operates affectively.

Ziomek says of *Hannibal* that "Cinematographic frames are focused on texture details, accentuated lighting and foregrounding silhouettes" (55) and that Hannibal "is granted a noticeable number of close-ups […] creating a more sympathetic portrayal of the villain" (55). Ultimately, "it is the artistic aspects of murders that allures the audience" (56). *It*, too, makes use of texture and lighting. As in *Hannibal*, these aspects draw in the viewers, but in *It* they also work to draw in prey. Klock claims that "*Hannibal* is defined by its deeply surreal images" (9), and that "[v]iolence on *Hannibal* is always quite beautiful" (15). In *It*, the surreality is created through the uncanniness of Pennywise and the mixed-period costume, and while the violence is not beautiful, the prelude to it is. Similarly, in reference to *The Handmaid's Tale*, Leyda says:

"it coerces viewers to watch its horrors and rewards them with its aesthetic accomplishments" (179) and "[t]he series employs close-ups and lush cinematography to draw viewers into Offred's experience" (181). It also uses close-ups and color to draw viewers in. Additionally, Nussbaum, in her review of *The Handmaid's Tale* in *The New Yorker*, claims that in the show "the emphasis is visual, making violence as beautiful as a nightmare: red dress, blue dress, white sheets, black van." Like the creators of *Hannibal* and *The Handmaid's Tale*, the creators of *It* have made use of the power of aesthetics to manipulate the audience. Through a similar use of contrasting color, lighting, and close-ups, in addition to costuming and movement that emphasizes the uncanny, and makeup and facial expressions that emphasize fear and childishness instead of aggression and danger, the creators of *It* have created an aesthetically appealing Pennywise who can draw both viewers and prey in.

Andy Muschietti, the director of the film, has explicitly discussed the design of and his vision for Pennywise, saying, "aesthetically, I don't dig the 20th century clown. I think it looks cheap, and it's too related to social events [...] but I'm more aesthetically attracted to the old time, like the 19th century clown" (qtd. in Foutch). When asked why the 19th century, he responded: "The aesthetics I guess [...]. I didn't think much about it. It was more of an instinctive choice" (qtd. in Foutch). His statement that it was an "instinctive choice" indicates something happening on an unspoken level, some central attraction to a design that provides a slightly uncanny, out of time feeling that can arouse curiosity first, and then fear. The look is uncanny because it is both familiar and unfamiliar; it is like a clown, but not quite like a clown; like a human, but not quite like a human. The uncanny is often associated with horror, Freud having claimed that "It undoubtedly belongs to all that is terrible—to all that arouses dread and creeping horror" (219), and connecting it to repressed childhood fears; however, it can also provide a positive feeling in its familiarity. Mangan says of the uncanny, "a strong feeling of rightness (a sense of integrated order) is conjoined with at least a tincture of wrongness (something in this order is unnatural, aversive)" (197). The sense of "rightness" can lead to an acceptance of what one sees, explaining why observers do not run away upon first experiencing Pennywise; it could further lead to a desire to uncover the "order" within it or a curiosity about its mixture of the familiar and unfamiliar. By de-emphasizing the expected, bright, baggy colorful contemporary clown costume, but retaining a familiarity of some earlier type of clown, perhaps some people's fear of Pennywise as a clown is diminished and their curiosity or interest is piqued.

To create this mixture of the familiar and unfamiliar, the costume designer, Janie Bryant, took Muschietti's ideas of a 19th-century costume and combined them with other period details, emphasizing the idea of Pennywise as a timeless element, as well as some of the uncanny aspects. Bryant "crafted a form-fitting suit that draws upon a number of bygone times—among them Medieval, Renaissance, Elizabethan, and Victorian eras"; it has "a classic Harlequin quality to the elegant red lines. [...] Every part of the costume is meant to suggest something both ancient and disturbed" (Breznican). Additionally, Bryant deliberately made various aspects of the costume toy-like or childlike: "The pants being short, the high waistline of the jacket, and the fit of the costume [...] gives the character a childlike quality" and "[e]ven the gloves are so tight and seamless they make his hands look like porcelain" (Breznican). These design decisions move away from creepy-killer clown territory, and even from haunted doll territory, to something else. He becomes a character who seems like a fragile delicate old toy and, therefore, not dangerous. The design invites the viewer to come closer to see just how delicate the costume is, to see the details of the design, to see how the various eras and costumes come together, and, perhaps also, because of the seeming fragility, to actually protect Pennywise. This sense of lack of danger and need for protection is also emphasized by the youthfulness of both the actor and the costume: "The costume accentuates his youth, making it look like The Blue Boy outgrew his dandy outfit" (Breznican). This "outgrown" costume isn't as bright and colorful as the 1990s one (which was mainly bright yellow, with orange pompom buttons, blue sleeves, and a multi-colored ruff), but its color, or lack thereof, works to greater effect here. This costume is mainly a gray white with a few splashes of color in the pompom buttons: "Bryant's version of the character prefers to camouflage himself and strike rather than lure children with lively plumage" (Breznican). The reference to camouflage suggests both danger and protection; being able to both protect and draw in. Seeing a brightly colored clown makes it easy to avoid if one is afraid of clowns. Due to camouflage, one could see subtle movement, have one's eye caught by an unexpected splash of color and be drawn in to investigate, perhaps to help something needing help, not realizing the danger until too late. The subtlety and simplicity of the costume works to appeal in a way that a more current, typical clown costume does not.

The costume itself seems less like a costume and more like regular clothes; notice the stains and damage to the ruffle, for example. The dinginess and dirtiness of Pennywise's costume could operate on an affective level, leading to a paradoxical appeal since, according to Brinkema, disgust and rot doesn't just repel, it attracts: "the disgusting is alluring while nevertheless remaining revolting" and "aversion to an object is superimposed alongside attraction toward that same object" (164). It is the formal qualities of disgust that create this affective aesthetic since they consist of "variation in coloration [...] a texture that takes on a sheen or moist glisten [and] the softening of edges" (170). Brinkema also indicates that a central quality of rot is that of changing, deforming, and reforming, in terms of both color and form itself

(171). Pennywise's changes of form, blurring of boundaries and colors, places him in this category of rot and disgust and creates a paradox of attraction and repulsion.

In addition to the costuming, the cinematography also contributes to Pennywise's appeal. According to Brinkema, a central desire of all film "is the wandering desire to see what is on the edge of vision" (90). While this relates explicitly to the edge of a frame of film, this desire can also be applied to wanting to better see things in shadow—like Pennywise—and, therefore, desiring to come closer. The cinematography also helps create Muschietti's aesthetic vision, the uncanniness of the character that will create curiosity in addition to or maybe even instead of fear. Muschietti says of the cinematographer for the film, "Chung is an artist who goes for a surrealistic element" and that "[w]e also discussed the balance of making something realistic, but with that element of intrigue—that something is not right" (qtd. in Dillon). By referring to the something being "not right" as "an element of intrigue," Muschietti implies the desire to have Pennywise be appealing. When someone is intrigued, they want to come closer; they are drawn in. Viewers are drawn to "a shine in the lower part of Pennywise's eyeball" (Dillon), which Muschietti requested. Coloring in post-production also focused on drawing attention to Pennywise's eyes, since, according to colorist Steve Nakamura, "we could crush the shadows and pull up the eyes, making him more contrasty and even creepier" (qtd. in Dillon). The shadow and color contrast is visually appealing in itself, while being also creepy, and it helps to focus the viewers' gaze on Pennywise's eyes.

Pennywise's eyes and facial expressions are the final aspects that (along with the costuming, the colors, the lighting, and the overall uncanniness of the character) lead to his appeal. Throughout the film, Pennywise, particularly when first appearing to the kids, holds his eyes, head, and mouth in a way that implies both submissiveness and youth. This, in turn, can imply not only a lack of danger but also a need for protection. Often, when Pennywise first appears his head is tilted down, but his eyes are looking up, which makes them appear larger, showing more of the white, and his mouth is open in a slight smile, but with no or just a brief glimpse of teeth. The deliberate shine in the white of the eye not only draws the viewers' attention to it, but also makes this portion of the eye look even bigger. In addition, in these scenes, he is either positioned beneath or at a distance from the character and is shot from above or almost straight on, in a medium or long shot, which makes him seem at first smaller than he is. According to Marsh, Adams, and Kleck these qualities imply someone who is: "pleasant, physically weak, socially weak or submissive" (74). In particular, "submissive parties [...] widen their eyes and raise their brows" (74) and more "babyish" faces have "large or round eyes and thick lips" (74). These qualities not only subconsciously indicate submissiveness, but also can indicate someone who is afraid since, "A person expressing fear [...] would acquire bigger and rounder looking eyes, higher and more arched brows, and a babyish flattened and smoothed brow ridge" (75). This description matches very closely the description of Pennywise in scenes where he first appears to someone, setting him up as an approachable figure, not only safe, but also needing help. It explains not only why the kids, particularly Georgie, won't just run away upon first seeing him, but also why audiences are drawn to him, at first.

Clearly, the creators of the film wished to create a Pennywise who would be creepy but intriguing, perhaps even approachable and appealing, to draw in not only Georgie but all of the prey, including the audience. Now that this appeal has been discussed in general, and in theory, specific scenes from the movie can be examined to illustrate how all of these factors come together in practice to create this appeal. The obvious scene to begin with is the first scene Pennywise appears in, his encounter with Georgie. In this scene, approximately five-and-a-half minutes into the film, we first just see the whites of Pennywise's eyes, then he leans forward and we also see the very white bottom half of his face and red lips, some whitish teeth, and the white ruffle. Pennywise is a moment of brightness in the darkness of the sewer and the grayness of the day. When he talks to Georgie, he is looking up from the sewer, but mostly with his eyes. He does not tilt his head up. It is a submissive look, a pleading look, which further emphasizes the whites of his eyes. His eyes don't seem to blink and his stare is intense, but not frighteningly so, due to the continued small smile, which reveals only a glimpse of the white of his teeth. There is a flash of his white hands occasionally. So far, Pennywise is not threatening. He is friendly and a matter of interest to Georgie. It is when Georgie reaches for the boat that the change comes: ragged teeth move further out of Pennywise's face, as if they are a separate creature lunging at Georgie, as if they are a snake coming from Pennywise to bite off Georgie's arm. As Georgie tries to run away, one white arm, longer than it should be, clearly not human, but still looking like an arm, comes out in a straight line to grab him. Pennywise is able to engage Georgie, in part due to Georgie's naiveté, but also because he doesn't appear threatening and, in fact, may be seen as a curiosity.

This scene is the subject of a comparison by Nelson Carvajal of the introductions of Pennywise with Georgie in both the miniseries and the film to argue that the 1990 version is more effective; however, several commenters disagree, with one in particular making an insightful argument regarding Pennywise's aesthetic, without putting it into those explicit terms. Tavis Northam states that "the 2017 Pennywise does a much better job of giving me the sense that something is off here" and implies that it is this sense of being "off," this uncanniness, that keeps Georgie there, contrasting it to

Curry's "more human" performance, where walking away from him would have no more "repercussions […] than dismissing an actual stranger" (qtd. in Winter). Northam goes on to say that "[t]he lighting and shooting in the 2017 version" creates something "like the sense of dread you get that immobilizes you or keeps your mind racing as you ask yourself 'what am I even experiencing here'" and "It is much more engaging in this way" (qtd. in Winter). Curry seems more like just a human stranger because the clown makeup is so stereotypical with the fully red bulb-like nose, the bright white makeup, drawn-on dark eyebrows, and bright red hair; he is a clown in the sewer—odd, yes, but Georgie could just say goodbye. As the lighting is bright in the miniseries and Georgie can see Pennywise clearly there is no need to linger, no need or curiosity to figure out what exactly that thing or person is. In the 2017 film, Pennywise is partially lit, helping to root Georgie to his spot, because he is intrigued by what he sees, which is the lower half of Pennywise's face with somewhat washed out white makeup and a bigger red smile than the Curry version. All of this makes the 2017 Pennywise more intriguing than a contemporary circus clown would be. With a contemporary circus clown there are the questions: How'd he get in the sewer? Why is he there? With the more surreal Pennywise, the questions become: Do I really see what I think I see? Is he a clown or something else? In addition, Pennywise's submissive facial expression adds to the innocence of the exchange, making Georgie, and the audience, willing to stay and engage with him. Pennywise does not always appear in this appealing way to the kids (notably, Stan and Beverly have quite different first encounters with him), but in most of the others' first encounters with Pennywise, there are the same contrast of simple colors, sense of the uncanny, and submissive head posture and facial expressions, which emphasize, even if only subconsciously, his appeal.

For example, although Ben first sees Pennywise in a non-clown form, as a headless figure chasing him, when he turns to look after hearing "egg boy," Pennywise appears in his clown form. It is a brief shot, from a medium-to-close distance, but the contrast of colors, since his face is brighter than the surroundings, is striking. His head is slightly tilted down, and, as in the sewer, he looks up. His mouth is open but no teeth are showing, just the red of lips around the darkness of open mouth. While he is actively pursuing Ben, and Ben's encounter is in that way very different from Georgie's, the headless body jerkily chasing after Ben is more menacing than this quick view of Pennywise.

A longer and slower encounter occurs later in the film when Pennywise appears to the bully Patrick. At first Patrick sees a bright red balloon, through which Pennywise can be slightly seen, then it pops, revealing Pennywise behind it. He is in half-shadows, light from above illuminating some of his head and shoulders, creating once again white against darkness. Once again his head is bowed slightly, with only his eyes looking up, revealing more white at the bottom of them. His mouth is open, revealing the white, but not the sharpness, of teeth. Red lines of makeup contrast his white face; his nose is a dark oval, and the red bottom lip stands out. His hair is carrot-red and shiny. Due to the light and the color, attention is drawn first to the hair and then down the face, following the streaks of red, until the focal point becomes his teeth, but they are not sharp and pointed, just a line of white. Then he quickly comes closer to the camera, moving from a medium shot to a close up. His movements are jerky, because his head is bobbling side to side, like a doll. As he approaches, his pointed teeth are revealed as he raises his head for a direct look, instead of keeping it bowed. As he comes in to attack Patrick, his arms stay straight at his sides. The bobbling head movements and the unmoving arms add to the uncanniness of the scene. In both this instance and the encounter with Ben, the first shape Pennywise takes (in this case, dead decomposing children) is more frightening than his clown shape. While Patrick has nowhere he can run when he sees Pennywise, he also is prepared to fight what is coming for him, but instead of immediately attacking the balloon or Pennywise, he stands still for a brief moment, as if taking in what he sees. Here, as in the encounter with Georgie, Pennywise seems at first to be non-threatening and then becomes swift in his attack.

The most developed aesthetic encounter with Pennywise occurs when he appears to Eddie, after he has first appeared as a leper who chases him. Eddie then turns and sees a triangle of red balloons with the bottom balloon, the point, covering Pennywise's face, a block of red leading the eye down into the white costume, all in front of the dark backdrop of the abandoned house. After this long shot, there is then a close up on just the bottom balloon as it floats up, revealing Pennywise's face: stark white with the red lips and red lines, red nose, and bright orange hair. His mouth is slightly open, but no teeth are seen; his head is tilted down, his eyes up. As the balloon rises above his head, he smiles, showing regular teeth; it almost seems as if the balloon string is pulling his smile up smoothly. In the next longer shot of Pennywise's full body as he speaks to Eddie, no balloons are in sight. One arm is straight at his side, while the other holds the balloon string with his arm bent in front of his body. His head is still bowed slightly, and he stands in a slight hunch, making him seem smaller. The only thing that moves while he talks is his mouth, and the lack of other bodily movements is uncannily creepy. There is a close up on his face again, emphasizing the contrasting colors and submissive positioning. This longer scene illustrates how the aesthetic aspects of Pennywise draw both his prey and the viewer in, making them linger. As with the encounters with Ben and Patrick, Pennywise first appeared in a clearly more menacing and disgusting form, making his appearance in clown form stand out even more and be a brief respite. The alternating of long and close shots mimics our being drawn in. In this scene, Pennywise is not explicitly frightening, but oddly disturbing and interesting.

The other appearances of Pennywise make less use of these techniques, perhaps having already established the subtle appeal; however, they do not disappear completely. For example, when Pennywise appears to Bill in the wet basement, again there is a contrast of color against the dark water and the uncanny jerky running. Additionally, Pennywise is still made to seem smaller than he is, particularly as he rises from the water. Contrast and size are used similarly when Mike is being beaten by the bullies and sees, in a medium shot, Pennywise in the woods, out of focus at first. Pennywise's white face and orange hair contrast the green and yellow of grass and flowers. The white ruffle has a red splash of blood on it now. His head isn't bowed, but he seems small among the tall grass. These techniques are even used in the projector scene, in which Bill's mom's long red hair blows back to reveal Pennywise with his white face. His head is bent slightly down and he is smiling. It's only when he comes out of the screen with all of the sharp teeth that it becomes truly terrifying; however, even in that instance, when he is huge, he crawls out of the screen like a child. He doesn't walk or run. The final scene in which these techniques are put to use is in the abandoned house, when Richie is in the room full of clowns. Pennywise jumps up from the casket as Richie slams it shut, and there is again a dark room contrasted with the white of his face and clothes. He jumps up like a jack-in-the-box and lands in a football type stance with his head slightly bowed, appearing more doll-like than human. He is more active here, but there is a bowed submissive head and uncanny movements, including when he runs toward Richie with his arms straight out and is moving so smoothly he looks like he is floating quickly towards him.

Pennywise's appearances increasingly leave behind the subtly uncanny and submissive aspects, as the kids and the audience have been lured in and there is no need to use the tricks anymore. The contrast of colors is often retained but even then seems to be somewhat subdued. For example, when Pennywise comes toward Eddie in the house, the room is lit more consistently and his costume seems more grey than white. When he walks towards Eddie, after untwisting himself, he is bowed slightly forward, but as the camera is looking up at him, the bow doesn't look submissive as much as it seems to indicate that he hasn't untwisted completely, and will ultimately loom over Eddie. Similarly, after Bev hits her father, Pennywise is behind her, looming, and, when she turns, he grabs her neck. There is a contrast of colors, his head tilted down, his mouth slightly open, but as he looks down, the camera under him, it isn't a vulnerable or submissive look, but is instead one of dominance. Not only is the submissive appealing Pennywise form not needed after a point, but by the final confrontation, the Pennywise form itself is not needed.

In the final fight he takes on many forms, none fully, until his face finally cracks away.

The aesthetic appeal of Pennywise is no longer needed by the end of the film; by that point, it has served its purpose. Inside the world of the film, he has lured victims in; outside of the world of the film, he has lured in viewers. This aesthetic appeal works on an almost subliminal level. It is doubtful that, when asked why they find Pennywise appealing, someone would respond it is because his facial expressions indicate submissiveness, but some might say they find the colors or costume interesting. Regardless of whether viewers are aware of it, these visual aspects (the coloring, the facial expressions, the makeup) may have helped create their interest in Pennywise, just as these aesthetic aspects are used to make the horror not only palatable but also beautiful in *Hannibal* and *The Handmaid's Tale*. Based on the trailers for *It: Chapter Two*, and the ideas discussed above, it would not be surprising if, while the contrast of the red and white is retained, Pennywise only takes on the appealing aesthetic form when luring in new victims, and appears more horrific to the Losers' Club, as well as the audience throughout the film. After all, we, like the Losers' Club, have already encountered him and been drawn in enough to return.

Works Cited

Barkan, Jonathan. "'It': Here's 'Pennywise' in Full Clown Costume and He's Definitely Freaky!" *Bloody Disgusting,* Aug. 16, 2016, bloody-disgusting.com/movie/3403108/heres-pennywise-full-clown-costume-hes-definitely-freaky/.
Breznican, Anthony. "Pennywise from It: See the clown's full costume from new Stephen King Film." *Entertainment Weekly,* Dec. 26, 2016, ew.com/article/2016/08/16/pennywise-costume-stephen-king-it-movie/.
Brinkema, Eugenie. *The Forms of the Affects,* Kindle Ed., Duke University Press, 2014.
Dillon, Mark. "*It*: Fear Itself." *American Cinematographer,* Oct. 19, 2017, ascmag.com/articles/it-fear-itself.
Foutch, Haleigh. "Andy Muschietti on 'IT' and Why Stephen King Wasn't Involved in the Film." *Collider,* Aug. 21, 2017, collider.com/andy-muschietti-it-movie-interview/.
Freud, Sigmund. "The 'Uncanny.'" *The Standard Edition of the Complete Psychological Works of Sigmund Freud, Volume XVII (1917–1919): An Infantile Neurosis and Other Works.* pp. 217–256, arch.mcgill.ca/prof/bressani/arch653/winter2010/Freud_TheUncanny.pdf.
It. Directed by Andy Muschietti, New Line Cinema, 2017.
_____. Directed by Tommy Lee Wallace, Lorimar Productions, Warner Brothers Television, 1990.
Klock, Geoff. *Aestheticism, Evil, Homosexuality, and Hannibal,* Kindle Ed., Lexington Books, 2017.
Leyda, Julia. "Hook and Eye." *Communication Culture & Critique,* vol. 11, no. 1, 2018, pp. 179–182, *Oxford Academic,* doi:10.1093/ccc/tcx 007.
Loughrey, Clarisse. "It interview: Director Andy Muschietti on staying true to the spirit of Stephen King." *The Independent,* Sept 8, 2017.
Mangan, Bruce. "The uncanny valley as fringe experience." *Interaction Studies,* vol. 16, no. 2, 2015, pp. 193–199, *PhilArchive,* doi:10.1075/is.16.2.05man.
Marsh, Abigail A., et al. "Why Do Fear and Anger Look the Way They Do? Form and Social Function in Facial Expressions." *Personality and Social Psychology Bulletin,* vol. 31, no. 1, 2005, pp. 73–86, *ResearchGate,* doi:10.1177/0146167204271306.

Medina, Joseph Jammer "Why They Changed the Look of Pennywise the Clown for the New IT Film!" *LRM*, Aug. 21, 2017, lrmonline.com/news/why-they-changed-the-look-of-pennywise-the-clown-for-the-new-it-film/.

Nussbaum, Emily. "A Cunning Adaptation of 'The Handmaid's Tale.'" *The New Yorker*, May 15, 2017.

Winter, Max. "Watch: What Stephen King's Pennywise Can Teach Us About Character Introductions." *No Film School*, Sept. 20, 2017, nofilmschool.com/2017/09/watch-stephen-king-pennywise-introduction.

Ziomek, Ewa. "Hannibal Revived: an Aestheticized Portrayal of Hannibal Lecter in NBC's TV Series *Hannibal*." *Crossroads: A Journal of English Studies*, vol. 23, no. 4, 2018, pp. 46–58, *Central and Eastern European Online Library*, doi:10.15290/CR.2018.23.4.04.

Derry's Subterranean Carnival in Stephen King's *It*

CONNY LIPPERT

Introduction

Derry, recurring bad place extraordinaire in Stephen King's small-town horror fiction and main locale of his 1986 bestseller *It*, has a "long history of gaudy sacrifices" (879) that intersperse the more mundane ups and downs of its existence. It is no ordinary town but the site of an ancient evil, often dormant and subterranean, sometimes catastrophically active and demanding tribute, yet always exuding a noxious influence, inciting violence. Fate draws together a group of pre-teens who encounter, fight, and ultimately vanquish, a malevolent creature that lives in the labyrinthine sewers under their hometown. Alienated from their parents, their peers, and society in general, the kids call themselves the Losers' Club and form a strong bond of love and friendship. Together, they survive battling the monster, but must return to Derry to finish as adults what they started as children. The story follows their collective hero's journey, which centers on the element of going underground to re-emerge victorious, transformed, and reborn. Within the tangles of the novel's dark tapestry, the discerning reader can make out the loosely linked subjects of carnival and rites of passage, woven together to create a horror narrative about growing up, about facing one's fears, and ultimately also *about* horror fiction.

Gothic Carnival

Reminiscent of the dark carnival in Ray Bradbury's 1962 coming-of-age classic *Something Wicked This Way Comes*, the creature in *It* sustains itself on human fear, feeding primarily on children because they believe easily, and their fears are less complex than adults'. The story's most memorable figure, and the eponymous creature's main avatar, is Pennywise the Dancing Clown. Tim Curry in the 1990 TV mini-series and Bill Skarsgård in the 2017 film respectively have delivered inspired and distinct portrayals of Pennywise. Meanwhile, the evil clown's incongruous visage has cemented its place as one of the iconic images of the horror genre. Pennywise furthermore often embodies its victims' current worst fears in the form of monsters drawn from popular culture, such as Dracula, the Werewolf, or the Mummy. In other words, the creature complements the darkly carnivalesque image of the evil jester by wearing the guises of figures King associates with what he sees, as will be shown, as a displaced version of festive misrule: the horror movie.

Horror's popularity as a genre is currently at a high point and a large variety of explanations of why and how horror fiction works have been brought forth by different critics over time. Mathias Clasen, for instance, is a recent proponent of what could be called the "rollercoaster theory." He argues from a bioculturally focused point of view, based in the evolutionary social sciences, and suggests that we seek out horror because it allows us the pleasure of experiencing intense emotions in a safe context, therefore facilitating what he describes as something akin to educational mental play behavior (Clasen 58, 59). Noël Carroll, in his seminal *The Philosophy of Horror* (1990), aims to provide an explanation from a philosophical perspective so basic and fundamental that it can cover all of what he calls "art-horror" (8), including media beyond that of narrative, such as pictorial fine art. He concludes that the monster, which always inspires fear and disgust due to its abnormality, engenders curiosity, drawing us to the genre. Along his journey to this conclusion, Carroll examines and dismisses as too narrow the hitherto most popular types of explanations for how horror works. These include theories revolving around religious awe or Lovecraftian cosmic fear, psychosexual and psycho-mythological Freudian or Jungian explanations, and the related "safety-valve theory," leaning on assumptions about the concept of catharsis. Engaging with horror fiction is seen as a way to excise negative emotions and contemplate a reversal of the accepted order, thus ultimately reaffirming normality and the status quo. This model is discussed, for instance, in Grixti and Botting, and similar explanations for the attraction of horror fiction have been offered by many other critics. Although widely contested and rightly seen as too narrow to cover all of horror, this theory has been persistent and pervasive. It is, furthermore, of particular interest here, as it supplies the core basis for a carnivalesque reading of Stephen King's *It*.

In anthropological and sociological readings of carnival, a similar argument is widespread. Chris Humphrey, for instance, explains that, while studies of medieval festive practices have been oscillating between a "subversion or containment" approach, the majority consensus is that carnival helps protect the existing order (ix). Lewis Hyde, in his writing on the figure of the trickster, also references this divide over whether carnival merely enforces the status quo or can actually disrupt it (187). He argues that the former is the case as long as stability is sought in a society, "but when the order is in fundamental crisis these rituals can become the focal points for change" (Hyde 188). In keeping with the safety-valve theory, then, not only the clown as a carnivalesque figure but also the monster and, with it, the horror genre are often regarded as agents of a guided release for all that is anti-social and repressed in every-day life. David Gilmore, for instance, writes: "In ritualized violence, such as occurs in gothic fiction, horror movies, and village festivals, the hypothetical *victime émissaire* (scapegoat or sacrificial victim) acts as a symbolic target for the therapeutic displacement of pent-up aggressions" (21). In other words, this theory submits that we release our aggressions and anti-social impulses in a guided, channeled, socially acceptable, and non-threatening form when we participate in carnivalesque festivities or consume horror fiction.

King himself has been a proponent of this idea and says—also referencing the notion of catharsis—that "the dream of horror is in itself an outletting and a lancing … and it may well be that the mass-media dream of horror can sometimes become a nationwide analyst's couch" (*Danse* 27). According to him, the horror film, and by association also his own narratives, allow the audience to "indulge in deviant, antisocial behavior by proxy" (King, *Danse* 47). He goes on to compare horror films to "lifting a trapdoor in the civilized forebrain and throwing a basket of raw meat to the hungry alligators swimming around in that subterranean river beneath" (King, *Danse* 205). Feeding the alligators below becomes a metaphor for venting aggression in a safe and guided fashion. Whether the safety-valve theory ultimately holds true for festive misrule *or* for horror fiction notwithstanding—and I am neither offering a defense nor repudiation of the model here—in his novel *It*, King portrays Derry's subterranean carnival as not only a gothic inversion of a cathartic ritual but also a comment on the perceived function of horror narratives overall.

It is not surprising that carnival imagery has been popular in the gothic and horror genre. In his study on the carnivalesque mode of reading gothic narratives characterized by a "wicked playfulness" (14), Timothy Jones highlights this return, particularly of American Gothic, to representations of the festive (206). He posits that carnival gothic, like carnivalesque practices themselves, is primarily playful and celebratory, thereby breaking somewhat with overly serious readings and interpretations of the genre. According to him, we enjoy a very specific kind of wickedness and vibe in our gothic fare, which falls away when the boundaries into the "wrong kind of wrongness" (Jones

94) are crossed. Jones believes that King searches for societal "phobic pressure points" (*Danse* 18) in a similarly ludic way, focused on generating affect rather than to determine why they exist or how to unravel them (Jones 163). Carnivalesque imagery, which is a recurring motif in Poe, Bradbury and King, has also found much resonance in horror film audiences. Perhaps evoking such wicked playfulness and a time when circus, carnival and clowning were not the tame affair they are now, the appearance of the clown or carnival in the gothic context, as a marginalized and unpredictable element in social interaction, is calculated to induce unease and conjure a specifically gothic affect. One example of the sought-after effect turning into horror instead of art-horror for a large portion of the audience is Tod Browning's 1932 film *Freaks*, which capitalized on the freak-show element of carnivals and used real-life performers from such shows as actors. While the sensationalist draw of the "abnormal," as described by Carroll, may well be part of what drives consumers of gothic and horror media to seek out carnivalesque imagery, Browning's spectacle, although considered a genre classic today, did not manage to hit a suitably wicked-playful tone with its contemporary audience (King, *Danse* 50).

As previously mentioned, the figure of the clown is now very well-established in the horror genre. There are a number of plausible reasons—or, as Clasen calls them, "evolved defensive dispositions" (44)—why people might feel disturbed by clowns. Firstly, face-paint that largely conceals the wearer's facial expressions and thus their emotions can have an alarming effect, like a mask used to hide evil intent. Bouissac agrees that "[w]hat results is an altered human face that verges on the alien and the uncanny" which usually frightens young children "until they learn that this peculiar face means play in the culture in which they live" (19). Another concerning aspect of the clown, much like the trickster, to whom we will return shortly, is his historical and mythological function as breaker of rules and taboos, and his resulting unpredictability. The "monstrum," as that which shows or warns (Gilmore 9), is by definition not so far removed from the clown, fool or jester, who mocks us and parodies us to reveal our shortcomings. If "the monster is a metaphor for all that must be repudiated by the human spirit" (Gilmore 12), the laughter evoked by the clown who mocks somebody's behavior or illustratively acts in socially unacceptable ways, similarly is a social deterrent, a warning to the deviant. Breaking taboos can make one seem ridiculous, even if it is not quite bad enough to make one seem monstrous.

The clown is in a position to speak truth to power, which can be seen as part of either the safety-valve *or* the revolutionary function of carnival as a whole. Bouissac summarizes that "the clown's performances deliver information that is so difficult to stomach that we have to laugh it off" (179). In several sexually-charged scenes in *It*, Beverly, as the only female member of the Losers' Club, contemplates the proximity of fear of the unknown and laughter. In one of the book's most controversial scenes, eleven-year-old Bev has intercourse with the rest of the Losers' Club in order to strengthen their bond after their first confrontation with the monster leaves them disoriented and lost in the sewers. She realizes then that, for many of her peers, sex is "some unrealized undefined monster" to which they refer as "It" and at which they giggle nervously because "what's fearful and unknown is also what's funny. You laugh the way a small child will sometimes laugh and cry at the same time when a capering circus clown approaches" (King, *It* 1065). Through Bev's eyes, we contemplate coming-of-age themes of impending maturity, liminality, and rites of passage, and their connection with mirth and transgressive laughter. Indeed, the Losers seem to be forever suspended between terror and glee, as, while they "were afraid all the time, [they] couldn't stop laughing" (King, *It* 386). Screams and laughter, seemingly antithetical, are put in a constant, intimate relationship and echo the "screaming and laughing down there in the pipes" (King, *It* 162). The suddenness with which one can turn into the other is disconcerting and, while the groups' collective laughter is also a symbol of their strength and causes the monster to recoil (King, *It* 850), Pennywise's devious glee and unpredictable mischievousness represent a distorted reflection of this and serve to make the creature appear all the more evil. The monstrous and the ridiculous are once again shown to be closely related.

Under the Surface

According to Bouissac "[s]ocieties are haunted by their clowns, who bang on the ground upon which we rest and make it sound hollow. It resonates with their sarcastic laughter" (179). This hollow-sounding ground reminds us of the narrative trajectory within Poe's "The Cask of Amontillado" (1846), with its carnival setting and its motley-clad fool, moving from the above-ground festivities into the subterranean crypt and "in doing so, [shifting] into a Gothic mode" (Jones 58). Not only the screams of unfortunate Fortunato, bound and walled up in the Montresor family crypt in Poe's story, but also his forced laughter at the cruel joke he assumes Montresor is playing on him, continue to echo throughout the genre.

King's small towns are often tainted by ancient artefacts or forces in the ground—a spaceship in *The Tommyknockers* (1988), Pennywise in *It*, or the sour earth in *Pet Sematary* (1988). Subterranean spaces, which Botting describes as a staple gothic ingredient, tend to be cold, dark, claustrophobic, damp and noxious, and full of gothic stock elements, such as ghosts, ghouls, and demons (44). Mythology and religion will give that which is below ground diabolic and infernal connotations. A haunted house without a dark and damp basement would truly be lacking a vital component, and basic human anxieties, such as fear of the dark, entrapment, and premature burial ensure that these sepulchral locales evoke an atmosphere befitting the gothic. Often, these are spaces of liminality and isolation, harboring subversive elements of, and reflecting, the normative, above-ground society. According to Pike, the underground "always includes a displaced vision of something that poses a crisis of representation in the world above" (*Styx* 2). In other words, those elements banished into subterranean spaces are often abject vestiges of upper society and, discarded and unregulated, they develop a meaningful existence of their own. Through a continuous referencing of H.G. Wells' *The Time Machine* (1953), and specifically its subterranean Morlocks, *It* similarly comments on the way in which Derry is being cannibalized by its own relegated elements.

Psychoanalytic readings of the gothic will perhaps always hark back to Freud's vertical topography of the mind, connecting the underground with the human subconscious. The leading image accompanying spatial and metaphorical depth in King's oeuvre is that of the previously mentioned subterranean alligators. To keep them fed is to keep the id satisfied, which is what supposedly happens when we participate in carnivalesque festivities or consume horror fiction. In *It*, the horror writer and protagonist Bill Denbrough, the book's thinly-veiled stand-in for King, is perceived to have a direct pipeline to the "sub-sub-conscious" (225), which allows him to write successful genre fiction. In the form of horror movies, genre fiction factors heavily in the plot, as well as the intertextual referentiality of *It*. The young protagonists, for instance, watch *I Was a Teenage Frankenstein* (1957), marveling at the alligators in the basement to which spare body parts are fed (King, *It* 363). These subterranean reptiles, reminiscent of the "lizard brain" and the darker impulses initiated by the id, are furthermore repeatedly paralleled in the description of Pennywise. The subterranean monster, which is consistently described as emanating a "cellar-smell," or in fact, "the stink of the beast," dwells in those places connected to drainage and sewage (King, *It* 26, 79). Giblett points out the connections between the portrayal of the alligator, its smell, and Freud's uncanny. He emphasizes the ways in which alligators and crocodiles embody human "fears of an oral kind, about who gets to eat and who gets to be eaten" (Giblett 300). In *It*, this is paralleled in the continuous repetition of the nursery tale "The Three Billy Goats Gruff," which poses the central question "would the monster be bested… or would it feed?" (King 186, 849, 1013). Mike Hanlon, as the town librarian and lay-historian, thinks to ask what is feeding in and on Derry (King, *It* 154). The town's id/It, we are given to understand, likes to open the metaphorical trapdoor itself, to periodically venture topside and collect its basket of raw meat.

Dirt and waste represent another immediate link with subterranean spaces prominently featuring in *It* through the centrality of sewage in the plot. Associations of the underworld as well as those focusing on the human bowels emphasize notions of odor, heat and depths (Hillman 183). In his reading of Rabelais, Bakhtin further links the carnivalesque atmosphere of Mardi Gras not only to revelry but also the "bowels [and] excrement, and other images of the material bodily lower stratum" (Bakhtin 223, 224). Waste, be it refuse, excrement, or exclusions from society and the world above, tends to be found underground. Hyde, somewhat paraphrasing Mary Douglas's seminal *Purity and Danger* (1966), suggests that "dirt and order are mutually dependent" (177). He proposes that purity and sterility threaten to result in stagnation, and that a little dirt—like a vaccination—can bring necessary change and renewal into a system (Hyde 188). In keeping with Bakhtin's reading, dirt is seen as "an essential element in the struggle against death" (Bakhtin 224). While Bouissac rightly warns against simply equating the figures of the trickster and the clown, he does point out that "very suggestive clusters of functional features" (132) can be identified in their respective narratives, of which this type of dirt-work is an example. Carnival, likewise, can be such an injection of unruly chaos—metaphorically speaking, dirt, as matter out of place—into order. In a designated time and space societal inversions can occur, allowing for release and renewal. In the carnivalesque spirit, authority can be mocked and temporarily subverted. Only the willingness to confront and deal with the abject and rejected elements of society enables the trickster-hero to bring about change. In order to confront the creature in its own lair, the Losers must take on certain trickster-like qualities and quite literally face their home-town's waste and dirt—by walking, wading and crawling through it. Horror tales themselves can also be seen as such dirt-rituals, as they allow the reader to confront and engage with individual as well as societal abject recesses. Dirt-rituals help to feed the alligators. The gothic tale can facilitate this type of carnivalesque work and the underground is clearly particularly suitable to accommodate it.

Hyde's dirt-worker, the trickster figure, appears in a myriad of different forms, depending on the cultural background. In Greek mythology, for instance, there is Hermes, in Norse mythology, Loki. In native North American contexts one can find various forms of animal-tricksters like coyote, hare, raven or spider. The trickster is a marginal and liminal character, and, among a myriad of other characteristics, he is a mischief-maker who often becomes the butt of his own jokes and pranks. He is chiefly guided by self-interest and his various appetites, as well as constantly provoking authority. According to Barbara Babcock-Abrahams, the trickster "lives in cells, caves, ghettos, and other 'underground' areas—like the spider inhabiting the nooks and crannies of social spaces" (155). Her point seems particularly significant when it is revealed that the creature's main shape, other than the clown, is a giant spider living in a cave underneath Derry's sewer system—a marginalized, liminal space. As Beverly says "It's everywhere in Derry.... It just fills the hollow places" (King, *It* 891). Pennywise the Dancing Clown, then, is the darkest possible version of a trickster figure and the Losers oppose it by learning a few tricks themselves. They, too, are somewhat marginal and liminal characters who like to dwell in underground clubhouses and play in the relegated Barrens. Richie in particular manifests many of the trickster-like qualities mentioned above. Eventually, the Losers defeat It by understanding how to effectively disrupt the creature's own order of fear through mirth, ultimately employing the metaphysical ritual of Chüd, which consists of telling riddles and jokes, to evoke genuine loss of control manifesting in laughter. Much like the smile carved on a bullet in Bradbury's aforementioned tale, the children, in true disruptive, carnivalesque fashion, manage to weaponize ludic laughter to defeat the clown.

There is one last function of the underground setting in *It*, which bears mentioning in the present context. Alongside Freudian notions of a vertical topography of the mind, King also connects the creature in *It* with the unvocalized and suppressed fears and realizations of burgeoning sexuality, as indicated above. Particularly subterranean waters and the sea are often linked to notions of the female. Perse, the demonic presence in King's 2008 seagothic novel *Duma Key*, for example, is named after Persephone, the Greek queen of the underworld, and closely related to the ocean. Perse's appearance is reminiscent of the female personification of death Coleridge's ancient mariner encounters. She "is a slumped thing in a hooded red robe" and, more importantly "It's a WOMAN!" (King, *Duma* 468). This capitalized exclamation parallels the revelation in *It* that the monster is not only female ("OH DEAR JESUS IT'S FEMALE") but also pregnant (King 998). The assumption that the subterranean and the subaquatic are associated with matters of female reproduction, motherhood, and associated rites of passage suggests itself (Goldmann 172). Beverly's worries regarding adulthood, sexual maturity, and womanhood can be read in this context and are clearly further framed by her father's violently obsessive anxieties concerning her innocence. The final confrontation scenario in which Bill penetrates the creature's body with his own (King, *It* 1073) is not only reminiscent of rape, but also of a gothicized Freudian attempt to re-enter the womb. As Giblett reminds us: "Our beginnings as individuals are in the watery world of the womb and our beginnings as a species in evolutionary terms are in the womby world of water" (309). Derry's metaphorical subterranean rivers do not only house alligators, but female ones, who are ready to spawn fresh, grotesque horrors.

The myth of Persephone carries further significance for a carnivalesque reading of *It*, investigating rites of passage. In it, the daughter of Demeter, goddess of the harvest, is abducted by Hades, ruler of the underworld, to be his reluctant bride. Due to her mother's resulting grief, the earth is plunged into sterility and faced with starvation and annihilation until, after threatening, negotiating and trickery, an arrangement is reached under which Persephone spends a part of the year with Hades and the rest with Demeter and the other gods. Her annual return to the surface heralds spring, and her subterranean months symbolize winter. She thus provides a neat representation of cyclical regeneration which, some argue, is also at the core of the pre–Christian origins of carnival as a spring festivity demarcating a cyclical rite of passage and renewal. Derry, of course, has its own version of this, with It as its twisted fertility deity, complete with gothicized and darkly carnivalesque, ritualistic blood offerings. In return for being Its "haunt" (King, *It* 153), the creature provides the town with economic prosperity. As the monstrous embodiment of the town and its aggressions, Pennywise is associated with the Kenduskeag river, and specifically the Canal running through the town, which can be read as an allusion to the town's monster being directly connected to the reason for its economic growth—the river on which logs of lumber once floated. The Canal Days, for instance, which conclude with Adrian Mellon's "ritual sacrifice" (King, *It* 33), celebrate Derry's rebirth in material prosperity, echoing the return of spring. The periodic reappearance of Pennywise at roughly every 27 to 28 years suggests a comparison to the menstrual cycle with its 28 days, as well as the average duration of a pregnancy at 280 days. Its ambiguous gender and the final realization that the monster is female and indeed pregnant strengthen this line of argument and firmly connect it to notions of birth, rebirth, and rites of passage. As Persephone and the rites associated with her periodic descent and re-emergence from the underworld mark the changing of the seasons, Pennywise's connections to matters of fertility engender a cyclical carnivalesque tribute in Derry.

Katabasis

A rite of passage commonly denotes a key transitional stage, such as a young person's journey from childhood to adulthood. In his seminal work on the subject, Arnold van Gennep delineates three phases of the process: separation, transition, and reincorporation. Emphasizing the importance of the transitional stage, he also calls them preliminal, liminal, and postliminal stages (Gennep 11). Going underground and emerging with new skills or insights can qualify as such a rite. The gothic potential lies within the numerous possible trials that may await a protagonist in the transition-stage of this progression. The idea of katabasis—descent—and emerging altered after a subterranean quest has been with us since antiquity. Prominent among those who have undertaken the underworld journey are, for instance, Hercules, Orpheus, Dante, and, of course, Persephone.

The aforementioned fairy tale "The Three Billy-Goats Gruff," which is so central to *It*, is a coming-of-age tale. The fabled and frequently-referenced troll under the bridge was, according to King's official website, the core idea for the story. Beneath the figurative bridge, Derry, are the sewers and tunnels housing the monster–King's equivalent of the troll. While most of Pennywise's activities are closely related to the Derry Canal and its waters, the murder initiating the final sacrificial cycle also takes place under a bridge. In the fairy tale, the bridge symbolizes a rite of passage—a journey over troubled waters from home to a better place, where the pastures are greener. The Losers' Club, consisting of the fairy-tale-number of seven children, does indeed manage to reach the other end of the bridge. However, they do so, not by crossing it, but by walking underneath, in order to confront the troll, and make normal passage possible again for future generations. The Losers undergo their trials in a locale closed off from the upper world and separate from the dwellings of humanity. The liminal underground space in which the children must make their stand is a cousin of the mythological underworlds of old.

King is particularly fond of the katabasis-motif and employs variations, followed by a figurative rebirth into another stage of life, in nearly every novel-length work. Journeys through dark and closed-off spaces feature as a key step in the protagonist's character-development. Magistrale defines the spatial manifestations of what Winter calls the "night journeys" (Winter 2) of King's characters more broadly, as the "image of the tunnel or narrow passageway" to symbolize "the emergence of a new stage in the development of the individual involved" (*Fear* 90). Jack Sawyer in *The Talisman* (1984) travels the dark and frightening Oatley Tunnel, while Larry Underwood in *The Stand* (1990) has a very similar experience with the Lincoln Tunnel. Gard in *The Tommyknockers* finds his heroic end after working his way into the spaceship buried in the Maine woods. Perhaps the most explicit example of this trope, however, can be found in the underground journey the Losers' Club undertake in *It*. It is katabasis as part of the hero's journey, and the protagonists must face their pursuer in order to emerge victorious and transformed. In Joseph Campbell's influential study on the monomyth of the hero's journey, *The Hero with A Thousand Faces* (1949), he summarizes this type of narrative, in which the mythological hero leaves, or is lured from, his familiar surroundings and heads into adventure. The hero either descends alive, or dies to do so, into the "kingdom of the dark" and "journeys through a world of unfamiliar yet strangely intimate forces […]. When he arrives at the nadir of the mythological round, he undergoes a supreme ordeal and gains his reward." After all this, the final task is to return, leaving the mystical powers behind, "from the kingdom of dread" to bring a boon which "restores the world" (Campbell 245, 246). The Losers, accordingly, go down into the sewers to find and battle "their clown" (King, *It* 715), do so successfully but at great cost, and struggle to return to the world above, which they have—at least temporarily—rid of Its presence. Because they have failed to prevent the monster from reappearing, however, the Losers are denied their rite of passage in full and must return twenty-seven years later to complete it.

The Losers are able to retrace their childhood journey into the underworld as adults because, due to their unfinished rite of passage, they have retained some of their juvenile attributes in adulthood. They have been marked by their ordeal. All seven of them, for instance, remain involuntarily childless. Although they have been blessed with wealth and material success—all apart from Mike, who alone stayed behind in Derry—parallels to their childhood selves are maintained and emphasized. While Beverly has married someone very much like her abusive father, Eddie has chosen a partner very similar in appearance and character to his overbearing mother, fearing that he has become "a clown in [...] a Freudian circus" (King, *It* 100). King describes them as explicitly childlike even as adults (*It* 117, 136). This, again, is very reminiscent of *Something Wicked This Way Comes*, in which Charles Holloway, idealized father of protagonist Will, is the perfect mixture of child and adult. The desperate outpouring of mirth and glee employed to fight off the carnival's dark influence at the end of the novel parallels the equally unruly ritual of Chüd. Charles ultimately finds the laughter needed to win their fight, just as Richie manages to use his rebellious humor and his silly voices to turn the tables on the monster. Bradbury's tale and *It* share a fair amount of narrative DNA but are most alike in their core representations of the myth of childhood. The darkly carnivalesque attractions the protagonists face in each story can only be handled and defeated by employing a mix of innocent, playful willingness to suspend disbelief and be foolish, and mature accountability and recognition of danger.

Conclusion

King, who describes his generation's cultural background as a "strange circus atmosphere of paranoia, patriotism and national *hubris*" (*Danse* 23), believes horror fiction to function primarily as an agent of the status quo (*Danse* 50). For him, real life fears can either temporarily be ignored, or the anxieties they engender can be excised, by consuming horror fiction. Facing horror's malleable, metaphorical representations that can be—like Pennywise—shaped into the reader's personalized emotional lightning-rod, guides the negative energy generated by real-life fears safely into the ground. According to King, the "magic moment of reintegration and safety at the end" (*Danse* 28) present in many horror narratives allows for feelings of relief, having faced the facsimile of danger without the actual peril. King's understanding of horror thus fuses the "roller-coaster theory" and the "safety-valve theory," imagining a horror audience that employs the genre for temporary and partial catharsis *and* as a mock rite of passage, in which the lauded feeling of reintegration echoes Gennep's third step of "reincorporation" (11).

In *It*, carnivalesque imagery, like the curiosity-driven draw of the circus or the freak-show, is employed to gothic effect and harks back to Bradbury's myth of "this small-town American boyhood" (King, *Danse* 371). While a cycle of bloodletting occurs periodically in Derry, the resulting violence is only an enhancement, not an inversion of the town's status quo. Instead of having a safety-valve or vent function channeling Derry's aggression and helping to disperse it, through the presence and influence of the creature, the town's meanness only accumulates through its rituals. It has grown to be a twisted place, built it Its image (*It* 989), and when Jake Epping visits Derry in King's 2011 time-travel novel *11.22.66*, he notices immediately that there is something very wrong with the town (108). By evoking and then abusing the carnival spirit, the monster in *It* manages to invert the expected cathartic function of ritual aggression into its very opposite. Derry's dark carnival is a perverted dirt-ritual, a period of gaudy misrule turned ugly, and a bloody rite of regeneration and rebirth.

It can furthermore be seen as a direct commentary on the chasm between what Carroll distinguishes as "art-horror" (8) and real horror, since Pennywise more often than not appears as a monster plucked straight from the movie screen. Monsters without a zipper running down their back are not carnivalesque—they are not safe—and only the realization of this fact can lead to salvation. One victim, even while being carried off by It in the shape of the Creature from the Black Lagoon, is still feeling for that zipper he is sure must be there (*It* 269). He thinks the creature looks like something "out of a horror comic or horror book or horror movie," maybe even "a bad dream or a fairy tale" (King, *It* 271), succinctly summing up fictional horror only to contrast it with the monster's twisted reality. The boy's refusal to differentiate between a real and a fictional threat causes him to fall prey to It. Where Jones distinguishes between a carnival gothic practice and the "wrong kind of wrongness" (94) of real horror, King unpacks the "paradoxical trick" of using horror to "destroy itself" (*Danse* 28). In other words, Derry's subterranean carnival is a metafictional, gothicized version of the use of horror fiction as interpreted by King. It is a catastrophic reversal of the expected letting-of-steam and excising-of-emotion, and instead festers into a culmination of violence, which can only be conquered by the emphatic dispersion of anxiety accomplished through unfettered mirth and laughter. Yet, in the process, the novel allows us, the readers, to feel relief when the monster is vanquished, and the status quo restored.

WORKS CITED

Bakhtin, Mikhail. *Rabelais and His World.* Indiana University Press, 1984 [1968].
Beahm, George, editor. *The Stephen King Companion.* Futura, 1989.
Botting, Fred. *Gothic: The New Critical Idiom.* Routledge, 1996.
Bouissac, Paul. *The Semiotics of Clowns and Clowning—Rituals of Transgression and Theories of Laughter.* Bloomsbury, 2015.
Bradbury, Ray. *Something Wicked This Way Comes.* Orion Books, 2008 [1962].
Campbell, Joseph. *The Hero with a Thousand Faces.* Pantheon Books, 1949.
Campbell Reesman, Jeanne. "Riddle Game: Stephen King's Metafictive Dialogue" *The Dark Descent: Essays Defining Stephen King's Horrorscape,* edited by Tony Magistrale, Greenwood Press, 1992, pp. 157–170.
Carroll, Noël. *The Philosophy of Horror: Or, Paradoxes of the Heart.* Routledge, 1990.
Clasen, Mathias. *Why Horror Seduces.* Oxford University Press, 2017.
Coleridge, Samuel Taylor. "The Rime of the Ancyent Marinere." *Romanticism: An Anthology,* edited by Duncan Wu, Blackwell Publishing, 2006, pp. 332–349.
Douglas, Mary. *Purity and Danger: An Analysis of Concepts of Pollution and Taboo.* Routledge & Kegan Paul, 1966.
Freaks. Directed by Tod Browning, Metro-Goldwyn-Mayer, 1932.
Freud, Sigmund. "The 'Uncanny,'" *Collected Papers: Volume IV.* The Hogarth Press, 1956, 368–407.
Gennep, Arnold van. *The Rites of Passage.* University of Chicago Press, 1960.
Giblett, Rod. "Alligators, Crocodiles and the Monstrous Uncanny," *Continuum: Journal of Media and Cultural Studies,* vol. 20, no. 3, 2006, 299–312.
Gilmore, David D. *Monsters: Evil Beings, Mythical Beasts, and All Manner of Imaginary Terrors.* University of Pennsylvania Press, 2003.
Goldmann, Heinrich. *Katabasis—Eine Tiefenpsychologische Studie zur Symbolik der Dichtung Georg Trakls.* Otto Müller Verlag, 1957.
Grixti, Joseph. *Terrors of Uncertainty.* Routledge, 1989.
Hillman, James. *The Dream and the Underworld.* Harper Perennial, 1979.
Humphrey, Chris. *The Politics of Carnival—Festive Misrule in Medieval England.* Manchester University Press, 2001.
Hyde, Lewis. *Trickster Makes This World—How Disruptive Imagination Creates Culture.* Canongate, 1998.
I Was a Teenage Frankenstein. Directed by Herbert L. Strock, Santa Rosa Productions, 1975.
It. Directed by Andy Muschietti, Warner Bros. Pictures, 2017.
Jones, Timothy. *The Gothic and the Carnivalesque in American Culture.* University of Wales Press, 2015.
King, Stephen. *Danse Macabre.* Macdonald & Co. Publ. Ltd., 1981.
_____. *Duma Key.* Pocket Books, 2008.
_____. *11.22.63.* Hodder & Stoughton, 2012.
_____. *It.* Hodder & Stoughton, 1986.
_____. *Pet Sematary.* Hodder & Stoughton, 1988.
_____. *The Stand.* Hodder, 1990.
_____. *The Tommyknockers.* Hodder & Stoughton, 1988.
_____, and Peter Straub. *The Talisman.* Penguin, 1995 [1984].
Kinser, Samuel. "Carnival." *Medieval Folklore—A Guide to Myths, Legends, Tales, Beliefs, and Customs,* edited by Carl Lindhal, John McNamara, John Lindow. Oxford University Press, 2002, pp. 58–61.
Kristeva, Julia. *Powers of Horror—An Essay on Abjection.* Columbia University Press, 1982 [1941].
Magistrale, Tony. *Landscape of Fear: Stephen King's American Gothic.* Bowling Green State University Popular Press, 1988.

Pike, David L. *Metropolis on the Styx*. Cornell University Press, 2007.
_____. *Subterranean Cities—The World Beneath Paris and London, 1800–1945*. Cornell University Press, 2005.
Poe, Edgar Allan. "The Cask of Amontillado." *Selected Poetry and Tales,* Broadview Press, 2012, pp. 372–378.
Spooner, Catherine. *Contemporary Gothic*. Reaktion Books, 2006.
Stephen King's It. Directed by Tommy Lee Wallace, Warner Bros. Television, 1990.
Strengell, Heidi. *Stephen King: Monsters Live in Ordinary People*. Duckworth, 2005.
Thoens, Karen. "It, a Sexual Fantasy." *Imagining the Worst: Stephen King and the Representation of Women*, edited by Kathleen Margaret Laut and Theresa Thompson, Greenwood Press, 1998, pp. 127–142.
Turner, Victor. *The Ritual Process: Structure and Anti-Structure*. Aldine Transaction, 2008 [1969].
Wells, H.G. *The Time Machine*. Pan Book Ltd., 1953 [1895].
Winter, Douglas E. *The Art of Darkness: The Life and Fiction of the Master of the Macabre: Stephen King*. Penguin Publishing, 1986.

Patriarchy and Abject Horror in Stephen King's *It*

Young Beverly Marsh's Search for Subjectivity

RALPH BELIVEAU *and* LAURA BOLF-BELIVEAU

In *It* (2017), Beverly Marsh first joins the Losers' Club in a chance meeting at the pharmacy. Beverly stands in front of a large display of feminine hygiene products, seemingly unsure of which to take. Choosing the iconic blue-and-pink Tampax box, she heads to the register only to stop when she sees Stan, Eddie, and Bill who are shopping for supplies to take care of Ben's injuries. Quickly hiding the Tampax box, Beverly listens to their problem—not enough money to purchase what they need—and intervenes. As she flirts with the pharmacist to distract him from the boys impending shoplifting, the Tampax box openly sits on the counter. The boys get away with their supplies and Beverly buys the tampons. She then runs into the boys, dressing Ben's bloody wounds. The Tampax, secure in a grocery bag, swings from her hand. As she asks if the boys need help, an interesting juxtaposition is evident: Ben's wounds are public and communal; however, her menstrual blood is private and internal (hence, the selection of tampons, not pads). This scene is just one way the abject—the horrific and disgusting things that must be excised to preserve the self—is evident in the film and Stephen King's 1986 novel.

By focusing solely on young Beverly, this essay interrogates how her body is made abject by three masculine entities: her father, Pennywise/It, and the boys in the Losers' Club. While our use of abject comes from Julia Kristeva's 1982 *Powers of Horror*, we will expand beyond her usual application of maternal abjection and suggest that Beverly's character in *It*—both in the novel and the 2017 film—is a struggle over object, abject, and subject. Ultimately, we assert that the abject horror space of *It* offers a complicated way of thinking about a young girl's agency, and a reading of young Beverly matters because patriarchy is often ubiquitous. Beverly is more than one of the gang; how she is constructed provides insight into the story world, and, potentially, today's world.

In King's novel, Beverly is not yet twelve. She lives with both her abusive father, Al Marsh, and an absentee mother, Elfrida. Beverly is known for her lovely auburn hair, but little is known of her physical development. At one point her mother looks "at the nubs in Beverly's sweatshirt" (King 408), but there is no indication she has met the level of physical development evident in the 2017 film. Played by Sophia Lillis, this young Beverly has clearly reached puberty (as evidenced by the shopping for tampons). Lillis herself would have been fourteen during filming, and her character's physical development is most prevalent when she swims with the boys at the quarry. In that scene, each boy is stripped down to his white briefs. None is physically developed. When Beverly arrives, she announces that she'd be the first to jump in, and she quickly takes off her dress. Her plain white bra and blue underwear cannot hide her mature figure. As she jumps off the cliff, Richie's comment, "What the fuck?" is clearly referencing more than her bold leap. Later, Beverly sunbathes as the boys stare at her prone body. She is both a member of the group—evidenced by her playfulness in the water—and prospective sexual interest. Beverly's body is likewise objectified by her father and Pennywise/It, and we quickly see that bodies matter in *It*.

Bodies are often contested sites and are fundamental to understanding the way we think, feel, and reason. Bodies are "constitutive of what we call the self" (Hillman and Maude 1). If the body is the self, then objectified bodies may pose challenges to identities and subjectivities. As Hill and Maude posit, embodied experiences such as sex, childbirth, eating, pain, desire, etc., are all aspects studied in literary studies (1). Literature and the body, part of Body Studies, began in the 1970s with the work of Michel Foucault. More contemporary approaches to the body in literature include a wide variety of theories (Hill and Maude 2). Literature can be, Hill and Maude suggest, the "body's closest companion" (3). But it is important to remember that bodies are mediated *through* representation. Medical, political, and other institutions often construct bodies certain ways; literature responds by deconstructing those myths: "[T]he body is never simply a passive depository of cultural fantasy or the workings of power; it resists all reification and fixivity" (Hill and Maude 5). Studying bodies in literature questions assumptions and discovers invisibilities otherwise overlooked. This is especially true when thinking about how Beverly's body is an ever-present marker of patriarchy. Through a discussion of the body and abjection, Beverly's character moves from an object to something different, something worthy of deconstruction.

Kristeva, the Abject and Horror Spaces

As a horror text, *It* achieves effect by creating anxiety and tension in readers and viewers. The anxieties have to do with the violation of boundaries in terms of the laws of real experience in the scientifically experienced world, the organization of culture into collective ideas of right and wrong, and the individual experiences of mental and embodied physical integrity. These boundaries are violated by the supernatural, acts of violence perpetrated on society, and threats to bodies and minds. The surroundings in which Beverly finds herself incorporates many of these bodily threats. At home, her father is physically and psychologically abusive. In the larger society of Derry, other children's and adolescent bodies are disappeared, killed, and mutilated. Pennywise, the "It" responsible for the child murders, attacks Beverly and the other members of the Losers' Club using a horrific set of ideas, sounds, and images that violate the boundaries and bodies of the natural world.

These violations and disruptions of order are at the center of Julia Kristeva's work on the process of abjection:

> The abject has only one quality of the object—that of being opposed to *I*. If the object, however, through its opposition, settles me within the fragile texture of a desire for meaning, which, as a matter of fact, makes me ceaselessly and infinitely homologous to it, what is *abject*, on the contrary, the jettisoned object, is radically excluded and draws me toward the place where meaning collapses [1-2].

Horror in *It* is about the destruction of meaning. In its most threatening sense, the child killings that produce soulless mutilated corpses are among the strongest representations of the abject; the meaning of a human life is destroyed.

Kristeva extends the abject beyond the decaying corpse that was once a body. It becomes more than the antithesis of living, meaningful bodies. The abject fills us with disgust, from spoiled food that triggers vomiting, to excretory functions that produce the solids and fluids that we want to get away from, that repel us. Science teaches that the abject substances are threats to our health and well-being. Culture, in return, produces complex reactions to the abject to maintain meaning in the face of disintegration and chaos. As Rina Arya writes:

> The abject then is that which traverses and transgresses; that which endangers a structure and finds itself on the wrong side of the boundary [...] The boundary is in place to safeguard systems and functions and to separate and demarcate different states, such as life and death, and the sacred and the profane. Without the boundary we risk the threat of slippage between order and disorder and its corollaries— form/formlessness and life/death [41].

Society ritualizes and mechanizes the processes of dealing with the abject as a way of maintaining cultural meaning. Horror texts, on the other hand, revel in the threats to meaning. We engage with complex representations of the abject in film, literature, music, and other media to reinforce our sense of meaning through seeing how it is threatened. We make meaning out of these representations of abject threats to explore and "play" with our knowledge of ourselves as meaningful.

Kristeva's abject is a powerful concept when applied to young Beverly in both versions of *It*. We see a progression from object to abject, certainly, but whether young Beverly ever arrives at her own subjectivity remains in question. When deconstructing Beverly's body, gendered ideologies emerge as her body experiences the horrors of her home (the bathroom, specifically) and her larger society (the sewers of Derry).

Although Kristeva's approach is grounded in a Lacanian psychoanalytic analysis, the power of the abject, with its focus on the violation of boundaries, bodily decay and excess, and efforts to arrive at subjectivity give it power beyond the psychoanalytic paradigm. Freeland has offered a critique of the limits of the psychoanalytic approach (198–203). Additionally, Tyler cautions against using abjection to further stigmatize the notion of the maternal. We adopt Tyler's notion that the abject is a useful analytic tool when thought as social abjection: "Abjection is not just a psychic process, but a social experience" (87). In her analysis, Tyler argues that the maternal abject is associated with the maternal as a body separated from its subjectivity:

> It is when the maternal is no longer recognizable as *a* body and thus as a subject that it/she becomes abject […] it is precisely the uncoupling of the maternal from maternal subjects that enables the production of 'her' as a thing of horror—a bloody mess of signs [86].

The abject maternal is the opposite of the female body working toward subjectivity. The horror in *It*—the horror to which Beverly is subject—is the attempt to deny her subjectivity. Studying two specific settings, Beverly's bathroom and Derry's sewers, both places of abjection, shows how Beverly's body moves from object to abject. The question remains, then, is her body ever a subject?

The Bathroom as Abject Setting

Beverly's bathroom in her apartment, small and dingy like the rest of the home, is a site where she encounters multiple male figures: her father, Pennywise/It, and the boys. King describes the place as hideous, cracked, faded, stained, and unpleasantly pungent with "a slightly fishy smell coming from the drain" (398–399). From this drain, she hears the voices of disappeared children. Then, a "gout of blood suddenly belched from the drain, splattering the sink and the mirror and the wallpaper with its frogs-and-lilypads pattern" (400). Without thinking, Beverly calls for her father, but he cannot see the blood; in fact, he calls her behavior "foolish." But

> Beverly felt as if her throat had been lined with slate. Her heart raced in her chest. She thought that she might vomit soon. There was blood on the mirror, running in long drips. There were spots of blood on the light over the sink; she could *smell* it cooking onto the 40-watt bulb. Blood ran down the porcelain sides of the sink and plopped in fat drops on the linoleum floor [King 401–402].

This site is bloody, certainly, but as Kristeva reminds us in her use of abjection, bodily fluids like piss and shit are also part of horror.

Standing in the room together, Beverly's father says:

> "I worry about you […] I don't think you're ever going to grow up, Beverly. You go out running around, you don't do hardly any of the housework around here, you can't cook, you can't sew. Half the time you're off on a cloud someplace with your nose stuck in a book and the other half you've got vapors and megrims. I worry" [King 402].

He punctuates this message with a punch to the stomach, and Beverly quickly lies and says a spider had climbed out of the drain. Her father's response is a smile and pleasure. After all, Al Marsh says, "'If you'd told me, Beverly, I never would have hit you. All girls are scared of spiders. Sam Hill! Why didn't you speak up?'" (403). Later, when she discovers that her mother also cannot see the blood, Beverly wonders: "*What am I going to do about this? Have I gone crazy? Am I imagining it?*" (King 410). Two possible subtexts emerge. It seems likely she is referencing the blood, but could she also be wondering about her father, his abuse, and, at a meta level, the way in which his words and actions inscribe a patriarchal positionality that keeps her an object of her father's world? The bathroom, which should be a sanctuary from her father becomes a reminder of her father's physical and psychological domination.

Pennywise/It, as a malevolent presence in the bathroom, is not as visually prevalent in King's novel. We only hear the voices whispering out of the drain. They initially call for young Beverly's help, but their voices take on the composite chant of It:

> "I'm Matthew…. I'm Betty…. I'm Veronica … we're down here … down here with the clown … and the creature … and the mummy … and the werewolf … and you, Beverly, we're down here with you, and we float, we change…" [400].

Once the blood belches up and her father confronts her, the only other reference King makes is how the drain gives a burping chuckle.

The 2017 film expands Pennywise/It's presence exponentially. After hearing the voices from the drain, Beverly takes her father's retractable measuring tape and uses it to penetrate the drain. As she pulls it out, the measuring tape pulls up what looks like hair, quite possibly her own since she recently cut it after her father touched it. The hair reaches out to grab her. Multiple strands wind around her arms, neck, head, and face, and the hair pulls her face closer to the drain. Then the blood comes, not as the belch from the novel, but as a torrential spray. Beverly is completely covered, as is every inch of the bathroom, and she screams. When her father opens the door in the film, much of the dialogue is the same; however, he touches her forehead, pushing away her matted hair, asking her, "Why did you do this to your hair? Makes you look like a boy." In both versions, Al Marsh's imposed ownership of Beverly's body is tied to Pennywise/It; the bathroom becomes a place of male presence and possession.

Unlike the novel, Pennywise the clown does make an appearance in the bathroom in the film. In the last forty minutes, Beverly is questioned by her father about a postcard he found in her underwear drawer. This card is from Ben, and has the now iconic poem: "*Your hair is winter fire, / January embers. / My heart burns there, too*" (King 192). Unlike the previous bathroom scene in the film, Beverly stands up to her father when he tries to claim her. After a scuffle, she flees to the bathroom, but he kicks in the door. Beverly hits him with the toilet lid, and he is incapacitated. As she moves toward the door to escape, Pennywise appears and grabs her by the throat. He says nothing to her but leaves a message for Bill: "You die if you try." Pennywise does not directly talk to Beverly in either bathroom scenes. This suggests that the malevolent force speaks through her father. Once he is gone, Pennywise must intervene directly. Beverly's father and Pennywise/It seemingly use the bathroom and blood as a way to abject Beverly and keep her from being a subject. If one's father is no longer a danger, It will still get you.

The boys from the Losers' Club also enter the bathroom, but they are there to confirm what Beverly sees and help her clean it up. Worried about leaving stains on the rags, young Beverly from King's book questions if the blood will wash out. Ben hysterically giggles in response, telling her that it doesn't matter; "they" (the adults) cannot see it. Unlike the fear of her father or of It's voices, Stan, Ben, and Eddie are male allies in the book. When they wait for the rags to finish washing at the laundromat, Ben tells Beverly, "'You're not alone'" (419). They share their stories, finish the laundry, and Beverly feels good, thinking that they "had *done* something about it, that seemed to be the important thing" (King 420). The film, while keeping the gist of the novel's bathroom scene, changes some significant elements, and, as a result, changes the object-abject relationship between Beverly and the boys.

The bathroom scene in the 2017 film takes place sometime after the Losers' Club spends the afternoon at the quarry. Beverly has already purchased the tampons, taken off her dress in front of the boys, and sunbathed under their gaze. She has been their object. Now most of the boys enter the apartment with Eddie asking, "Are you taking us to your bathroom?" He muses about the sanitary conditions of the bathroom—how the bathroom is a site of injuries. Eddie's comments connect the bathroom to abjection. As Bill opens the door, they become bathed in red light and see what Beverly does: a bathroom drenched with blood. Bill says, "We can't leave it like this." There is a video montage of them cleaning; donning yellow plastic gloves, they clean, mop, wipe, and completely clean the bathroom until it is exactly as before. The end of the scene has a telling moment where Bill and Beverly talk—really flirt—about the Derry Fair. Beverly tells Bill, "It's not true, you know. What they say about me. I was only kissed by one guy. It was a long time ago. It was a nice kiss though." She references her own kiss with Bill in a third-grade play. This moment, now that the blood is gone, finds Beverly seeking her own agency. She's not the "slut" the girls so cruelly call her. She reminisces about a chaste kiss from long ago. After her speech, she says "January embers." Perhaps she can find subjectivity if Bill is the one that wrote her the now blood-stained postcard with the poem about her hair. But Bill is confused and says that he doesn't know much about poetry. She tells him not to mind, and they return to the group.

The bathroom, one of two places that represents the abject, is connected by blood to Beverly's father, to Pennywise/It, and to the boys. This blood could be read as menstrual and represent the end of her purity for her father (in the film, upon discovering her box of tampons, Al smells her hair and says, "Tell me you're still my little girl."). For It/Pennywise, blood comes up from the vaginal drain (with a fishy smell)—and suggests that when something is inserted (i.e., the tape measure), one will be punished with the revelation of the abject maternal hair and blood and the sound of lost children. As Barbara Creed notes, we see abjection at work in horror where the child struggles to break away from the mother: "In the child's attempts to break away, the mother becomes an 'abject'; thus, in this context, where the child struggles to become a separate subject" (12). Beverly struggles against the drain, where Pennywise/It obscenely violates the boundary of the maternal. The boys of the Losers' Club, especially in the film, work to remove the abject blood from the bathroom only to reclaim Beverly as an object, both love interest and then damsel in distress, as they must look for her in the underground realm of Derry.

The Sewers as Abject Setting

The other major site of abjection in *It* takes places in the sewer works. The connection between bathrooms with drains, sewers, and the service tunnels beneath the town of Derry is how they service the removal of the abject from our bodies. The anxiety and disgust we feel for bodily excretions and other waste products are removed by these engineered systems. We flush the abject away. When Beverly and the Losers' Club clean the Marsh bathroom, encounter the drain in Neibolt Street, and eventually go in the sewers, they are entering the sites of abjection, placing themselves in danger to confront the ultimate abomination of *It*.

King plays off notions of abject connected to liquids. In these places, Pennywise/It can lure children and then disappear. It can hide bodies in the sewer system or use the sewer entrance for access to the Denbrough's basement where Bill sees the first apparition of the murdered Georgie in the 2017 film. This location of horror also clearly links to the sink drain in the Marsh apartment, where Beverly encounters her own apparition of Pennywise/It. In the novel, the link between the Losers' Club and Pennywise/It becomes clear when they explore the basement in the Neibolt Street house where it disappeared. Downstairs they find a bathroom where the toilet has exploded into porcelain shards, and they find a drain hole that makes the same sounds that they have heard in the Barrens. As they are watching the drainpipe, they hear the sound of It approaching. It bursts through, immediately taking the form of a werewolf pulled from their memories of a recent film.

Pennywise/It exists in the spaces of the abject, but in reverse. Instead of the usual processes of sinks, toilets, and drains that take away the abject, they offer It access. The Losers' Club's ability to survive the threat comes as a result of their solidarity and through Beverly's skills. Previously they determined that Beverly was the most effective with the slingshot. When Pennywise/It shoots out of the drain as the werewolf, Beverly fires silver ball bearings with the slingshot, wounding the werewolf form. Their collective belief in the "magic" of silver against the threat gives them power. They drive Pennywise/It back down into the drain, back into the place of abjection, by their collective will to have Beverly shoot and kill it.

This leads the group to enter the sewers below Derry, and eventually beyond. They go down into the sewers after Pennywise/It, but they eventually go past the sewers, into a section of underground passages that are more of a mineshaft than an extension of the sewers. But this is not a relief: the smell of sewage is replaced by a more horrifying smell, arising from the lair of It, but It influences each differently. Beverly associates the lair with the smell of her father's sock drawer. At other times, though, the appearance of It is fixed in the group's collective experience; together they see It as a giant eye. Because of their collective recognition of the monstrous eye, they are strengthened to fight and subsequently defeat it. In the fight, Eddie calls out that his aspirator is now filled with battery acid, which he shoots into It's eye, causing It to recoil. Belief is critical to the struggle against It, which had used the imaginations of people against them, to manipulate their desires. King writes: "*together they had discovered an alarming secret that even It had not been aware of: that belief has a second edge. If there are ten thousand medieval peasants who create vampires by believing them real, there may be one—probably a child—who will imagine the stake necessary to kill it*" (1033). Beverly's part in this path into abjection and toward potential empowered subjectivity requires a belief in her own active and imaginative agency. She brings this with her as she accompanies the others in their venture into the abject space in the sewers under Derry.

One of the ways that the abject manifests its power is in the quest for subjectivity. Much of horror works because of the way our ideas about our subjectivity, our very selves, are under threat. Beverly's desires to gain power in her own subjectivity are under several different kinds of threats, all of which produce different modes of abjection. One threat is patriarchy, the institutional maintenance of control over women. But the influence of the mother can also become abject if the father's control subjugates the influence of the mother. Beverly in the novel has a weak and absent mother, a mother who is aware of the dominance of Beverly's father over her. The mother even asks Beverly at one point whether the father touches her, suggesting the mother suspects sexual abuse. The power Beverly's mother has is severely limited. Where abjection would normally diminish the power of maternal influence, in the novel Beverly's mother is not a challenge to the power her father has over her. Alternately, in the film, Beverly's mother is already absent. There is no mention of the circumstances of this absence; Beverly makes no mention of it. The abjection of the mother has already taken place. In the novel, Beverly admits to both loving and hating her father. The suggestion of sexual abuse is never specifically confirmed, but we clearly see and hear psychological and physical abuse. Beverly's efforts to arrive at an empowered subjectivity are held captive through her father's domination.

Patriarchal rule would also normally be aligned with the order imposed by the rules, laws, and ideologically reinforced understandings that perpetuate a patriarchal society. In *It*, we see familiar signs of adults and authority figures who remain uninvolved. The world of adults seems oblivious to the very public bullying of the Losers' Club. As Beverly is chased by Henry and the other bullies, right after she is chased by her father, there is no suggestion that a bystander will say something or do something. This reinforces the idea that the adults in Derry do not even see what is happening to their town, whether through the supernatural horror of Pennywise/It or through turning a blind eye to the violence happening in their culture.

Beverly's efforts to become an empowered subject are challenged by the rule of her father, the dominance and threat of sexual and physical violence from the bullies, and the confrontations with It. In the film, when she finally strikes out against her predatory father and kills him, she is grabbed by Pennywise and taken down into the abject spaces of the sewers beneath the town where the monster has its lair. Even though this takes a different story path from the novel—where Beverly and the rest of the Losers' Club are chased into the sewers by the bullies and toward their confrontation with It—the path still takes her to the space of the abject. But in these spaces, there are repeated instances where her participation in the group is more empowered than her other circumstances. The power of the seven members of the Club, especially their imaginations, provides the power to successfully send It back to its hidden space. Where previously It's murderous reign ended with a large-scale massacre, this time It is thwarted by the seven members working together. The power comes to them and through them when they are working, imagining and willing together.

This leads to one of the most controversial and complex elements of the novel. After the young members of the club have defeated It, they become lost and disoriented in the underground labyrinth. Although not necessarily the sewers, this place is, nonetheless, abject and what happens to Beverly's body is horrific in the way it is objectified. Once It has been defeated, Richie asks the group, "'What now, Bill?' [...] Bill listened to the distant mocking thunder of the water and tried to have the idea that Eddie—all of them—had a right to demand. Because, yes, correct, he had gotten them into this and it was his responsibility to get them back out again. Nothing came. Nothing" (King 1093).

Beverly breaks the silence with "'I have an idea" (King 1093). She begins undressing, telling the boys:

> "I know something [...] I know because my father told me. I know how to bring us back together. And if we're not together we'll never get out [...] Something that will bring us together forever. Something that will show—[...] that I love you all [...] that you're all my friends [...] Who's first?'" [King 1093–1094].

Bill's leadership of the group is stagnant, and it is the sole female of the Losers' Club who sacrifices her body for their future. This idea, which she credits to her father, this taking of each boy into her body in this abject place, is both moving and disturbing.

At one level, we see this sacrifice as innocent, for Eddie, who is first, does not have the knowledge to know what to do. Beverly tells him to put his thing in her. Her knowledge of sex, too, seems unformed. King describes the surface beneath her back legs and the thunder of the distant water as drowsy and soothing. Then her father's face appears to her with a chilling line: "I want to see if you're intact" (King 1099). But this is Eddie, a friend, someone for whom she has pleasant memories. This first time is painful for her, King writes, but she tells him to go slower so it will be easier for *him* to breathe. Here we have two male characters—first her father's demand to see if she's a virgin and then Eddie's reluctance to take away that virginity—juxtaposed in a way that moves from objectification to potential subjectivity. Her father claims her body as his to possess and then she gives that possession to Eddie. As Eddie is close to climax, King remarks:

> She senses that this is something for him, something extraordinarily special, something like … like flying. She feels powerful: she feels a sense of triumph rise up strongly within her. Is this what her father was afraid of? Well he might be! There was power in this act, all right, a chain-breaking power that was blood-deep. She feels no physical pleasure, but there is a kind of mental ecstasy in it for her [1100].

Sex with Eddie ends with him telling her that he loves her.

As she thinks about repeating the act with the rest of the boys, her consciousness breaks, and King does not narrate the conversations taking place among the boys. Instead, Beverly thinks that she must create "[…] *this essential human link between the world and the infinite, the only place where the bloodstream touches eternity*" (King 1100). With Ben, whose penis is the largest, she orgasms. With Bill, the final to have sex with her, she senses his eagerness but realizes, King says, that none of them must speak of this ever again. And then it is over. King writes: "*There is an emptiness down there now, and although she is glad that her sex is her own again, the emptiness imparts a strange melancholy which she could never express*" (1104). In a way, the novel has been about her innocence, about her father's insistence that she stay pure for him. This underground place where she unifies them through sex, so different from the bathroom where her father invades, has an ethereal quality, one she connects to bare trees and melancholy winter skies and seems to move from the abject to the subject. Whereas, her father objectifies her body, in the abject space underground, after the "defeat" of It, she takes ownership of her body and willingly gives it to the boys. Bill could not think of a way out, so she finds one. She appears to have acted under her own volition.

This scene from King's novel is not repeated or even hinted at in the 2017 film. Jung, writing for *Vulture* in 2017, quoted an earlier forum where King addressed this part of the book:

> I wasn't really thinking of the sexual aspect of it. The book dealt with childhood and adulthood—1958 and Grown Ups. The grown ups don't remember their childhood. None of us remember what we did as children—we think we do, but we don't remember it as it really happened. Intuitively, the Losers knew they had to be together again. The sexual act connected childhood and adulthood. It's another version of the glass tunnel that connects the children's library and the adult library. Times have changed since I wrote that scene and there is now more sensitivity to those issues.

Upon asking for verification of this earlier statement, *Vulture* quotes King: "'That sounds like my statement.' He added: 'To it I'd just add that it's fascinating to me that there has been so much comment about that single sex scene and so little about the multiple child murders. That must mean something, but I'm not sure what.'"

Abject, Subject and Patriarchy

Beverly Marsh instigates her own struggle toward agency by moving through the places of abjection. From one direction she struggles against the boundary violations of the abject. From the other direction the forces of patriarchy assert that her subjectivity must be controlled by her father, by the bullies, and by Pennywise/It.

Is her struggle toward a maternal subjectivity? The mothers in the novel and in the film are quite negative portrayals. On the one hand, like the rest of the adults and the police in Derry, they seem unable or unwilling to protect their children—especially, as Linda Anderson points out, against domestic violence by men (115). And perhaps the greatest story element against this is the revelation that Pennywise, usually coded as male (or the masculine name Bob Gray), otherwise referred to as a neutral-gendered monster, turns out in the final manifestation to be a monstrous, egg-laying female spider. While there is plenty to suggest that this is not It's true form, that It's true form is more ambiguous, the horror of the image is related to the gendered notion of the horrific archaic mother idea. As Karen Thoens writes, "The world order at the culmination of King's epic gender myth is nostalgic. The patriarchal hierarchy is restored; pliant, submissive females dedicate themselves to their men, who alone possess the secrets of the universe" (139). This is certainly a valid criticism in terms of how successful Beverly is at reaching her subjectivity. She has endured a great deal of the labor for the Losers' Club, survived paternal abuse, maternal neglect, and the terrors of a child-murdering supernatural shape- and gender-shifting being.

Still, we can see how King's novel and the film about young Beverly present bridges that hold out hope for an arrival at subjectivity. The bridge between the child and adult sections of the Derry Public Library are one of several bridging figures in *It*. The drains, sewers, and underground labyrinths are a bridge that Beverly and the Losers' Club must cross to confront Pennywise/It. Beverly's instigation of intercourse with the boys acts as a bridge between their childhood and adulthood. Even the manifestations of It serve as a bridge between the identifiable horror and the less identifiable and indescribable place where "the deadlights" exist as It's true form. But perhaps the idea of identifying the truth of It's form is as ambiguous as the effects of the abject on Beverly's own subjective power. She will still be contained in a patriarchal world, where she will have to bridge back though the reality of her body as the object of others' perceptions.

On his website, King has said that the seed for *It* was planted by a somewhat terrifying trip alone, after an auto breakdown, across a bridge, alone in an unfamiliar place. He thought of "The Three Billy Goats Gruff" tale, the troll under the bridge, and a connecting bridge in a Connecticut library joining the adult and children's sections: "[T]he corridor was also a bridge, one across which every goat of a child must risk trip-trapping to become an adult" (King "IT: Inspiration"). The process Beverly Marsh endured to survive the summer of 1958 contained perhaps the hints of what would be needed for her to achieve complete subjectivity. Certainly, her experiences of abjection offer a direction. But the context of Derry—of patriarchal America—in the late 1950s should be thought of less with nostalgia than as a cautionary tale where female subjectivity is rare, damaged, or worse, suspended in a web of monstrosity. Perhaps that is what horror tales can offer us.

WORKS CITED

Anderson, Linda. "'OH DEAR JESUS IT IS FEMALE'; Monster as Mother/Mother as Monster in Stephen King's *It*." *Imagining the Worst: Stephen King and the Representation of Women*, edited by Kathleen Margaret Lant and Theresa Thompson, Greenwood Press, 1998, pp. 111–125.
Arya, Rina. *Abjection and Representation*. Palgrave Macmillan UK, 2014.
Creed, Barbara. *The Monstrous-Feminine Film, Feminism, Psychoanalysis*. Routledge, 1993.
Freeland, Cynthia. "Feminist Frameworks for Horror Films." *Post-Theory: Reconstructing Film Studies*, edited by David Bordwell and Noel Carroll, University of Wisconsin Press, 1996, pp. 195–218.
Hillman, David, and Ulrika Maude, editors. *The Cambridge Companion to the Body in Literature*. Cambridge, 2015.
It. Directed by Andy Muschietti, performances by Bill Skarsgård, Jaeden Lieberher, Wyatt Oleff, Jeremy Ray Taylor, Sophia Lillis, and Finn Wolfhard, New Line Cinema, 2017.
Jung, E. Alex. "Stephen King: 'It's Fascinating' People Are More Offended by *It's* Child Orgy Than Its Child Murders." *Vulture*. 8 Sept. 2017. Accessed 31 Jul. 2019.
King, Stephen. *IT*. Scribner's, Paperback Edition, 2017.
_____. "IT: Inspiration." https://www.stephenking.com/library/novel/it_inspiration.html, no date. Accessed 15 June 2019.
Kristeva, Julia. *Powers of Horror: An Essay on Abjection*. Translated by Leon S. Roudiez, Columbia University Press, 1982.
Magistrale, Tony. *Landscape of Fear: Stephen King's American Gothic*. Bowling Green State University Popular Press, 1988.
_____. *Stephen King: The Second Decade, Danse Macabre to The Dark Half*. Twayne Publishers, 1992.
Sears, John. *Stephen King's Gothic*. University of Wales Press, 2011.
Thoens, Karen. "*It*, A Sexual Fantasy." *Imagining the Worst: Stephen King and the Representation of Women*, edited by Kathleen Margaret Lant and Theresa Thompson, Greenwood Press, 1998, pp. 127–140.
Tyler, Imogen. "Against Abjection." *Feminist Theory*, vol. 10, no. 2, 2009, pp. 77–98.

From Page to Screen
Troubled Domestic Space in the It *Franchise*

Rebecca Janicker

By the time that *It* appeared in 1986, Stephen King had established himself as a bestselling novelist with numerous film and television adaptations to his name. Consequently, as long-time King scholar Tony Magistrale puts across, the author had become "not merely a literary juggernaut, but a cultural phenomenon as well" (*America's Storyteller* 11). In keeping with King's formidable reputation, *It*—an unusually expansive novel, even by King's standards—boasted an impressive panoply of horrors. Garyn G. Roberts sees *It* as "an affectionate tribute to all the monsters that have haunted the movie screen, mass market novel and other popular media for decades" (88). Focusing on a core group of seven protagonists, exploring key episodes from their childhood and the legacy for them as adults, the novel moves between multiple perspectives and various points across time. The group, known as the Losers' Club, is united by a common enemy, a monster that preys on their hometown of Derry and emerges every twenty-seven years to feed. Having vanquished this monster as children, they reunite as adults in a bid to end It once and for all. It thrives on their fears, polluting the entire town and tainting the lives of all its residents; however, despite the wide array of frights on offer here, it is perhaps the everyday horrors, and especially those pertaining to house and home, that loom the largest. King's works have been adapted for screens large and small since his earliest years as an author and some have been redone for different formats. Analyzing aspects of the three texts in the *It* franchise to date, novel (1986), miniseries (1990), and film (2017), my intention here is to explore the treatment of domestic space across these different formats.

It will first be helpful to make some contextualizing remarks about the house in American Gothic. Early European Gothic novels placed significant emphasis on setting. As a creative response to changing modes of explanation driven by Enlightenment thinking, Gothic literature offered a critique of recognized social institutions (Edmundson 20). In tales driven by the villainous actions of aristocrats and clergy, evocative backdrops such as decaying castles and remote monasteries served not only to heighten atmosphere but also to make such critique explicit. Yet certain European Gothic conventions had to be adapted for the New World and setting was chief amongst them. Sylvia Grider, in her survey of the haunted house in literature and culture, explains that the dearth of medieval architecture in America turned attention instead onto the mansions built in the 19th century (180). Such buildings, though marked out by their opulence, are, nonetheless, recognizably domestic spaces. Over time, and with the genre's shift from the old world to the new, the haunted house has become the archetypal Gothic setting (Crow 177; Savoy 9). In "The 'Uncanny'" (1919), a work often discussed in relation to the Gothic, Sigmund Freud elucidates that the "uncanny" pertains to a fearful sense that something, or someone, is both familiar and unfamiliar at the same time (220 and 224). Haunted house stories have special potency because the home is so familiar—the place in which we should feel safest—and a threat to the home, which renders it unfamiliar, is fundamentally destabilizing (Mariconda 268). The familiar can become unfamiliar "through the process of repression" (241), so a source of fear may actually be something once known and since forgotten rather than something unknown. An "uncanny" effect or sensation, thus, stems from "something which ought to have remained hidden but has come to light" (241), which translates into the Gothic preoccupation with the past invading the present. Haunted house tales, with their literalized incursions of past trauma, are bound up with the Gothic trope of the return of the repressed (Clemens 3–4). King distills such sites, steeped as they are in deeply held superstitions, down to their simplest state with the remark that "we might call this particular archetype the Bad Place" (*Danse Macabre* 296). Exploring tropes of bad places and haunted houses, this essay argues that *It* centers on domestic spaces like homes and houses, and on threats of a domestic nature, with each version of King's story offering a medium-specific engagement with this theme.

Homey Horrors in King's Novel

In the first instance, I want to consider the role of the haunted house and the treatment of domesticity in King's novel. Heavily descriptive and character-driven, the novel contains an extensive and detailed exploration of the impact of It, not only on the lives of the Losers, but on the whole of Derry. King employs the time-honored Gothic device of the haunted house to convey the nature of the threat to the town. His novel is divided into five parts separated by *Interludes* comprising extracts from Mike Hanlon's unpublished work, *Derry: An Unauthorized Town History*.[1] The first interlude opens this record with Mike's unsettling rumination on his findings: "Can an *entire city* be haunted? / Haunted as some houses are supposed to be haunted? / Not just a single building in that city, or the corner of a single street [...] but *everything*. The whole works. / Can that be? [original emphases]" (153). Overtly invoking the image of the haunted house,[2] King sets the scene for the tale of a troubled place in which past traumas continually resurface to disturb the present. As Mike comes to understand, Derry is a town "haunted by its own violent history" (Mercer 319) and the novel supplies many illustrations, from a homophobic attack to a mass shoot-out. These anecdotes weave a rich tapestry of the countless ills plaguing Derry. Yet, although It's nightmares take many forms, *It* can be understood, at least in part, as a tale about troubles of a particularly domestic variety. A small town, Derry functions as the home writ large and the novel oscillates between horrors both communal and personal. When concentrating on the Losers, King utilizes settings such as houses and homes to portray their private ordeals and offer a critique of domestic abuse.

Having cast Derry as a larger version of the haunted house trope, the novel does much to reiterate the hold that domestic spaces exert over the imagination. One such example is a sinister old house out by the trainyards that features repeatedly and comes to seem a fundamental part of the novel. At one time "a trim red Cape Cod" (373), by 1958 the house at 29 Neibolt Street is "old and boarded up, its porch gradually sinking back into the ground, its lawn an overgrown field" (308) and, thus, redolent of "that atmosphere of gloom and decay which adheres to the crumbling abbey and the ruined castle in the gothic novel" (Bailey 4). Given the absence of a stated history for this house or for its inhabitants, John Sears's assertion that this is "a weak version of the motif" (162) is understandable; however, its dilapidated appearance epitomizes the haunted house motif and its recurring presence in the novel—which effectively bestows a history upon it—serves as a constant reminder of It's capacity to strike at the very heart of home. The site of several terrifying encounters, the "damned old house on Neibolt Street" (156) looms over the Derry of the Losers' childhood and retains its daunting power on their return. Eddie is traumatized by two childhood encounters at the house, one with a disfigured hobo and another with It. At the reunion, Mike's disclosure that the body of a young boy who "quite literally died of fear" (505) was found at the house causes Eddie great distress. Bill and Richie are attacked there by Pennywise as children and the Losers subsequently go to Neibolt Street to confront It, finding the already spooky house imbued with additional menace, as though "encased in a poisonous envelope" (841), due to It's uncanny ability to make the familiar monstrous. As a symbolic and literal exemplar of the "Bad Place," this location emphasizes the repeated link between horror and domesticity in King's novel.

The impact of It starts to crystallize once Mike contacts the adult Losers. Although they have left the troubled space of Derry far behind, forgetting much of their childhood in so doing, it transpires that they are haunted by It and this has had harmful repercussions for their home lives. One by one, Mike's calls paint a picture of their individual domestic situations. Although they all enjoy considerable professional success, their private lives are rather less fulfilled, which seems indicative of It's maligned reach. For instance, Stan and Patty Uris have a nice suburban home "set tastefully back behind low yew hedges" (52) yet, to their regret, remain childless. Eddie and Myra Kaspbrak, inhabiting a similarly comfortable Long Island home, are also without children. Rich in detail, the novel provides plenty of opportunities for introspection and Mike's call reminds Eddie that home has always had unpleasant connotations. Eddie's conscious memories of his mother are of an overbearing woman whose public insistence on the inherent frailty of her son repeatedly humiliated him and curtailed his childhood freedom. In consequence, Eddie has long nurtured the suspicion that, in marrying the overweight Myra, "he had, in a sense, married his mother" (94). After the call, his childhood comes to seem darker still. Entering a Gothic reverie, in which long-repressed memories begin to resurface, Eddie realizes that "*I am remembering my boyhood at last* […] *Oh God if I could only forget it all again*" (110). Eddie's reflection that "*Home is the place where when you go there, you have to finally face the thing in the dark*" (101) draws attention to It's potential to undermine the safety of the domestic sphere.

As other flashbacks disclose, for some of the Losers, their childhood home is more of a battleground than a refuge. For Tony Magistrale, "*It* is a novel about child abuse" (*The Second Decade* 106) and, as Sara Martín Alegre discerns, in some cases It effectively makes family strife manifest (110). Although It is the chief cause of Bill's unhappy home life, there are other facets to his suffering. King describes how the parents come to neglect their remaining son because they are trapped in their own grief for George. One especially lonely occasion sees Bill recall how his home used to be: "There had been a time when the TV room opening off the kitchen would have been full of talk and laughter, sometimes so much of both you couldn't hear the TV at all" (247). King's prose couches Bill's sense of loss in the language of haunting, explaining how the younger boy's absence has come to leave its mark on Bill's home life: "Georgie was still there, only now it was a Georgie he couldn't see" (248). For Bill, home is hardly a sanctuary. The case of Beverly Marsh is even starker, because she endures her father's physical and emotional abuse for much of her childhood. Like Eddie, Beverly is forced to deal with dark memories as she is drawn inexorably towards her childhood residence on her return to Derry. Revisiting the bathroom in which she experienced a bloody confrontation with It as a young girl, Beverly's sensation "that the old nightmare had gripped her again" (563) has a Gothic quality of haunting tied to a mundane, domestic locale. Pennywise here destabilizes Beverly's childhood memories, luring her into an appealing "trim and tidy" (562) version of her former home, only to unveil the sordid reality of a building that is actually "crumbling and deserted" (568). It's uncanny power works to insinuate that Beverly's home might, at last, be a comfortable refuge, before cruelly snatching this away. Overall, then, the novel's use of troubled homes and menacing houses works to communicate the theme of troubled domesticity.

Domestic Dread for the Domestic Medium

In 1990, *It* was adapted into a two-part miniseries for television by ABC, a commercial network with a long history of Stephen King productions (Magistrale, *Hollywood's Stephen King* 174). By this time, King's brand of horror had been shown to be as successful on the screen as it was on the page. Brian De Palma's *Carrie* (1976) and Stanley Kubrick's *The Shining* (1980) established King's first and third novels as cinematic events, whilst *'Salem's Lot* (1979) brought his second novel to the small screen in what was to be the first of many TV adaptations. Writing in much more recent years, Lorna Jowett and Stacey Abbott claim that, although King has personally been critical of television in the past, especially as far as the horror genre is concerned, "his name has, in recent years, become indelibly linked to TV horror" (71). From the choice of subject matter to the nature of the format itself, there are reasons why *It* might work especially well on TV, as the following examples drawn from the miniseries aim to demonstrate.

Following Helen Wheatley, I argue that the television format enhances the overall effect of King's novel because the domestic nature of the medium brings home (so to speak) the domestic focus of the narrative. For Wheatley, "Gothic television is understood as a domestic form of a genre which is deeply concerned with the domestic, writing stories of unspeakable family secrets and homely trauma large across the television screen" (1). The novel incorporates many momentous events in Derry's past, including a terrible fire and a tragic explosion, but, as discussed above, *It* also features numerous examples of domestic turmoil throughout. It is important to note that the program focuses more on the private and domestic than it does on the public and dramatic in terms of choices about theme, narrative and setting. To take one example, in a change from the novel's opening, the miniseries ensconces the viewer in a reassuring, domestic environment before undermining this in the most brutal way. The opening credits play out over a nostalgic montage of old photographs of young children and suburban dwellings, culminating in an exterior shot of Derry's Paramount cinema in its heyday and shoring up a cozy view of mid-century small town America. When the static shot comes to life and shows the same cinema in a state of disrepair, this sends a signal that the action has moved to the present day. In the suburbs, children play in the streets as a mother exhorts her young daughter, Laurie Anne, to come home and avoid the brewing storm. This homey scene is torn asunder with the arrival of Pennywise. An initially attractive figure, lurking playfully in the laundry billowing on the clothesline, the clown quickly turns savage. The mother comes outside to see Laurie Anne's abandoned tricycle, wheels still spinning, then her gaze shifts off-camera and she begins to scream. From the outset, the miniseries prioritizes the novel's disquieting theme of violence against children, "one of the long-standing taboos of Standards and Practices" and, therefore, a challenge for the adaptation process (Brown 158), and brings it right into the viewer's own home. Although compiled from minor incidents in the novel,[3] the fate of Laurie Anne makes an effective televisual introduction because it forges a clear link between Derry's past and present in showing that It's threat to the home, symbolized by the death of an innocent young girl, is still active.

Once the peril posed by It has been highlighted, the miniseries adheres more closely to the novel. The regimented nature of commercial television demands "episodes of precisely prescribed lengths, often with required breaks for advertisements" (Mittell 33). In accordance with this industrial imperative, the miniseries uses Mike's phone calls as a device to both introduce the adult Losers and convey their childhood experiences via a neat sequence of self-contained, yet interrelated, flashback scenes.[4] Exhibiting fidelity to the source material in its depiction of Bill's story, the program reproduces the details of George's death and its aftermath and reiterates the devastating consequences for Bill's home life. Akin to Eddie, Bill finds that Mike's phone call triggers repressed childhood memories and these are shown in the form of flashbacks. Following George's funeral, a forlorn Bill leafs through a photo album in the younger boy's now-empty bedroom. In a startling sequence, lifted from the novel but most effective in a visual format, a recent photo of George winks horribly and then oozes blood, causing Bill to fling the album across the room. When his parents seek out the cause of the commotion, it becomes apparent that they are unable to see the gore that so horrifies Bill. Rather than offering comfort or reminiscing about their mutual loss, Bill's parents chastise him and render the subject taboo, effectively estranging their older son. The Denbrough home deteriorates here, as it does in the novel, from a nurturing family environment to a haunted, lonely place that chimes with Wheatley's characterization of Gothic television as a medium for telling tales of "homely trauma" (1). The use of "visual 'tags'" (Browning 25), specifically here the replication of Bill's childhood expression and posture by the adult Bill during the transition from flashback to present day, provides visual confirmation of the resurfacing of these repressed events.

Conspicuously, Beverly's story—both past and present—is steeped in domestic violence and preserved largely intact across all three versions of *It*. Following introductory scenes of Beverly as an adult, showing her relationship with her partner to be physically and emotionally abusive, the TV flashbacks make it plain that her father was similarly violent and controlling. The miniseries makes much of a horrific episode that further destabilizes the young Beverly's already-troubled domestic existence. An evening incident, striking in its evocation of mid-century American home life, sees Beverly's father watching ABC's popular *77 Sunset Strip* (1958–1964) whilst she uses the bathroom. On hearing children's voices drifting from the drains, Beverly's tentative "Is someone there?" is met with the sight of a balloon that swells up out of the plughole and bursts, filling the sink with blood and spattering the surrounding area. Echoing the bloody photo of George, this is another eye-catching incident that—in keeping with the constraints of network television censorship—poses no immediate danger to Beverly but nevertheless puts across the threat of It even within this private domestic space. Given that Beverly's troubled home life has been replicated in her adulthood, it is perhaps unsurprising that she seeks to confront the domestic terrors of her childhood by revisiting her family home on her return to Derry. In a replay of the novel, Beverly drinks tea with the kindly old woman who has made the house into a pleasant home. This sequence works well in an audio-visual format, as the woman is bodily transformed into a nightmarish figure that speaks with her father's voice and pursues the terrified Beverly to the door. Once they are outside, the creature is revealed to be Pennywise and the house is shown to be boarded up, derelict, and inaccessible, as the *mise-en-scène* neatly imparts the uncanny power of It to make this homey environment an enduring site of horror for the traumatized Beverly.

The miniseries is fairly faithful to the novel with selected strands of the narrative, but one notable omission is the sustained, shadowy presence of the house on Neibolt Street. Conflating the childhood experience of Ben, who meets It as a mummy, with Eddie's horror of Neibolt Street, Stan's encounter with It is entirely different in the TV adaptation and sees him trapped in a spooky house. Though an even weaker version of the haunted house than that of Neibolt Street (Sears 162), since we learn nothing about the history of the place, it is telling that this Gothic device still retains a degree of prominence in the miniseries. Lured into a grand house, Stan finds the door slammed shut behind him and is transfixed with horror as a mummy descends the stairs. A classic scary scenario, complete with nightmare logic and a B-movie monster, it seems fitting that such an event should play out in an archetypal house of horrors that chimes with King's "Bad Place." The inclusion of such a setting, albeit in a different way to the book, utilizes the haunted house device in a novel manner and emphasizes the domestic theme once more. Mark Browning suggests that "the limited budget forces some creative thinking and produces [some] powerful effects" (23) in the TV version. Though the ordeals of the children are relatively low-key, consisting largely of implied threats, they are still productive of effective scares because they take place in the children's neighborhood and often in their own homes, places in which they should feel safest, undermining their security and serving as a chilling reminder of the domestic abuse at work in Derry. Stan's childhood ordeal has a horrifying impact on his adult home. Arguing that TV has ever been a natural home for horror (161), Lisa Schmidt notes that seriality, which clearly pertains to the miniseries format since it has more than one episode, ensures that "the viewer will be that much more invested in the character's situation" (166). In *It*, the cliffhanger between Parts One and Two is the revelation of Stan's suicide, prompted by Mike's call. Coming at the end of the first installment, by the time of this very domestic horror scenario (Stan is found in his own bath) the viewer is familiar with the Losers' childhood history, as well as their goal of reuniting to confront It as adults, and, thus, able to fully appreciate the significance of this loss. By focusing on domestic narratives and threats, the miniseries offers a distinctly televisual take on the novel, infuses it with episodic suspense and screens this version of the story within the very domestic environment that (as *It* implies) is replete with Gothic potential (Wheatley 18).

Cinematic Spectacle in It *(2017)*

Twenty-seven years after the miniseries, *It* was released in cinemas. The Hollywood treatment and cinematic release meant a bigger budget and the potential to achieve a more forceful treatment of It. An interview with director Andrés Muschietti and cinematographer Chung-hoon Chung stresses the quest to make a "darker, R-rated version more in keeping with modern horror aesthetics" and in accordance with Chung's surrealistic style (Dillon 47). Divided into two cinematic releases, the 2017 film is set principally in 1989 and shows the Losers defeat Pennywise as young teens. The second film, released in 2019, portrays their reunion as adults. Although this strategy undoubtedly streamlines the narrative even further than the miniseries, it also means a loss of thematic potency for the version of events offered in chapter one. This is because the relationship between past and present, exemplified throughout by the use of flashbacks to convey the gradually resurgent memories of the adults (in both novel and miniseries), is entirely absent from the first film. Whilst *Chapter Two* addresses this theme through the gradual introduction of flashbacks, key ideas about memory and haunting, which are so integral to the Gothic notion of the return of the repressed, are diminished considerably in the 2017 film; however, though there are many deviations from the source material, the first film does see the reinstatement of content not included in the TV adaptation. Once again, a preoccupation with domestic horrors is in evidence.

Interestingly, the house at 29 Neibolt Street, missing from the miniseries, plays a central role in the big screen version. Following Eddie's personal experiences there, which mirror those in the novel, the Losers realize that this is the site of the old well house, part of the sewer system and It's main point of access to Derry. Here, the house is re-imagined to become a rather stronger version of the motif, crucial to It's reign of terror in the town, and the Losers determine to go there to meet It head-on. These scenes are very compelling in a visual format, as the house makes for a suitably imposing horror setting. Framed by a gnarled tree and rusted fencing, shot from below to enhance its bulk, this edifice looks every inch the haunted house. King describes the house in Lovecraftian terms, a place where "the *angles* were wrong, the perspective crazy" (846). In addition to a murky *mise-en-scène* complete with cobwebs and dead leaves, the use of dolly zooms and canted angles creates a disturbing ambience that heralds the imminent showdown with the clown; moreover, though the children fear the supernatural energy of this place, in a grim reminder of the more mundane domestic horrors portrayed in the film, Bill declares that his home life is so unhappy since George disappeared that "walking into this house, for me, is easier than walking into my own." Reinstating elements of King's novel, and using cinematic techniques to augment the thematic concerns, thus, brings the Gothic device of the haunted house back to the forefront of the tale in visual, as well as narrative, terms.

Bill's story, though initially handled in the same way as in the other versions, takes a different tack that drives home his domestic woes. Consistent with the desire for a "darker" vision, Bill's ghastly experience certainly amplifies the tension in a truly cinematic fashion whilst also giving weight to the theme of troubled domestic space. When George fetches wax to waterproof the paper boat, around two minutes are devoted to his anxious descent into the gloomy basement, where he discerns what appears to be a pair of gleaming eyes watching him. Though this is revealed as illusory, the threat is now apparent and George is killed in the streets shortly afterwards. Bill is subsequently forced into a vivid confrontation with the irrevocable damage to the home caused by George's absence. Waking in the night, Bill sees George, dressed as when he left to sail the boat, and follows his younger brother into the basement that so troubled him. A more ambitious version of the bleeding photo of the book and miniseries, this scene sees George become monstrous, rapidly decaying and raging at his older brother, until Pennywise appears and chases Bill upstairs. In another terrifying sequence, and in a departure from his settled home life in the novel, Mike's vision of people trapped in a burning building re-enacts the horror that befell his family home when his parents died in a house fire. As with the reinterpretation of the house on Neibolt Street, these new additions to the story offer lavish, cinematic viewing experiences, although the emphasis on domestic horror still endures.

Finally, as mentioned above, the childhood story of Beverly Marsh remains essentially the same across all three versions of the story, concentrating on domestic abuse as well as on the invasion of It. In the film, the inside of the Marsh family home is foreboding, contrasting starkly with the bright exterior. The latent sense of menace is made manifest by the intrusive behavior of Beverly's father, who exerts his hold over her by smelling her long hair and saying, "Tell me you're still my little girl." Though she acquiesces, Beverly retreats to the bathroom where she cuts the length of her hair away as though to exorcize his presence. This private space is coded as a refuge for Beverly, one in which she transforms her appearance in defiance of her abuser and visits to re-read the haiku sent to her by an admiring Ben. Her peace is shattered in the film's recreation of a key scene from both the novel and the miniseries. As her father slumbers in front of the TV, which now plays only static, Beverly approaches the sink after hearing children's voices floating up from the drain. Tendrils of hair snake out, yanking her towards the plughole and holding her in position as gouts of blood gush relentlessly upwards. This memorable scene is not only retained but heightened considerably for the film as the entire bathroom is rendered incarnadine. The scale of the damage, to which her father is once again oblivious, is accentuated by the extensive cleanup operation performed by the Losers. Commensurate with the scale of a Hollywood project, and as hoped for by the filmmakers, *It: Chapter One* mobilizes the "formal, technological and industrial" resources typically associated with cinema (Schmidt 160) to provide a more lavish entry in the *It* franchise.

Conclusion

From neglectful and abusive parents, through to B-movie monsters and the ultimate adversary in the form of Pennywise the clown, horrors both ordinary and extraordinary combine here to assail the inhabitants of small-town America. The *It* franchise exploits a range of shocking creatures and scenarios with which to terrorize its child and adult protagonists, as well as horror fans, alike. From King's novel through to adaptations for screens large and small, the tales told of It are ever laced with everyday menace, featuring bedrooms, bathrooms, basements, and other everyday spaces made sinister, showing the domestic focus to be integral to *It*'s continued relevance and appeal. Inspired by King's epic novel of battling overwhelming odds, drawing on the creative possibilities offered by different media formats, the *It* franchise makes for a gripping case study of how the abiding American Gothic preoccupation with troubled domestic space has been re-imagined, across multiple media platforms, over the decades.

Notes

1. Mary Jane Dickerson argues that, echoing William Faulkner and in employing Mike, who is African American, as historian, "King insists that the story of the black American permeates the history of the American northeast as much as it does the history of the south" (178).

2. My monograph, *The Literary Haunted House: Lovecraft, Matheson, King and the Horror in Between* (2015), examines the haunted house motif in three of King's novels, *The Shining* (1977), *Christine* (1983), and *Bag of Bones* (1998).

3. In the novel's "Second Interlude," Laurie Ann Winterbarger is a five-year-old girl who disappears while sledding outside her home in 1985. Her character's fate is re-imagined for the miniseries, as the circumstances of her death seem to echo those of the book's three-year-old Matthew Clements who dies in 1958. In one of the novel's numerous historical scenes, he rides his tricycle outside his home as his mother does laundry. The sight of "his overturned trike on the grass" (188) prefigures the discovery of his body the following day.

4. The first part of the miniseries is essentially devoted to covering flashback stories for six of the adult Losers: Bill, Ben, Beverly, Eddie, Richie, and Mike, in a systematic fashion. Stan is the seventh Loser to receive a call, although his experience with It is only recounted later on, towards the middle of the second installment.

Works Cited

Alegre, Sara Martín. "Nightmares of Childhood: The Child and the Monster in Four Novels by Stephen King." *Atlantis*, vol. 23, no. 1, 2001, pp. 105–114.
Bailey, Dale. *American Nightmares: The Haunted House Formula in American Popular Fiction*. Bowling Green State University Popular Press, 1999.
Brown, Simon. *Screening Stephen King: Adaptation and the Horror Genre in Film and Television*. University of Texas Press, 2018.
Browning, Mark. *Stephen King on the Small Screen*. Intellect, 2011.
Clemens, Valdine. *The Return of the Repressed: Gothic Horror from "The Castle of Otranto" to "Alien."* State University of New York Press, 1999.
Crow, Charles L. *American Gothic*. University of Wales Press, 2009.
Dickerson, Mary Jane. "Stephen King Reading William Faulkner: Memory, Desire, and Time in the Making of It." *The Dark Descent: Essays Defining Stephen King's Horrorscape*. Ed. Tony Magistrale. Greenwood Press, 1992. 171–186.
Dillon, Mark. "Fear Itself." *American Cinematographer*, vol. 98, no. 10, 2017, pp. 46–55.
Edmundson, Mark. *Nightmare on Main Street: Angels, Sadomosochism, and the Culture of Gothic*. Harvard University Press, 1997.
Freud, Sigmund. "The 'Uncanny.'" *The Standard Edition of the Complete Psychological Works of Sigmund Freud: An Infantile Neurosis and Other Works* Vol. 17 (1917–1919). Translated by James Strachey, Vintage, 2001. 217–256.
Grider, Sylvia. "The Haunted House in Literature, Popular Culture, and Tradition: A Consistent Image." *Contemporary Legend*, 2, 1999, pp. 174–204.
It. Directed by Andy Muschietti, Warner Bros., 2017.
It: Chapter Two. Directed by Andy Muschietti, Warner Bros., 2019.

Janicker, Rebecca. *The Literary Haunted House: Lovecraft, Matheson, King and the Horror in Between*. McFarland, 2015.
Jowett, Lorna, and Stacey Abbott. *TV Horror: Investigating the Dark Side of the Small Screen*. I.B. Tauris, 2013.
King, Stephen. *Danse Macabre*. 1981. Warner, 1993.
_____. *It*. Hodder & Stoughton, 1986.
Magistrale, Tony. *Hollywood's Stephen King*. Palgrave Macmillan, 2003.
_____. *Stephen King: America's Storyteller*. Praeger, 2010.
_____. *Stephen King: The Second Decade, "Danse Macabre" to "The Dark Half."* Twayne Publishers, 1992.
Mariconda, Steven. "The Haunted House." *Icons of Horror and the Supernatural: An Encyclopedia of Our Worst Nightmares* Vol. 1. Ed. S.T. Joshi. Greenwood Press, 2007. 267–305.
Mercer, Erin. "The Difference Between World and Want: Adulthood and the Horrors of History in Stephen King's *It*." *The Journal of Popular Culture*, vol. 52, no. 2, 2019, pp. 315–329.
Mittell, Jason. *Complex TV: The Poetics of Contemporary Television Storytelling*. New York University Press, 2015.
Roberts, Garyn G. "King and the Heritage of Horror." *Readings on Stephen King*. Ed. Karin Coddon. Greenhaven Press, 2004. 81–89.
Savoy, E. "The Face of the Tenant: A Theory of American Gothic." *American Gothic: New Interventions in a National Narrative*. Eds. Robert K. Martin and Eric Savoy. University of Iowa Press, 1998. 3–19.
Schmidt, Lisa. "Television: Horror's 'Original' Home." *Horror Studies*, vol. 4, no. 2, 2013, pp. 159–171.
Sears, John. *Stephen King's Gothic*. University of Wales Press, 2011.
Stephen King's It. Written by Lawrence D. Cohen and Tommy Lee Wallace, ABC, 1990.
Wheatley, Helen. *Gothic Television*. Manchester University Press, 2006.

The Truth Inside the Lie
It *and the Evolution of the Serial Killer*

Rebecca Frost

It feeds on popular culture just as much as It feeds on fear. When, in the novel, It summons the adult Losers back to Derry to enact revenge, It resumes many of the physical forms It took to frighten them when they were children, a large number of which were associated with the monsters in horror movies from their childhoods. While It can and does assume guises related to more personal fears of the children, It's main source of inspiration seems to come from the children's own imaginations, so It feeds largely on the popular culture that the children consume.

The miniseries placed the adult characters in a contemporary setting with the book. This meant that the changes to It's various monstrous forms was more dependent upon technology's ability to reproduce them onscreen than generational differences between King's original audience, the original timeline of the story, and the updated filmed version. The more recent 2017 movie shifts the timeline by almost as much time as It's own sleep cycle, positioning the Loser's childhood in the late 1980s. This is a much more drastic repositioning of the story, filmed at a time when CGI techniques were far less of a limiting factor in the choice of It's public faces, and so the fears that originated within the novel have been largely changed to new forms that reflect this generational change. It feeds on children and cultural myth, allowing for the main characters—and the intended audience—to have an entirely different set of fears at their disposal in 2017 than they did in earlier decades.

Horror in Cycles

The original plot of It already positions the story as adaptable to new decades and generational expectations. As Karen Thoens points out, King's contrasting of the murder of Georgie Denbrough in 1957 with that of Adrian Mellon in 1984, each the opening horror of the next cycle, is already "a signifier of social change" (128). The shift from the innocent child in the 1950s as circumstantial victim of Pennywise in clown form to a gay man attacked by a number of young men from town who offer him as a sort of sacrifice to It already shows the ways in which It is adaptable to new circumstances, including new prejudices and new fears. Although in-text Mike Hanlon later describes Mellon as "a gay and rather childlike man," his childlike attributes matter less than his sexual orientation when it comes to distinguishing Mellon as the chosen victim (King 477). The victims of It are generally childlike in some way, but what makes Mellon stand out—and positions him solidly in the 1980s as opposed to the 1950s—is his sexual orientation and the public response to it.

King has already established the ability of It to respond to new cultural fears and play on contemporary tensions each time It surfaces for the next killing cycle, using concerns about racism in the destruction of the Black Spot or righteous feelings of vigilante justice during the shooting of the Bradley Gang prior to tapping into fears of homosexuality and AIDS. Those concerns would certainly be on the minds of his readers in the mid–1980s, many of whom could also likely be counted on to remember the apparently more idyllic period of the 1950s. Just as a postwar childhood could be remembered as having been carefree, full of paper boats and simpler pleasures, the current situation in the 1980s could be seen as a threat from outsiders, a period of unrest and new fears of Baby Boomers watching their own children grow up in the midst of rising threats. While the miniseries kept the main characters within roughly the same generation as the Losers in the book, the movie has once again provided a shift in the timeline of It's attacks.

In the movie, the initial encounter the Losers have with It as children now happens in the 1980s, positioning the new main characters as a generation younger than those in the book or miniseries. While the original Losers are roughly King's own age and, therefore, have the full benefit of his own childhood experiences—especially fears grounded in horror movies of the 1950s—the new movie draws on the childhood and life experiences of those who grew up in the 1980s, during which AIDS was not the only new real-life horror. The figure of the serial killer rose in public and popular consciousness in the 1980s, as well.

Investigative historian Peter Vronsky argues that "an enormous glut of serial killers" grew up as contemporaries of the book and miniseries Losers, either during or within the decade and a half after World War II (*Sons of Cain* 310). Because those groups of fictional children experienced childhood before the so-called Golden Age of serial killers—indeed, the term itself was not coined until the 1970s and does not appear once in King's book—the figure of the serial killer, in either his factual or fictional form, does not menace the children of the book or miniseries. The various forms It takes to scare them are, by and large, creatures not immediately recognizable as human—or rather, creatures immediately recognizable as inhuman. Like the werewolf or the mummy, they may have once been people, but have now clearly been changed into the supernatural.

Audience members who grew up during the period of the 1980s and 1990s, however, experienced the American true crime boom in which the genre "both created and assuaged fears about serial killers, and it educated consumers of pop culture" about the criminals themselves, as well as the procedures useful in catching them (Murley 3). Thomas Harris introduced the world to serial-killing cannibal Hannibal Lecter in 1981, and his 1988 novel—which became the Oscar-winning 1991 movie—*The Silence of the Lambs* countered Hannibal with the figure of the FBI agent proficient in criminal profiling. Between the miniseries and the movie, the serial killer as a mythic figure exploded into popular consciousness as a public fear validated by the FBI and multiplied through both factual and fictional retellings in which real-life figures such as Ted Bundy spawned fictional offspring in the form of Lecter, Dexter Morgan, and various sweeps-week characters on shows such as *CSI: Crime Scene Investigation* and other forensic procedurals. Even though the 2017 movie is set before *The Silence of the Lambs* was released, it is still addressing an audience for whom dueling serial killer and FBI profiler is a popular narrative trope.

King's original text mentions mass, spree, and copycat killers, but does not even reference "Killer Clown" John Wayne Gacy—this connection only comes in his 2001 novel *Dreamcatcher*, in spite of Gacy's arrest having been prior to the publication of *It* (*Dreamcatcher* 550). The serial killer is not part of the conscious or subconscious fears of the original Losers, nor likely of the audiences of the book and the miniseries. The 2017 movie, however, was filmed in a world where the serial killer is such a commonly accepted figure that "we find it irrelevant to distinguish between a Ted Bundy (a real serial killer) and a Hannibal Lecter (an imaginary one)" (Arntfield and Danesi 140). Common knowledge of the serial killer moves between the factual and fictional almost seamlessly so that knowledge of one figure is considered tantamount to knowledge of all, and fears of serial killers have coalesced not around an eyeball, a plastic statue of Paul Bunyan, or even a teenage werewolf who is, after all, usually human. Instead, the new fear is of the Ted Bundy or the Hannibal Lecter: a figure who presents himself as normal enough—although likely charming, urbane, and an apparent cut above so many others—but whose monstrosity is hidden inside.

A More Human Threat

The guises It takes in the book and miniseries vary from the relatively human Pennywise the Dancing Clown, played onscreen by Tim Curry, to the horror movie monsters taken from onscreen portrayals originated by men in heavy makeup and costumes; to the spiderlike "true form" It takes when the Losers go into the sewer. Because It has the ability to shapeshift into what It knows will scare the children the most, it is difficult to categorize It's many forms into a single category, but Linda Anderson points out that most of It's guises "are explicitly defined as male" (Anderson 111). There are, of course, a few exceptions—the genderless eye or Mrs. Kersh—but the generality holds. This is also a generality that can be applied to serial killers, marking one way in which It is positioned to be easily adaptable to this new site of fear.

Tony Magistrale also observes that "King approximates the medieval perception that evil [...] exercised the ability to modify its shape to one essentially human," seen especially in the figures of Pennywise and Mrs. Kersh (*Second Decade* 106). The 2017 movie adds to the array of more-or-less human forms, tuning Mike Hanlon's fear from an oversized bird to the door behind which his parents and others were trapped in a fire; Ben's horror-movie mummy into a headless boy from the Kitchener Ironworks explosion; and Patrick Hockstetter's death from flying leeches into undead children and Pennywise himself. The other forms of It that undergo a marked change from the original text are the one that threatens Stan, shifting from the unseen drowned children to a painting of a woman; and Richie's fear shifting from the plastic Paul Bunyan statue to clowns. Since Bill is menaced by the appearance of his younger brother, Georgie, and Eddie by a leper, only Bev's encounter with blood coming out of the drain retains the non-human face on their individualized horror. Even the final confrontation between the Losers and It at the end of the childhood cycle has them facing Pennywise instead of It's spiderlike "true" form.

It could be argued that the humanization of It's forms in the 2017 movie is also a response to the lessening of the human menaces from the book. Karen Thoens argues that the parents in Derry are just as responsible for the fates of their children as the monster Itself, focusing on the neglect inherent in Derry's mothers since the abuse inflicted by Derry's fathers is overt. Beverly Marsh, the only female in the Losers, "comes to identify masculinity with monstrosity" because of the physical abuse she suffers at the hands of her father (Magistrale *America's Storyteller* 128). While Bev's father is indeed shown within the 2017 movie, many of the Losers' other parents are only referenced in passing. This emphasizes the neglect Thoens highlights, a more passive threat in the face of It's active pursuit.

The active human threat is, however, still present, although the dangers in this case "bear the disguise of other children" (Beahm 262). While the bullies from the book and miniseries, led by Henry Bowers, continue to pursue and attack the Losers, their female classmate, Greta Bowie, is also given a more active role especially in the persecution of Bev and the humiliation of Eddie. While in the book Greta is merely guilty of ignoring Eddie when he happens to cross socio-economic lines on a walk past her house, in the movie she is responsible for writing the word "loser" in large letters on his cast. Even though she is pretty and popular, Greta becomes another one of the characters who "turn out to be monsters beneath their human exterior," no longer a passive female character but actively targeting some of the main characters (Strengell 210). The Derry of the movie is still just as dangerous as the Derry of the book, although not every hoodlum wears a leather jacket.

The various new faces of It, as well as the expansion of bullying to girls as well as boys, increase the human aspect to the threats faced by Derry's children. The emphasis of true crime—and crime fiction—on "the dangers of the ordinary, the trusted, and the prosaic" come through in the updated film version of the 1980s as the iterations of It, while still monstrous, tend more toward the human (Murley 159). Monstrosity no longer has to be completely inhuman, since everyday people have proven themselves to be just as terrifying—and not purely part of a child's overactive imagination.

Hiding Behind a Human Face

Since It lives alone in the sewer with nothing but the eggs of It's children and only emerges to feed, It needs not concern Itself with looking or acting human on a day-to-day basis. It is also assisted by the fact that adults in Derry hardly ever see It—and, if they do, they rarely speak about the sighting or react in a way that would threaten It. It, like the serial killer, only reveals Itself to It's victims; although, again, the forms It chooses to take evolve between the book, the miniseries, and the movie. Children of the 1980s have been taught to fear people more than movie monsters, because the people could easily be monsters in disguise.

Tony Magristrale's previous analysis of It's clown form as "an adult in elaborate makeup—who is capable of disguising monstrous intentions" lends itself to both the argument of the evil being human, as well as the adaptability of the creature's faces across generations (*Landscape* 113). Already the clown, in the form of Pennywise, plays with the idea of the contrast between surface appearance and possible intent. The painted clown puts on an accepted false face to appear in public and fulfill a certain expected role, one which itself holds the dual possibility of inspiring amusement or fear. Clowns, like It and like serial killers, apply a specific outer appearance to assist them with their intended purpose. The form of Pennywise already contains within it this idea of the human form in a mask, although the different costuming styles of Tim Curry and Bill Skarsgård once again show a shift from the more playful, Ronald McDonald style and coloring to a more old-fashioned, monotoned costume. Pennywise is not masquerading as an entirely "normal" adult, but the updated costume does allow him to blend in more and become more of a menace because he is more difficult to spot. This Pennywise interacts with the Losers on more of a personal level, approaching them instead of taunting them from a distance.

The threat has become less obvious. Like Ted Bundy, It's tricks are harder to recognize immediately and, once spotted, it might be too late for the intended victim. Even though "the children are fully aware that there is something more sinister going on" than a series of murders or copycat killings, and the Losers have the added benefit that their recognition does not come immediately before their deaths, they still find themselves at a loss for how to respond (Jenkins 17). Horror movies might have taught the earlier generation of Losers that silver bullets will work against a werewolf, but how can the updated group triumph over a creature that generally looks more or less human without the built-in weaknesses of the earlier supernatural forms?

The difference between It and a serial killer is, of course, that It's mask includes that of humanity–It is always an inhuman creature, albeit, one that can and does adopt the guise of a person. A serial killer is a human who is described using the language of monstrosity but is, in fact, still a human being, albeit, one marked as deviant. Each pretends to be something he or It is not to get closer to his chosen prey. This disguise is only identified by a small number of people, and then often only shortly before those people become the next victims. It takes a special adversary, or perhaps group of adversaries, to identify them, stand against them in battle, and bring them to justice, whether that group is made up of specialized law enforcement officials or Losers.

Since the serial killer has become such a fixture in popular culture, it makes sense that It would borrow lessons learned from both factual and fictional characters since those fears have been cultivated in the children who have grown up with that popular culture. Aside from It's adaptability as a monstrous creature of many faces, "[t]he contemporary view of murderers as 'monsters' also comes from the gothic tradition," a tradition upon which King himself often draws (Arntfield and Danesi 59). It is positioned to easily take on aspects of the serial killer while still maintaining the feel of the original creature from the book. It is, after all, meant to adapt to the fears of whichever children It encounters during this murderous cycle, and shifting from one aspect of gothic tradition to another is a small change—and yet one that can mean the difference between inspiring fear in It's victims or encountering confusion or even disdain over something too old-fashioned and uninspiring. As the popular culture that feeds our fear changes, so must It change in order to adapt and likewise feed.

Where It has the advantage over the serial killer, however, is in It's basic monstrosity. A bullet would serve as defense against a serial killer, whether or not it was made of silver so long as the defender recognized the basic danger, but what defense do the Losers have against It when It takes the form of the undead? Ben's personalized horror is especially troublesome, since the general rule of thumb to defuse a zombie is to damage its brain or remove its head, but the child Ben sees in the library is already decapitated. The book especially emphasizes that It is bound by the beliefs surrounding the physical form It chooses to take, meaning that the werewolf is indeed harmed by the silver slug the Losers cast, although numerous other forms have no such obvious defense. What, for example, would repel a supernatural leper? Without a solid form of defense, or a convenient bag of sneezing powder, must the Losers simply run?

It attacks children because their fears can indeed be summed up in such almost simplistic physical forms: the mummy, the leper, the creature from the lagoon. The threat they pose is immediately recognizable and sparks terror from a distance, prolonging it through the chase. Adult fears are too nebulous to be presented so clearly so, although It is moved to encourage grown men to violence against others, It does not prey on adults as It's main source of nourishment, and the book suggests that this is because It likes the way flesh tastes when it is infused with fear. The single-image fears of children make it easier for It to flavor It's food.

Even though It has functioned alongside Derry for centuries, adapting to changes in cultural fears, were It to regenerate in another reboot after *Chapter Two* (2019), It may find Itself struggling to continue to dine as It has been accustomed. Advances not only in technology, leading to more realistically rendered violence and monsters in film media—the appearance of It at the end of the miniseries being an infamous example of technology's inability to portray the artistic vision—alongside greater access to information and media, again through technology and media infrastructures, has led to laments that children grow up far too quickly. The fear of the visually different Other—that which leads to many of It's guises within the book—is childish. The fear of the monster who looks exactly the same as everyone else is more adult.

It *and the Evolution of Fear*

It is not Stephen King's personal statement on serial killing—that comes later with the novella "A Good Marriage"—although the figure of It has indeed been adapted to address such fears. The very basis of a menace that goes through cycles of hibernation and wakefulness timed to approximate the human generation, one that is able to change It's outward appearance, easily allows for such adaptation. The It of the book is clearly set up to respond to the changing fears of It's preferred prey, children, and It's guises evolve in response.

The Losers of the book and the miniseries grew up around the same time as King himself, and their fears were stoked and supplied through various monster movies. It took some of It's forms directly from the big screen, shown especially when Bill and Richie encounter It as a werewolf shortly after Richie saw a horror double-feature that included the teenage werewolf. Even when the Losers return as adults, their returning memories help them regress to childhood and the forms It takes relates to their earlier fears in spite of their chronological ages. These Losers, then, grew up in an era where those fears coalesced around monsters and inhuman beings whose difference was notable even at a distance. Although the adults and bullies of Derry provided their own sites of abuse and neglect, they were not the physical manifestations of the Losers' fear.

Peter Vronsky points to Ted Bundy as the turning point in perceptions of real-life dangers, since "he was not one of 'them' but one of 'us'" (*Serial Killers* 6). For the Losers of the book and miniseries, this shift happened during their lifetime, and popular culture still relied largely on the inhuman and recognizable Other as the overarching menace. In spite of the way phrenology and Lombroso's theory of anthropological criminology had fallen out of scientific favor since the 19th century, there was still the public perception that criminals—especially violent serial criminals—would somehow be recognizable Other and otherwise deficient in comparison to the average citizen. Bundy, however, came across as approachable and normal, an image further emphasized during Mark Harmon's performance in *The Deliberate Stranger* (1986) and one that continues today with both Netflix's *Extremely Wicked, Shockingly Evil and Vile* (2019) starring Zac Efron as Bundy and its docuseries *Conversations with a Killer: The Ted Bundy Tapes* (2019). The movie Losers, then, were growing up in a world where the serial killer was not only gaining a cult following, but where Bundy had already been played by a young heartthrob whose outward appearance stood in direct contrast to the threat he presented. Public fears and popular myths were shifting from the outwardly monstrous to the apparently normal—or at least the apparently human. Although a leper is not considered "attractive" and a headless boy is clearly not entirely human, the basic shapes of these monsters indicate humanity. The way Ben's headless boy is filmed, for example, saves the supernatural reveal for the very end so that, at first, he seems to be confronted by a child not much unlike himself.

Since the 1980s, the threat of the apparently "normal" person has all but saturated the media market. Anthony Hopkins' award-winning performance in *The Silence of the Lambs* shows that the serial killer, at least as the urbane figure Hopkins presented, indeed had a place in the mainstream market. *Law & Order* (1990) began the process of introducing the public to the scripted legal procedural, and *CSI: Crime Scene Investigation* debuted in 2000 and paved the way for myriad spinoffs and other shows dedicated to the more forensic aspect of criminal cases. These shows not only present the everyday responses to crime, but also depict the criminals—the threats—as everyday people. Serial killers are not as frequent an occurrence as many of the crimes depicted and because of this their appearance in the shows is generally relegated to sweeps week in intermittently recurring roles, but the face of danger is still now markedly human.

The audience for the 2017 movie would have been exposed to such representations of danger and violence for decades and, in case of those who had grown up in the 1980s, since childhood. The curfew imposed on the original Losers was seen as laughable even at the time, but the thought that no adult would harm a child simply because it was daylight was gone by the 80s. Strangers were indeed considered to be dangerous, no matter how kindly they may have looked or acted, and children were taught less to respect them than to be wary of them. Fears and cultural perceptions of danger have shifted, and It shifts with them: the adaptable monster that is capable of putting on a more human face in order to align with updated cultural fears.

Works Cited

Alegre, Sara Martín. "Nightmares of Childhood: The Child and the Monster in Four Novels by Stephen King." *Atlantis*, vol. 23, no. 1, 2001, p. 105–114.

Anderson, Linda. "'OH DEAR JESUS IT IS FEMALE': Monster as Mother/Mother as Monster in Stephen King's It." *Imagining the Worst: Stephen King and the Representation of Women*, edited by Kathleen Margaret Lant and Theresa Thompson, Greenwood Press, 1998, pp. 111–125.

Arntfield, Michael, and Marcel Danesi. *Murder in Plain English: From Manifestos to Memes– Looking at Murder Through the Words of Serial Killers*. Prometheus Books, 2017.

Beahm, George. *The Stephen King Companion: Four Decades of Fear from the Master of Horror*, Thomas Dunne Books, 2015.

Conversations with a Killer: The Ted Bundy Tapes. Directed by Joe Berlinger, Netflix, 2019.

The Deliberate Stranger. Directed by Marvin J. Chomsky, Warner Bros. Television, 1986.

Douglas, John E., and Mark Olshaker. *Mindhunter: Inside the FBI's Elite Serial Crime Unit*. Scribner's, 1995.

Extremely Wicked, Shockingly Evil and Vile. Directed by Joe Berlinger, Netflix, 2019.

Frost, Rebecca. "A Different Breed: Stephen King's Serial Killers," *Stephen King's Contemporary Classics: Reflections on the Modern Master of Horror*, edited by Philip L. Simpson and Patrick McAleer, Rowman & Littlefield, 2015, pp. 117–132.

Harris, Thomas. *The Silence of the Lambs*. St Martin's Press, 1988.

Heldreth, Leonard J. "Rising Like Old Corpses: Stephen King and the Horrors of Time-Past." *Journal of the Fantastic in the Arts*, vol. 2, no 1, 1989, pp. 5–13.

It. Directed by Andy Muschietti, Warner Bros. Pictures, 2017.

_____. Directed by Tommy Lee Wallace, Warner Bros. Television, 1990.

It: Chapter Two. Directed by Andy Muschietti, Warner Bros. Pictures, 2019.
Jenkins, Jennifer. "Fantasy in Fiction: The Double-Edged Sword." *Stephen King's Modern Macabre: Essays on the Later Works,* edited by Patrick McAleer and Michael A. Perry, McFarland, 2014, pp. 10–23.
King, Stephen. *Dreamcatcher.* Pocket Books, 2001.
_____. *It.* Viking, 1986.
Magistrale, Anthony. *Landscape of Fear: Stephen King's American Gothic.* Bowling Green State University, 1988.
_____. *The Moral Voyages of Stephen King.* Wildside Press, LLC, this edition 2006. 1989.
_____. *Stephen King: America's Storyteller.* Praeger, 2010.
_____. *Stephen King: The Second Decade, Danse Macabre to the Dark Half.* Twayne Publishers, 1992.
Manos, James, Jr., developer. *Dexter.* John Goldwyn Productions, 2006.
Murley, Jean. *The Rise of True Crime: 20th-Century Murder and American Popular Culture.* Praeger, 2008.
Penhall, Joe, creator. *Mindhunter.* Netflix, 2017.
Rule, Ann. *The Stranger Beside Me.* W.W. Norton & Company, 1980.
Russell, Sharon A. *Revisiting Stephen King: A Critical Companion.* Greenwood Press, 2002.
_____. *Stephen King: A Critical Companion.* Greenwood Press, 1996.
The Silence of the Lambs. Directed by Jonathan Demme, Orion Pictures, 1991.
Strengell, Heidi. *Dissecting Stephen King: From the Gothic to Literary Naturalism.* The University of Wisconsin Press, 2005.
Thoens, Karen. "It, a Sexual Fantasy." *Imagining the Worst: Stephen King and the Representation of Women,* edited by Kathleen Margaret Lant and Theresa Thompson, Greenwood Press, 1998, pp. 127–140.
Vronsky, Peter. *Serial Killers: The Method and Madness of Monsters.* Berkley Books, 2004.
_____. *Sons of Cain: A History of Serial Killers from the Stone Age to the Present.* Berkley Books, 2018.
Wolf, Dick, creator. *Law & Order.* Wolf Films Universal Television, 1990.
Zuiker, Anthony E., creator. *CSI: Crime Scene Investigation.* Jerry Bruckheimer Films, 2000.

Wuh-We Do It

The Losers' Club and Collaborative Leadership in It

André Loiselle

> "Look," he said. "Boards here and here. You stick em in the streambed facing each other. Okay? Then, before the water can wash them away, you fill up the space between them with rocks and sand—"
> "Wuh-Wuh-We," Bill said.
> "Huh?"
> "*Wuh-We* do it."
>
> —Stephen King, *It* (229)

In this passage, bullied outsider Ben Hanscom gives advice to his new acquaintances and fellow students at Derry Elementary School—Bill Denbrough and Eddie Kaspbrak—on how to build a dam in the creek that runs through the "Barrens," a forested area on the edge of town. This is an important turning point in *It*. The brief exchange expresses the self-conscious sense of togetherness starting to emerge among the members of what would soon become the Losers' Club. As we slowly find out, the Club is "dedicated to killing the monster ... whatever the monster really was" (King 677): It, as the Losers eventually start calling the child-killing thing (479). While the dam scene is omitted from the big screen version of *It* (Andy Muschietti 2017), it does appear in the more structurally faithful 1990 television series, where the impression of a growing friendship is palpable, albeit, less evocatively developed than in the novel. But beyond this sense of a nascent relationship among the boys, this brief exchange also points toward an important aspect of the Losers' Club: the *collaborative* perspective asserted by Bill. This essay will examine Bill's role as the collaborative leader of the Club and contrast the

Losers' cooperative problem-solving approach to that of the gang of bullies led by Henry Bowers. I will also discuss how Bill and the Losers succeed in undermining the monster's own brand of chaotic leadership through their concerted efforts.

Linguists Willie van Peer and Eva Graf interpret the exchange about building a dam as an astute rhetorical strategy on King's part to use Bill's stuttering as a means to express the boys' cognitive construction of a space of their own. Wuh-Wuh becoming *We* "shows the creation of a metaphoric interpersonal space based on the boys' relation to each other" (135). The shift from "you" to "we" in the conversation creates a shared space based on a new relational closeness. "This change in their relationship, linguistically marked in the changed pronouns, is something consciously observed by the boys: Ben feels very happy and realizes that he now forms part of a circle or union, a metaphorical 'We-space'" (137). The inclusiveness of the "We-space" that van Peer and Graf identify is crucial to the way the Losers conceive of their relationship as a collaborative space *for action*. "*Wuh-We* do it" does not refer merely to an emerging "we," but also to the fact that we *do it*. Throughout the narrative, the Losers act collectively within the "We-space" enunciated by Bill. While van Peer and Graf do not elaborate on this, it is significant that in this brief but momentous exchange among the boys it is Bill who modestly, but resolutely asserts the *we* that governs the group's actions. As the meek, understated but acknowledged leader of the Losers' Club (King 303), Bill establishes through these few stuttered syllables the modus operandi of the group: collaborative action under his leadership. The three versions of *It* discussed here explore the underlying theme of Bill's collaborative leadership style primarily by setting it against other kinds of leadership.

The most obvious opposition in terms of leadership styles in all versions of *It*, is the drastic contrast between Bill's emphasis on a collaborative "we" and the psychotic authoritarianism of Henry Bowers, the Derry school bully who leads his pack of thugs with violent despotism and pathological egotism. Henry always needs to be in charge; he is the one who gives the orders; the others must follow *him*, never the other way around. For instance, in a passage where one of his underlings, Victor Criss, takes the lead in malignant pursuit of some Loser, "Henry pushed him aside so savagely that Victor skidded to his knees" (King 938). While such authoritarianism might seem to represent strength and willpower, it is, in fact, a mode of leadership that often fails, especially under extreme conditions such as those depicted in horror narratives like *It*.

As I have discussed elsewhere (Loiselle 69), the state of dire crisis that tales of terror present might seem to allow for only one style of leadership: authoritarianism—a coldblooded military-like single-mindedness focused exclusively on destroying the enemy, whatever the human cost may be. But horror's scary scenarios do provide numerous options other than authoritarianism for individuals or groups who are presented with monstrous challenges. As Michael Regester and Judy Larkin suggest in *Risk Issues and Crisis Management in Public Relations* (2008) even crisis situations must allow for the emergence of various kinds of leadership. The authoritarian leader might initially arise as the one who is most able to act decisively in the face of a lethal threat; however, autocratic leadership also has serious shortcomings that might prove detrimental in times of crisis. Regester and Larkin note that the authoritarian's uncompromising stance inhibits creativity and imagination in the group and this might thwart the ingenuity necessary to find innovative solutions to extreme circumstances; furthermore, for Regester and Larkin, authoritarian leaders tend to demotivate team members who might feel powerless in determining their own fate especially when they disagree with the leader's decisions. The ensuing decline in morale can lead to devastating outcomes for the group (214).

Bowers always behaves in a radically authoritarian way when he leads his ruffians into the battlefield of schoolyard bullying. But as all versions of *It* make clear, this approach undermines the cohesiveness of his gang. During one of his more insane bouts of bullying, Henry pulls a knife on a terrified Ben Hanscom, ready to carve his name on the chubby kid's belly. This crosses the line even for his moronic followers, Victor and "Belch" Huggins, who urges him not to use the weapon: "'*Jeezum-crow Henry don't really cut im!*' Belch screamed, and his voice was high, almost a girl's voice" (King 190). Though he loses the support of his fellow bullies, who seem as terrified as Ben, Henry proceeds to cut his victim. He only has time to carve "H" above the rotund boy's belly button before Ben manages to escape and eventually stumble across Bill and Eddie in the Barrens, where they strike a new friendship.

The most memorable representation of Bowers' inability to maintain ascendance over his band of idiots appears in the screen versions of "The Apocalyptic Rockfight" chapter, when he uses a ruthless divide-and-conquer tactic that disastrously fails to weaken the cohesion of the Losers' Club. All versions depict an epic stone-throwing battle between the Losers and the bullies. As Henry's feeble-minded posse is pursuing Mike Hanlon, the only black kid in Derry, shouting racial slurs at him, they encounter the Losers who are hanging out in the Barrens. As he catches sight of the small group of inoffensive kids looking at him almost expectantly, Mike screams "help." Within seconds, Henry Bowers sees that "Mike was now standing beside and slightly behind Bill Denbrough, panting rapidly" (King 661–662). Surrounded by his dim-witted minions, Henry cockily blurts out: "I got bones to pick with a lot of you, but I can let that go for today. I want that nigger. So you little shits buzz off" (662). The Losers refuse to surrender Mike to the bully and Bill tells Henry and his gang to leave the Barrens. "'Who's gonna make me?' he asked. 'You, horsefoot?' / 'Uh-Uh-*Us*,' Bill said" (662). The contrast between Henry's "who's gonna make me" and Bill's stuttering "Uh-Uh-*Us*" is significant here for it evokes the power of the Losers' unwavering collective action against the misguidedly individualistic bravado of Bowers. Bill and then all the Losers start throwing rocks at Bowers and his brutes, who quickly flee. Henry is left alone to threaten the Losers. But his threats fall flat as the Losers stare him down and the stuttering leader says, "I think the s-s-six of u-us can p-put you in the huh-huh-hospital"; "seven" adds Mike, the newest member of the Club (665). Here seven against one does not come across as an unfair advantage. Rather it demonstrates the moral imperative of taking a collective stand against oppressive authoritarianism. Henry looks for his craven acquaintances, but "there was no help there; no help at all" (666). So, the bully-in-chief must sheepishly walk away.

In both screen versions, this moment is visually arresting and, indeed, more effective than in the novel. Having been pummeled by the Losers, and abandoned by his gutless entourage, Henry (Jarred Blancard/Nicholas Hamilton) is seen compositionally isolated and performatively impotent. The contrast between the cohesive group of Losers, who share a "We-space" shown mainly in ensemble shots, and the isolated bully speaks volumes on the opposite outcomes of collaboration and authoritarianism. The Losers are an unflinching cohort of fierce friends, who might be individually innocuous but are formidable when acting in unison. The self-centered authoritarian, on the other hand, is left to his own ineffectual devices. In the 2017 film, the opposition is even more conspicuous than in the television series, as Henry is seen alone, passed out on the barren shore of the Barrens creek, while the Losers are observed helping each other walk away from the scene of the battle. Looked down upon from a bird's eye view, Henry appears utterly defeated, lying on the ground in a quasi-fetal position. This is one of the very few moments in the film when the spectator might feel sorry for him, as he clearly has no one in the world who cares about him. Bowers will continue to bully the Losers and will return twenty-seven years later as Its spineless puppet, after escaping from the mental institution where he was incarcerated for his father's murder and the Derry child killings. But at that moment in the narrative it becomes evident that Bowers has no power. He is nothing but a wretched loser who has no support from his peers. Conversely, Bill never loses the support of his friends.

Attracted to Bill, perhaps strangely comforted by his stuttering, and feeling a deep sense of empathy for the loss of his little brother Georgie at the hands of Pennywise the Dancing Clown, the other Losers naturally follow him: "Bill was their leader, the guy they all looked up to. No one said so out loud; no one needed to" (King 303). Bill adopts what David Wilkinson, in

The Ambiguity Advantage: What Great Leaders Are Great At (2006), describes as the fundamentals of collaborative leadership: "inclusive practices [...] which] emphasize the need for shared vision and values, and a real sense of 'team'" (96). Through his simple "*Wuh-We* do it," Bill displays his ability to bring his friends together and self-effacingly take charge, a skill he shows from the very beginnings of the Losers' Club, at their "first meeting as a complete group in July of that year, that meeting of which Bill had taken such complete and effortless charge" (King 536). At each of their gatherings, ideas on how to defeat the monster, or Bowers' gang, come from each of them at different times or all of them at once. The shared vision among the seven Losers is so profound and intense that they can "read each other's minds" (805).

Scholars of leadership under pressure argue that qualities such as empathy, inclusiveness, and emotional intelligence are critical for those who lead groups experiencing extreme stress. In his contribution to the anthology of essays *Leadership in Extreme Situations* (2017), Eraldo Olivetta argues that in the context of dire conditions such as military campaigns, the most imperative skill for a leader is not unwavering decisiveness and callous determination, but rather emotional intelligence. Olivetta emphasizes the vital importance for the military leader to have empathy, to understand what soldiers are feeling and thinking. For Olivetta, the military leader working in a highly stressful environment must be able to tune into a wide range of emotional signals, capturing the unspoken but perceptible emotions of the individuals or group. By *listening* carefully, by *seeing* what is affecting the members of the cohort, the leader can grasp the group's perspective and act as a catalyst to move the group most effectively towards effective action given the collective state of mind (Olivetta 2017, 87–88). These are qualities that Stuttering Bill possesses, but that the self-centered Bowers sorely lacks.

Under Bill's collaborative leadership the Losers' can survive the dastardly attacks from Bowers's gang. When Bill starts the rockfight at the Barrens, his quiet authority is evident: "'Ch-ch-charge them,' Bill said in a low voice, and not waiting to see if they would or not, he ran forward. / They came with him, firing rocks not only at Henry now but at all the others" (King 663). Beyond "The Apocalyptic Rockfight," the Losers' unity also remains solid throughout the Club's long day's journey into the putrid bowels of Derry on July 25, 1958, "[t]he day that the Losers' Club finally met It in face-to-face combat, the day It almost had Ben Hanscom's guts for garters" (815). Though the novel provides a detailed and riveting account of the Losers' challenging struggle against It, the most succinctly effective and powerful expression of the Club's collaborative cohesion occurs in *It* the movie, near the end of the narrative. At the climactic moment of the confrontation, Pennywise (Bill Skarsgård) manages to grab Bill (Jaeden Martell) and separate him from his friends. Like Henry in "The Apocalyptic Rockfight" segment, the Clown seeks to use a divide-and-conquer tactic to splinter the group by offering to let the other children go: all It wants is to feast on Bill's flesh and feed on his fear. Bill urges the other Losers to leave: "I'm the one who dragged you all into this. I'm sorry. I'm so sorry. Go." Richie (Finn Wolfhard), the foul-mouthed, bespectacled joker of the Club, is the first one to respond to the Clown's offer to let them go: "I don't want to die." At this point in the film, it appears that Pennywise has managed to terrify the children to such an extent that they might be willing to turn on each other. Richie continues, addressing Bill with understandable resentment: "You punched me in the face. You made me walk through shitty water. You brought me to a fucking crackhead house, and now—"; he pauses briefly, takes a baseball bat, and exclaims his real purpose: "I'm gonna have to kill this fucking clown. Welcome to the Losers' Club, asshole!" He whacks Pennywise in the face, as the other children join in, pummeling the Clown to "death." Freed from the creature's grip, Bill stands before the vanquished monster and declares that the Losers are no longer afraid of It, sending Pennywise crawling back into a bottomless pit of starvation; a victory, for sure, but a temporary one as It will reemerge in twenty-seven years.

The Losers remain united before both Bowers and Pennywise because of the emotional capital Bill has managed to invest in each of his friends. Throughout all versions, Bill is shown to have the ability to create a sense of togetherness. From their first encounter, Ben experiences a deep connection with Bill, primarily because of the shared joy he could feel with his new friend. Specifically, Ben enjoyed the way Bill's laughter sounded with his: "It was a sound he had never heard before: not mingled laughter—he had heard that lots of times—but mingled laughter of which his own was a part. / He looked up at Bill Denbrough, their eyes met, and that was all it took to get both of them laughing again" (King 227). On his way back to Derry to reconnect with his childhood friends after having heard from Mike Hanlon that It has returned twenty-seven years after the Losers first defeated the Clown, an adult Eddie reminisces about his best buddy: "*He remembers that he loved Bill Denbrough; he remembers that well enough. Bill never made fun of his asthma. Bill never called him little sissy queerboy. He loved Bill like he would have loved a big brother ... or a father*" (278). Similarly, Beverly Marsh, the only girl in the group, whose abusive father set her up in adulthood to choose an abusive mate, recalls her close connection to Bill as she is flying back to Derry: "*there was a time when an eleven-year-old girl named Beverly Marsh loved Bill Denbrough*" (375). Stuttering Bill's authority differs markedly from her father's despotic control over her: "it was authority that listened" (536). Richie also recognizes Bill's different sort of authority: a caring, implicit leadership that everyone understood and respected. The novel's omniscient narrator describes Richie's thoughts about his best friend in these terms: "in some odd way they all sensed something comfortingly adult about Bill—perhaps it was a sense of accountability, a feeling that Bill would take the responsibility if responsibility needed to be taken" (303). Bill's ability to take responsibility, to gain the respect and love of the other Losers through his stuttering kindness, and to engage everyone in a "We-space" where a genuine bond of shared leadership can be achieved, all this reflects his deep emotional intelligence; or as expressed through the thoughts of his little brother Georgie, "Bill was good at *seeing*" (5). His ability to see and listen renders Bill a paragon of collaborative leadership.

But as a collaborative leader, Bill never claims to have all the answers, or to be immune to fear and despair. There are several moments in the novel and the screen versions when Bill needs his friends as much as they need him. This is especially true after intense confrontations with Pennywise. In a segment that appears only in the novel, Beverly espies a mentally disturbed Patrick Hockstetter being attacked by leeches flying out of an abandoned refrigerator in the Barrens. Convinced that this horrible scene is the work of It, Bev calls on the other Losers to investigate. As a thunder-and-hail storm rages, the fridge door swings open to reveal a message from the Clown:

STOP NOW BEFORE I KILL YOU ALL
A WORD TO THE WISE FROM YOUR FRIEND
PENNYWISE [King 802].

This message petrifies and infuriates Bill, who rages against It and seems to be on the verge of losing his sanity. In dire need of support, he cries to his friends,

"P-P-Pl-Please. H-H-Help m-m-me."
"We will," Beverly said. She took Bill in her arms. She had not realized how easily her arms would go around him, how thin he was. She could feel his heart racing under his shirt; she could feel it next to hers. She thought that no touch had ever seemed so sweet and strong.
Richie put his arms around both of them and laid his head on Beverly's shoulder. Ben did the same from the other side. Stan Uris put his arms around Richie and Ben. Mike hesitated, and then slipped one arm around Beverly's waist and the other over Bill's shivering shoulders. They stood that way, hugging, and the sleet turned back to driving pouring rain, rain so heavy it seemed almost like a new atmosphere. The lightning walked and the thunder talked. No one spoke [803].

This moment of unity and solidarity epitomizes the sense of collective purpose and engagement at the heart of collaborative leadership, where individual weaknesses are redeemed through shared strength. The 2017 film offers a similar illustration of the Club's unity through a group hug while the children are deep in the sewer system. Separated from the others, Bev is captured by the Clown and is exposed to the *"deadlights which were Its eyes"* (965).

She falls under Its malefic spell and is seen floating in a state of altered consciousness. Somehow, Ben (Jeremy Ray Taylor) miraculously manages to liberate Bev (Sophia Lillis) from her trance with an innocent kiss. The Losers hug each other in a moment of collective rejuvenation prior to the final confrontation with Pennywise. The vaguely sexual undertone of this moment suggests that this group hug might also be Andy Muschietti's way to provide a family-friendly evocation of probably the most controversial section in the novel: the gangbang scene.

Following their victory against It, the children try to find their way out of the tenebrous sewer system back to the world of light and normality. As they navigate aimlessly through the darkness of the cesspool, Bill becomes concerned about his capacity to maintain the Club's cohesion: "they were falling away from each other. The bond that had held them all this long summer was dissolving. It had been faced and vanquished [...] the fellowship was ending ... it was ending and they were still in the dark" (King 1029–1030). This is when Bev suggests a way to ensure that the group will remain united by being brought together via her body. All Losers lose their virginity at the same time when Bev invites each of her six male friends to have sex with her (King 1035–41). At the moment when Bill seems to be losing his ability to lead the group, Bev's solution is to use her body as an object of exchange among her male friends. This is a radical form of collaborative leadership, and a deeply problematic one.

Although King generally shows great empathy for female characters in his novels, this section betrays his deep entrenchment in a pervasive patriarchal mythology that confines the collaborative role of women to that of medium for interactions among men. As Gayle Rubin explains in her landmark article "The Traffic in Women: Notes on the 'Political Economy' of Sex" (1975), within male-dominated cultures, women serve as a channel for bolstering relationships among men, as they are used as an object of exchange from one man to another rather than a subject engaged in that exchange: "if it is women who are being transacted, then it is the men who give and take them who are linked, the woman being a conduit of a relationship rather than a partner to it" (174). By having sex with all six of her friends to "bring us back together" (King 1031), Beverly allows her body to become a vehicle for the boys to express their commitment to each other, but in the process loses her status as an equal member of the Club; furthermore, King might also be using the sex scene, again rather conventionally, to alleviate the risk that the stigma of homosexuality could be affixed upon the male members of the Club, who speak of loving each other and having been labeled "*sissy queerboy*" by local bullies. As Frann Michel points out in her reading of repressed homosexuality in Mary Shelley's *Frankenstein* (1818), "The repression of homosexual desire in men evidently heterosexual redounds upon women: as conduits or objects of exchange between men whose desire for each other is repressed" (Michel 248). While Bill, Ben, Richie, Eddie, Stan and Mike are having sex with Beverly, they are also symbolically having sex with each other.

While this section of the novel is successful in creating a bizarre sort of transcendental connectivity among the group, needless to say both screen versions stay away from this ethically dubious segment of the book and try to find other ways to express Beverly's collaborative role in the Club. As performed by mousy Emily Perkins in the 1990 miniseries, young Beverly occupies a rather secondary function in the narrative. Much is done of her unmatched ability to use a slingshot with lethal precision. But this skill only marginally increases the importance of her contribution to the defeat of the monster. Sophia Lillis as Beverly in *It* is a more charismatic figure, giving the tween girl a prominent role in the group as the most mature, intelligent, and resilient of the Losers. The sexual overtones of some of the scenes in the 2017 film, especially the awkwardly liberating kiss in the sewer system and the sequence at the quarry swimming hole where the boys are in awe before Beverly diving in the pond in her undergarments, approximate the purpose of the communal sex scene in the novel, where Beverly's body functions as the erotic gravitational pole that anchors the collaborative ethos of the Club. But through Lillis's arresting presence, the film does manage to enhance Beverly's role beyond that of mere vessel by making her a full-fledged partner in the seven-member crew. And that there are seven children in the Club is no coincidence: there has to be seven *diverse* kids, there has to be a girl, a black kid, a Jewish kid, a chubby kid, a sickly kid, a joker, and there has to be a leader.

For Richie, *seven* is "the magic number. There has to be seven of us. That's the way it's supposed to be" (712). Aptly, managerial guru Mark Oliver argues teams in a corporation should have seven members to be effective and sufficiently diverse, for "seven is the ideal number in terms of span of control and effectiveness of the organizational hierarchy" (228). But more importantly, even for the monster itself, the fact that the Losers' Club has seven members is especially meaningful. "[T]*he mystical talismanic quality of seven*" (King 973) is what gave the children their power to defeat It in 1958; however, when they come back as adults, the magic number has been broken. Stan Uris commits suicide upon hearing of Its return and Mike Hanlon is sent to the hospital by the monster. Feeling that the Club has now lost its talismanic power, It believes that the group can be defeated much more easily. In fact, the Club's only remaining strength is their leader. It feels that *"when their precious 'Big Bill' was dead, the others would be Its quickly"* (975). Its approach to vanquishing Bill is to capture his spouse Audra, so he would go *"half-mad for his wife"* (975). As such, Its main strategy to defeat what remains of the adult Losers is to sow chaos and confusion in Bill's mind. In the process, the Creepy Clown resorts to what Alain Joxe calls, in a different context, "leadership through chaos" (213).

To understand Its peculiar kind of leadership through chaos, we must remind ourselves that the monster is not merely "Bob Gray, also known as Pennywise the Dancing Clown." The Creepy Clown is only the most iconic form that It has come to assume through the screen adaptations. In the novel, when It is given its voice to reflect on Its experience with the Losers' Club, It appears as an ancient, shapeshifting cosmic creature from the "macroverse." It can be a witch, a leper, a giant spider, a werewolf, a mummy, Frankenstein, Dracula, Beverly's father, a shark, or a Doberman pincher in a clown suit. It is "[s]*omething with as many faces as Lon Chaney*" (King 278), that can speak in a "'whole slew of voices, all of em babbling together'" (147) to confuse and confound Its victims. "It worked Its will on us, just as It has worked Its will on this whole town" remarks an adult Mike (491). It incessantly tries to confuse the adult Losers and undermine their sanity as a means to destroy them. For instance, as an adult Ben nostalgically finds his way to the Derry Public Library where he spent many hours as a lonely child, he experiences a disturbing sense of déjà-vu: as he stands inside the door, Ben feels "literally lost in time, not really sure how old he was. Was he thirty-eight or eleven?" (512). This seemingly inoffensive confusion increases as he delves deeper into the Children's Library section. Soon "[t]hat feeling of *déjà-vu* swept him again. He was helpless before it, and this time he felt the numb horror of a man who finally realizes, after half an hour of helpless splashing, that the shore is growing no closer and he is drowning. [...] *Is something really stapling the past and present together here, or am I only imagining it?*" (514–515). But it is not his imagination. It is working Its uncanny will on Ben to confuse him. A grotesque version of Pennywise stands before him, with a mouth covered in blood-red lipstick and "empty sockets where his eyes should have been." Ben fears that he might be losing his mind.

To confuse and terrify are the main tactics of a chaos leader like Pennywise, to destabilize and disrupt the opponents to such an extent that they can no longer tell what is true and what is false; what is reality and what is fantasy. While chaos leadership is not a thoroughly theorized concept yet, it has been discussed as a mode of disruption in complex environments (Brafman & Pollack; Wheatley). Although disruption can sometimes have a positive impact, chaotic leadership is generally seen as a means to destabilize everything and demoralize everyone, with the endgame of toppling all established systems and structures. "Chaotic leaders are like Loki, the trickster of Norse mythology, who sows the seeds of confusion and discord" says leadership pundit Theodore Kinni:

> These are leaders who have a fetish for defying expectations [...] They say things that they don't mean and mean things that they don't say. They jump the rails of process and take off for territories unknown on a whim. They fire people for not following orders and for following orders. They refuse to acknowledge any authority—such as the values of the organization or its board—as greater than their own. This inconsistency and unpredictability results in a high-stress environment in which even highly motivated people burn out [Kinni 2018].

Significantly, It is convinced of Its absolute authority in the macroverse. The only other "thing" the monster acknowledges as a predecessor is the Turtle. But the Turtle withdrew in its shell a long, long time ago and is ultimately powerless (King 965). It functions as a chaotic leader who is infinitely egocentric, answers to no one but Itself, and thrives on confusing everyone and feeding on their petrified bewilderment.

But this confusion is not enough to undermine the collaborative force of the two remaining adult Losers who manage to corner It and destroy Its eggs (973–974). As Bill and Richie confront It as a giant spider in the Derry sewers, they strike "together with their right fists, but Bill understood it was not really their fists they were striking with at all; it was their combined force [...] it was the force of memory and desire; above all else, it was the force of love and unforgotten childhood like one big wheel" (1046). What managed to send It crawling in a hole in 1958 was: "*the bonding of seven extraordinarily imaginative minds.*" If they had been alone, "*It surely would have picked them off one by one* [... b]*ut together they had discovered an alarming secret that even It had not been aware of: that belief has a second edge*" (974). The seven's power of collaborative imagination defeated It in 1958. Not surprisingly, imagination remains crucial for the Losers in their adult age, especially for their leader Billy, now a famous writer, but also for Beverly, a fashion designer, Ben an architect, and Richie a disc jockey and impersonator "known as the Man of a Thousand Voices" (467). Imagination remains as central a part of their collaborative genius in 1985 as it was in 1958.

David D. Chrislip and Carl E. Larson's 1994 study of "how citizens and civic leaders can make a difference" in their book *Collaborative Leadership* explains that successful collaboration is facilitated by "catalysts—one or more people who had the clear vision, or the energy to get people moving, or the words to inspire imagination" (83). Back in 1957, the year when *It* commences, Chris Argyris had already discovered in his psychological study *Personality and Organization* that the collaborative leader can serve "as a catalyst in the group, mirroring back the members' thoughts and feelings" (197). This has been Bill's role in the Losers' Club as a collaborative leader: the one who could imagine a group of Losers working together to vanquish a formidable monster and a pack of bullies; the one who could mirror their thoughts and feelings to inspire the Losers to "'Ch-ch-charge them.'" His "*Wuh-We do it*" encompasses inclusiveness (we), optimism and vision (do it), but also compassion and humanity, as the very hesitancy of his speech (Wuh-Wuh-We) opens up a space for the redemption of weakness and the forgiving of errors. "All the attributes of any collaborative leader must be underpinned by a willingness to truly listen and be open-minded to the views of others" (Archer and Cameron, 213); a leader with an "authority that listens" and who is "good at seeing" will always be able to bring out the best in people, even losers, empowering them to meet any challenge … whatever It is.

WORKS CITED

Archer, David, and Alex Cameron. *Collaborative Leadership: Building Relationships, Handling Conflict and Sharing Control*. London: Routledge, 2013.
Argyris, Chris. *Personality and Organization: The Conflict Between System and the Individual*. New York: Harper, 1957.
Brafman, Ori, and Judah Pollack. *The Chaos Imperative: How Chance and Disruption Increase Innovation, Effectiveness, and Success*. New York: Crown Business, 2013.
Chrislip, David D., and Carl E. Larson. *Collaborative Leadership: How Citizens and Civic Leaders Can Make a Difference*. San Francisco: Jossey-Bass, 1994.
Joxe, Alain. *Empire of Disorder*. New York: Semiotext(e), 2002.
King, Stephen. *IT*. New York: Signet, 1987.
Kinni, Theodore. "Chaos Is Not a Viable Leadership Style: Sowing Seeds of Confusion and Discord Is No Way to Run an Organization," *Strategy+Business Magazine*, 19 July, 2018.
Loiselle, André. "Tackling Wicked Monsters: The Horror Film as an Experiment in Leadership." *The Journal of Leadership Studies*, vol. 12, no. 1, 2018, pp. 68–79.
Michel, Frann. "Lesbian Panic and Mary Shelley's *Frankenstein*." *GLQ: A Journal of Lesbian and Gay Studies*, no. 2. 1995, pp. 237–252.
Oliver, Mark. *The Seven Motivations of Life: Taking Your Leadership to a Higher Level*. Ashburton: MarkTwoConsulting, 2018.
Olivetta, Eraldo. "Leadership, Morale and Cohesion: What Should Be Changed?" *Leadership in Extreme Situations*, edited by M. Holenweger, M.K. Jager & F. Kernic. Cham, Switzerland: Springer, 2017, pp. 75–92.
Regester, Michael, and Judy Larkin. *Risk Issues and Crisis Management in Public Relations: A Casebook of Best Practice*. London: Kogan Page, 2008.
Rubin, Gayle. "The Traffic in Women: Notes on the 'Political Economy' of Sex," *Toward an Anthropology of Women*, edited by Rayna Reiter. New York: Monthly Review Press, 1975, pp. 157–201.
Van Peer, Willie, and Eva Graf. "Between the Lines: Spatial Language and its Developmental Representation in Stephen King's *IT*," *Cognitive Stylistics: Language and Cognition in Text Analysis*, edited by Elena Semino and Jonathan Culpeper. Amsterdam: John Benjamins Publishing, 2002, pp. 123–152.
Wheatley, Margaret J. *Leadership and the New Science: Discovering Order in a Chaotic World*. San Francisco: Barrett-Koehler Publishers, 2010.
Wilkinson, David J. *The Ambiguity Advantage: What Great Leaders Are Great At*. New York: Palgrave MacMillan, 2006.

The Clown Will Eat You Now

Brian W. Smith

Upon the release of the R-rated theatrical adaptation of Stephen King's *It* (2017), it became common among fans on social media to debate over which Pennywise performance was the best or most effective: Tim Curry in 1990 at age forty-four or Bill Skarsgård in 2017 at age twenty-seven.[1] Skarsgård's portrayal of Pennywise, as directed by Andy Muschietti, could be seen as a type of upgrade, or Pennywise 2.0, to Curry's original incarnation. He seemingly represents a reinterpretation of both King's novel version and Curry's miniseries version, delivering much more of the violence depicted in the book. Curry's and Skarsgård's performances were twenty-seven years apart and, coincidentally, mirror the character's hibernation period. There are notable differences in their portrayals that complement each other rather than compete. There is an evolution of the Pennywise character evident in their work behind the makeup. What follows is an examination of the approaches these actors used to bring the character to horrifying life on screen. A look at what makes each incarnation effective in their own right.

Tim Curry, a versatile character actor, had many iconic roles before landing the part of Pennywise: the flamboyant Dr. Frank N. Furter in the sexy, macabre, genre-bending stage and film musical, *The Rocky Horror Picture Show* (1975). Curry's portrayal of the "sweet transvestite from Transylvania," is a bold, brash performance that calls to mind that of the Chief Blue Meanie from *Yellow Submarine* (1968). Curry also shared the screen with legendary comedienne Carol Burnett as her intensely child-threatening con artist brother Rooster Hannigan in John Huston's *Annie* (1982). One of his most striking visual roles was as Darkness in Ridley Scott's *Legend* (1985), wearing elaborate makeup created by Rob Bottin. Curry brought both seductive grace and menace to the part. Another popular role included the enigmatic butler Wadsworth in Jonathan Lynn's slapstick mystery comedy *Clue* (1985). These combined experiences made his casting as Pennywise a no-brainer for those familiar with his work. Other actors considered for Pennywise were Roddy McDowall, Alice Cooper, and Malcolm McDowell.[2] Today, a look back offers a colorful and veritable rogue's gallery of eclectic personalities Curry managed to conjure through wardrobe, makeup, and a complete immersion into the mind and body of these characters.

Swedish actor Bill Skarsgård comes from a respected acting family with an increasingly impressive body of work, including his father Stellan and brother Alexander. Bill, a relatively young actor with model looks, has had a few genre credits, including *Hemlock Grove* (2013–2015), *Allegiant* (2016), and *Atomic Blonde* (2017). None of these earlier roles could predict the complete immersion into Stephen King's monstrous creation. *It* executive producer Seth Grahame-Smith could tell from Skarsgård's audition that he was right for the part. "What I remember most about seeing his audition was that he put the makeup on and I don't remember anybody else putting the makeup on…. Passion often wins the day and Bill brought incredible passion. He chased this role. He knew he could do it and he was going to make us understand that he could do it."[3]

They're All Gonna Laugh with You

To give context to the genre timeline before both the publication of the novel and the television adaptation, it helps to look back on the possible cultural influences on the Pennywise character. Wes Craven wrote and directed *A Nightmare on Elm Street* (1984) which birthed the creation of Freddy Krueger (Robert Englund), a child murderer who was burned alive by vengeful parents in the town of Springwood. His spirit continued to haunt the town's teenagers in their dreams. When the victims died in their nightmares, they died for real. Throughout the decade, Freddy became an unlikely household name. As further sequels were made, his character's popularity rose to the point where he became a wisecracking slasher, given to ironic one-liners as he killed hapless youths. Over the course of the decade, the influence of Freddy could be found in such films as *Hello Mary Lou: Prom Night II* (1987). This sequel in name only, is one of the rare horror films with a snarky female villain seeking vengeance for a fiery prank gone wrong. In *976-EVIL* (1988), directed by Robert Englund, a tormented high school geek is transformed into a murderous demon with Freddy-style insults for his prey. Finally, there was *Wes Craven's Shocker* (1989), which unleashed the soul of an executed killer to body jump through various characters and continue his murder spree. Each of these roles were played with sly and over-the-top campy fervor.

You'll Float Too After These Messages: It *1990*

Somewhat condensed but faithful to the Stephen King novel, the 1990 ABC two-part miniseries adaptation of *It* concerns Pennywise the Dancing Clown, a shapeshifting otherworldly creature that feeds off of flesh and fear, preferably that of children in the town of Derry. His true form is unknown to the seven young members of the Losers' Club he terrorizes and they refer to him as an "it." The film was directed by Tommy Lee Wallace, no stranger to small-town boogeymen with his prior work as a production designer and editor on John Carpenter's *Halloween* (1978) and *The Fog* (1980).

Tim Curry displays the duality of the Pennywise character very early on in the opening moments. A young girl in her backyard is called inside by her mother. The girl notices a clown dressed in eye-catching primary colors in the distance behind the linens swinging in the breeze. He waves cheerfully and greets her. She smiles back, but as the wind blows the laundry, she sees Pennywise again, looking volatile and hungry. It is the last we see of her. Pennywise's evil scowl is a cold and frightening sight to behold. His eyes and demeanor no longer relatable as human, but rather animalistic in nature. Pennywise as a predator of children calls to mind very real monsters and threats in our society, from strangers to family friends to notorious serial killers like John Wayne Gacy.

One of the most pivotal moments in the book concerns the death of George Denbrough, Bill's younger brother. While racing a paper boat down the street in a rainstorm, the boat slips into a storm drain. Georgie, distraught and believing he has lost the boat his brother worked hard on, is suddenly approached by a clown in the sewer drain. Curry infuses the role with the classic energy of a circus clown typical of the era. Curry plays up the old-fashioned, brash-style clown voice—theatrical, persuasive and with a big smile on his face. When he recites the signature line, "Oh, yes, they float," the sneering curl of his lips is visually reminiscent of his work in *The Rocky Horror Picture Show*. The menace starts to show itself until finally he shouts, "You'll float too!" His booming, operatic voice causes young Georgie to scream as it kills him offscreen. "My job was to give Tim the stage and not get in his way too much," director Tommy Lee Wallace recalled to *The Hollywood Reporter* in 2017: "He brought a spontaneous improvisation to the part."[4]

On a panel at the 2017 Fan Expo Canada, Tim Curry recounted to a lively crowd of adoring fans about his time on set shooting the sewer scene with Tony Dakota, the young actor who played Georgie. When Curry got really intense, Dakota said, "Tim you're scaring me." To which Tim replied, "I'm sorry, but that's what I'm supposed to be doing."[5]

You'll Float Two

The most notable difference between the Curry and Skarsgård approaches to Pennywise is in the level of menace and evil infused into the character. Curry's interpretation comes across like simply a man in a clown suit that occasionally bares his fangs to scare his prey. Curry's Pennywise appears to taunt each of the main characters and exploit their fears. He is often seen in the distance, on the side of the road clutching balloons as a car passes by or heard as a disembodied voice, a bunch of floating balloons providing the visual scare. Skarsgård is operating on a completely different level, bringing years of practicing an eerie grin and control of his lazy eye to create a unique cinematic villain. Skarsgård, makeup-free on *Conan*, displayed these traits to the host and audience.[6] Skarsgård's Pennywise is an otherworldly being merely wearing the guise of a human that is, in turn, wearing a clown suit. Pennywise is a bottom feeder, with his bright and striking costume greatly contradicting his dark and dank sewer dwelling. A similar example of this type of character approach is brilliantly portrayed by Vincent D'Onofrio in the sci-fi comedy *Men in Black* (1997) as Edgar the Bug, a giant alien cockroach that wears the flesh of a farmer it murders. The alien villain spends much of the running time of the film adjusting its uncomfortable skin suit.

In the notoriously horrifying opening storm drain sequence, Skarsgård strongly plays the subtext of Pennywise's intentions, like a wolf in sheep's clothing. Drops of drool on his blood-red lips are evident as he delivers his lines. There is no doubt the character is barely able to contain its hunger for the unsuspecting Georgie. Skarsgård's understanding of the character makes for quite the unique cinematic villain. "You're playing an entity that's playing a clown, so it's like these kinds of steps, and I wanted to get that into the character that there's kind of glitches almost. That it's not just a clown, it's something off. Something weirder. Something even more sinister."[7]

Pennywise's sinister nature is evident and startling upon every first glance by potential victims. In true horror movie fashion, Pennywise gives Georgie a jolt by flashing glowing yellow eyes from the darkness in the sewer drain. Remaining in the shadows and keeping a low voice, Pennywise oddly charms young Georgie with talk of the circus, cotton candy, and popcorn. Disarming Georgie with fits of giggles, Pennywise goes deadly serious for an extended, unnerving beat with a growl, Skarsgård seemingly channeling a cold-blooded predator that can practically taste the meat and blood of its unsuspecting victim. It is a chilling detail the actor utilizes and it quickly establishes his Pennywise as the stuff of nightmares. This is the stranger you warn your kids about. Luring Georgie further with the promise of returning his boat, Skarsgård grins wickedly, drawing out the suspense. In a swift move, Pennywise reveals the monster within and Georgie's fate is sealed in gory detail. Without

Skarsgård's commitment to the nuanced, predatory nature of Pennywise, the payoff of the scene might not have worked; however, it is the eyes, voice, and drool that telegraph to the audience (but not poor Georgie) that danger is imminent.

For most of the film, much like the 1990 counterpart, Pennywise is encountered as a taunting vision in the distance. In other cases, Pennywise is a fleeting glimpse. One scene finds the clown on the heels of Ben Hanscom, at first running away from a pursuing headless apparition in the library bookstacks. Another scene shows Pennywise cheerfully waving with and munching on a severed arm as Mike Hanlon is tormented by town bully Henry Bowers and his cronies. By far the most surprising and eye-popping moment is a contemporary take on the photo album scare. A large, monstrous Pennywise lunging out of the slideshow screen in Bill Denbrough's garage provided a memorable twist to a classic scene.

An intriguing aspect of the 2017 film is the way in which certain Derry townsfolk resemble Skarsgård's Pennywise, playing into the notion as expressed in the original book that It is everywhere. Eddie Kaspbrak's mother Sonia (Molly Atkinson), pharmacist Mr. Keene (Joe Bostick), Henry Bowers (Nicholas Hamilton) and librarian Mrs. Starret (Elizabeth Saunders) all seemingly share impish facial similarities and the staring eyes of Pennywise. Mrs. Kaspbrak is controlling over Eddie. She keeps him protected and guarded from sicknesses he might not have or ever catch. She contributes to his many anxieties and phobias. Mr. Keene has a creepy and leering vibe when chatting with young Beverly at his counter. His eyes linger a bit too long on her after she compliments him on his glasses. Henry Bowers has a threatening and murderous disposition. He is also easily manipulated by Pennywise to murder his own father. Mrs. Starret stares at Ben at the library as he reads about the explosion.

One of the main set-piece chapters from the book is adapted to the screen in the confrontation in the house on Neibolt Street. After Eddie Kaspbrak falls through a cracked floor to a kitchen table below and injures his arm, Pennywise unfurls from a nearby refrigerator. For the first time, we get a sense of Skarsgård's imposing stature. "Time to float," he threatens to Eddie. Skarsgård's body language, including a fluid-like dance as if to rev up for the impending kill, offers a delicious blend of creepiness and humor. Pennywise toys with Eddie who suffers an asthma attack. Skarsgård, as the clown, mocks Eddie's whimpering and breathing with villainous glee. Skarsgård seemed to enjoy the role: "It mentions in the novel somewhere, Pennywise is IT's favorite form. He really enjoys doing the clown, so that was something I wanted to play up as well, that he's having fun while he's doing this."[8]

Near the climax of the film, Skarsgård displays both impressive physicality and depth. Kidnapping and trapping young Beverly Marsh (Sophia Lillis) in his underground sewer lair, Pennywise dances a spirited and manic jig on a makeshift stage. The dance led to a number of music remixes and gifs online. Beverly makes an escape attempt, but Pennywise leaps off the stage and grabs her by the throat, holding her up to look her in the eyes. Beverly, a fighter, defiantly declares she is not afraid of Pennywise. Skarsgård holds on this, then shakes if off, showing a vulnerability in the character, a crack in the armor. It is the first instance we see a glimpse of the sniveling, weakened Pennywise about to be defeated. The Losers' Club might just have a fighting chance.

The climactic battle between the Losers' Club and Pennywise sees Pennywise desperately try to scare the kids with each of their worst fears. In a last attempt to claim Bill as a meal before returning to his twenty-seven-year slumber, Pennywise is quite literally backed into a corner, his voice quivering. The sinister, shapeshifting interdimensional being, suddenly reduced to just a guy in a clown suit is beaten by the group of kids, causing it to retreat further into his lair. Powerless against their combined strength and resolve, Pennywise falls into his pit to either starve or die ... until *It: Chapter Two*, that is. "I think this is probably the most exhausting character I've ever played." Skarsgård reflects. "Every scene is just 100% energy at all times. So, it wasn't easy at all."[9]

Curry and Skarsgård each brought their talents and strengths to the portrayal of Pennywise. Curry played the traditional jovial trickster, while Skarsgård played something darker and ancient and more akin to the sewer-dweller as described in the novel.

Notes

1. Rooney, Matt. "Face-Off: Pennywise (Curry) vs. Pennywise (Skarsgård)." JoBlo.com, 16 Jan. 2018.
2. Higgins, Bill. "Hollywood Flashback: Tim Curry Played 'It's' Scary Clown in 1990." *The Hollywood Reporter*, 7 Sept. 2017.
3. "It Pennywise Lives!—Bill Skarsgård." YouTube, Warner Bros. New Line Cinema, 20 Dec. 2017. Blu-Ray featurette.
4. Higgins, Bill. "Hollywood Flashback: Tim Curry Played 'It's' Scary Clown in 1990." *The Hollywood Reporter*, 7 Sept. 2017.
5. "Tim Curry Talks IT at Fan Expo Canada." YouTube, Bloodbath and Beyond, 10 Sept. 2017.
6. "It Pennywise Lives!—Bill Skarsgård." YouTube, Warner Bros. New Line Cinema, 20 Dec. 2017. Blu-Ray featurette.
7. "It Pennywise Lives!—Bill Skarsgård." YouTube, Warner Bros. New Line Cinema, 20 Dec. 2017. Blu-Ray featurette.
8. "Bill Skarsgård's Demonic 'IT' Smile—CONAN on TBS." YouTube, 12 Sept. 2017.
9. "It Pennywise Lives!—Bill Skarsgård." YouTube, Warner Bros. New Line Cinema, 20 Dec. 2017. Blu-Ray featurette.

Works Cited

Clown. Directed by Jon Watts, Dimension Films, 2014.
Curry, Tim, performer. *Annie*. Directed by John Huston. Columbia Pictures, 1982.

_____. *Clue*. Directed by Jonathan Lynn. Paramount Pictures, 1985.
_____. *It*. Directed by Tommy Lee Wallace. Warner Bros. Television, 1990.
_____. *Legend*. Directed by Ridley Scott. Universal Pictures and 20th Century Fox, 1985.
_____. *Rocky Horror Picture Show*. Directed by Jim Sherman, 20th Century Fox, 1975.
Hello Mary Lou: Prom Night II. Directed by Bruce Pittman, The Samuel Goldwyn Company, 1987.
It. Directed by Andy Muschietti, Warner Bros. Pictures, 2017.
_____. Directed by Tommy Lee Wallace, Warner Bros. Television, 1990.
Men in Black. Directed by Barry Sonnenfeld, Sony Pictures Releasing, 1997.
A Nightmare on Elm Street. Directed by Wes Craven, New Line Cinema, 1984.
976-Evil. Directed by Robert Englund, New Line Cinema, 1988.
Poltergeist. Directed by Tobe Hooper, MGM/UA, 1982.
Skarsgård, Bill, performer. *Atomic Blonde*. Directed by David Leitch. Focus Features, 2017.
_____. *The Divergent Series: Allegiant*. Directed by Robert Schwentke. Lionsgate, 2016.
_____. *Hemlock Grove* (TV series). Created by Brian McGreevy, Gaumont International Television, 2013–2015.
_____. *It*. Directed by Andy Muschietti. Warner Bros. Pictures, 2017.
Wallace, Tommy Lee, editor, production designer. *The Fog*. Directed by John Carpenter. AVCO Embassy Pictures, 1980.
_____. *Halloween*. Directed by John Carpenter. Compass International Pictures, 1978.
Wes Craven's Shocker. Directed by Wes Craven, Universal Pictures, 1989.
Yellow Submarine. Directed by George Dunning, United Artists, 1968.

Appendix: Interview with Erik Junnola

Ron Riekki

Ron Riekki: Why did you get involved with the clown horror genre?

Erik Junnola: I got involved with the clown genre unintentionally. The first audition was going by the pseudonym *Largo* for *It: Chapter Two*, so I didn't actually know what I was auditioning for till later.

What are your top ten horror films outside of the clown horror genre?

My favorite horror movies are *The Conjuring* series, which would probably come first, then *Annabelle*, the *Insidious* movies, and *The Exorcist* movies are obviously big ones.

What's your favorite film of all-time outside of the horror genre? And what's your favorite scene from that film?

My favorite film is a movie called *Cloud Atlas*. This movie really moves me and changed my view on life and love in many ways. It's about afterlives and how your past life could affect your future life in this world. The actors play many different characters so it was really an actor's dream movie to work on. There's a scene in the movie that stands out among many others when Robert Frobisher gets told by his dad that he'd amount to nothing but a single drop in a limitless ocean and, to this, he replied, "What is an ocean, but a multitude of drops?"

What are the clichés to avoid in the clown horror genre?

Clichés to avoid? I'd say are the red nose. Puffy hair generally looks a bit silly if you're going for scary. It all depends on the approach. I do feel Andy the director of *It* nailed it perfectly with Pennywise, look and all.

What direction do horror movies need to go in the future? How can the genre be improved?

I'd say horror needs to find some new ways to approach scary and to scare the audience. Horror needs to build into character more to draw the audience in.

Who is the best horror director in your opinion? What's the best cinematographer in the horror genre?

James Wan is probably my favorite horror director. I find he's always trying to find new ways to push the limits of horror from the past projects I've seen of his. As for best cinematographers, I'd say John R. Leonetti. He's done some of the best horror movies over the years.

What's the most scared you've ever been in your actual life?

I can't recall many times I've actually been scared in life, but one I was able to think of was when I was about to go bridge jumping into a river for fun and I knew the tide was a bit low but did it anyway. That moment before was extremely scary because you never know how deep a river can truly be until you go into the water prior to testing it, which we did not. I do not advise doing this to anyone. Check the river first if you feel you have to do it.

Interesting, especially considering the bridge scene opening of It: Chapter Two. *What was the hardest thing about the scenes you filmed?*

The shoot for *It: Chapter Two* was a bit of a tough one overall, but I've experienced more physically demanding shoots. The hardest part of the shoot was probably the fact that it was four nights back-to-back of night shooting, that means the moment the sun goes down at the time, 7 p.m., till the moment the sun starts to come up, 7 a.m. This meant that my sleep schedule had to be switched around. I had to sleep during the daytime and set my alarm every morning I got home for 4 p.m. that same day, so I had time to wake up, shower, eat. Luckily the hotel they put me in was a five-minute walk away, as the producers obviously considered that. Physically, I had to do a stunt that, unfortunately, didn't even make it into the film, where I was getting kicked off the bench that me and the rest of the actors were sitting on in scene one of two that were located inside the Derry Fair. We did about fifteen takes of that. Luckily, the main stuntman gave me some padding to put under my clothes there, but this didn't stop my hip and the side of my arm from getting bruised for a few weeks after that. At the end of the day, if a shot didn't make it into a film or show I'm in, I totally understand. As a director myself, I know that in theory some shots and scenes seem great but when pieced together, they just don't add up as well as you originally thought. That's the way the business is.

Can you describe the set the first time you walked onto it for the filming?

Before I describe my first experience on the set of *It: Chapter Two*, I will have to back it up a bit. I got a glance at what I didn't know to be the set at first when I was getting driven to the location of the shoot in Port Hope two weeks prior to the filming to get my costume fitting done. I saw what looked to be a fair getting constructed, of large proportion, and I asked the driver what it was they were building, and my guess was right. They were constructing a fair, but I still had no idea it was meant for my scenes. I couldn't really imagine a set of that size being constructed for scenes I was in. I didn't get the script at that point as it was all highly confidential. Fast-forward two weeks and I drive to location, and there it was, the fair. I nearly died of a heart attack. When I was called onto set, I was quite nervous. I had a tough time not smiling because I was so happy about everything and couldn't fathom a set of this size and 245 extras working around the scenes that I was cast in. It was truly insane and a moment I will never forget, seeing the rides going, smoke from the smoke-makers, 245 extras all in costume and an AD leading me and the other bullies to the set location. It all happened in slow motion probably because my adrenaline was rushing so fast.

What impressed you most about being on the film? Was it the set design? Or maybe even something else that even impressed you more?

Everything about being on the film impressed me. I have been on many low-budget films before and been the leads of some short films that had good budgets (for short films), even some extra work many years ago on big-budget films, but nothing of this caliber. Especially this being my first union gig at the time. I've booked other union gigs since the shoot. I had no idea what to expect. I feel everyone involved in the shoot was amazed at being in this massive fair to film something. Most who were acting with me seemed to have also never been on a set of this size with so many extras. It's not every day an actor gets this chance, even an extremely successful actor. Extras numbering 245 is a ton of people for any shoot, let alone a full scale fair with working rides. I was impressed by how many massive trailers there were, how the ADs would keep on top of my every move and let someone know if I would even leave the trailer. I was impressed with working with multi-praised and award-winning director and actor Xavier Dolan, and also with the lead of the Netflix show *Animal Kingdom*, Jake Weary. I was impressed with them putting me inside a five-star hotel that was seen in both *It* films. And also impressed with working with the biggest horror director ever, Andy Muschietti. The whole experience was, to say the least, impressive and once in a lifetime.

What has been the reaction of friends and family who've seen the film?

The friends and the *It* fans that have reached out to me have been countless and it has been a bit overwhelming. It's amazing the responses I've been getting and I'm thankful to have them. It's great to have some sort of support network, or recognition for any work you do, especially on such touchy subjects, as it's tough sometimes to come to terms with playing roles like that. By the way, my favorite quote from the film is probably one of the most famous quotes: "Swear, swear, that if It comes back, we'll come back too" sends shivers down my spine every time. When I got to see *It: Chapter Two* the first time, which was a week before the release date, I was truly amazed by what Andy put together. In my eyes, it was a masterpiece. The balance of comedy and horror, in my opinion, was perfect. I was laughing, crying, and jumping throughout the film. Some of the monologues in the film really hit home and I think it struck a chord with a lot of the audience as well. Seeing people react to the scenes that I was in was shocking. Some people were covering their eyes, literally, and I don't blame them from how brutal it was, but that's how it was. My favorite part of the movie would be when the Losers were all at the dinner table and reminiscing, making fun of each other and lastly, coming to terms with their new current dilemma.

Do you see yourself as a horror actor now?

I don't see myself as a horror actor, no. I just see myself as a serious and motivated actor. I've acted in many horror and thriller movies in the past, so dramatic acting is kinda my thing. But, at the same time, I audition for every type of role under the sun. I'm lucky enough to have earned and worked myself into a position with casting directors that I'm called to audition for every type of character, boy-next-door, killer, lover, nerd, psycho, jock. I do love to act in horror though, playing the guy who's scared and confused about what's happening around him, not understanding one's situation; I find those types of scenes and stories really interesting and fun to be involved with and I would say are up my alley in terms of preference. As long as there's a challenge for me in playing a character and the character is complex, I'm in and I'm invested.

What research did you do for Scuzzah? How did you get ready for the role?

For research into Scuzzah and the scenes I was involved in, I dove into the history of it all. The scenes I was involved in are very sensitive and based on the real-life killing of Charlie Howard, a gay man, in 1984, in Bangor, Maine. The murder happened almost exactly how the assault happened in real life, a bunch of bullies following a gay couple out of a fair, to a bridge, beating them, and then throwing one over the bridge. Finding this out shocked me. I felt nervous to do the scenes and wanted to approach it with as much respect and professionalism and realism as I could, in hopes to shed light to more people that this still happens in real life. This is not an issue of the past, but an ongoing one that needs to be dealt with, and that people need to step in and stop if they see these types of horrible things happening in person.

About the Contributors

Ralph **Beliveau** teaches at the University of Oklahoma. He coauthored *Digital Literacy* (2016), and coedited *International Horror Film Directors* (2017). He has written about network society, documentary rhetoric, horror media, *The Wire*, African American noir, Alex Cox, *Supernatural*, Richard Matheson, Shirley Jackson, and Paolo Freire and media literacy. He previously taught broadcast journalism, popular culture, and rhetoric at the University of Iowa, taught high school in the Chicago area, and worked in film and television.

Laura **Bolf-Beliveau**, Ph.D., is a professor of English at the University of Central Oklahoma where she regularly teaches classes in secondary methods, young adult literature, multicultural women's writing, and first year composition. She is a former high school teacher with more than fifteen years of experience in urban, rural, and suburban districts. In addition to publications in the areas of social justice, identity, and feminism, she has given numerous national presentations about young adult literature and media integration.

Jason V. **Brock** is a writer, editor, filmmaker, composer, scholar, and artist. His fiction and nonfiction works have appeared in many venues, such as *Weird Fiction Review*, *Fangoria*, and others, and include a monograph about horror and science fiction in culture called *Disorders of Magnitude*. He has been nominated for several honors, including twice for the Bram Stoker Award. His documentary about Forrest J Ackerman, *The AckerMonster Chronicles!*, won the Rondo Hatton Classic Horror Award for Best Documentary in 2014.

Rebecca **Frost** works and teaches at Keweenaw Bay Ojibwa Community College in Baraga, Michigan. She received her Ph.D. in rhetoric, theory, and culture from Michigan Technological University in 2015. She studies representations of crime with a special focus on the rhetoric surrounding narratives of serial killers and victims. She is the author of *The Ripper's Victims in Print* (2018) and *Words of a Monster* (2019).

Cory R. **Goehring** is an assistant professor of English at Waynesburg University. He received his Ph.D. from the University of Pittsburgh in 2010. His literary interests include Romanticism and its various "hideous progeny," including Gothic literature, children's literature, the American Renaissance, and, of course, Frankenstein and other monsters of our own creation.

Michelle Leigh **Gompf** is a professor of English and chair of the Department of Humanities at Concord University in Athens, West Virginia. In addition to writing on and teaching British literature from the 17th through 20th centuries, her interests include the anti-hero, Sherlock Holmes, and the weird tale. Her book *Thomas Harris and William Blake* was published in 2013 and she is working on a book examining the aesthetics and philosophy of the TV show *Hannibal.*

Dominick **Grace** is a professor of English at Brescia University College in London, Ontario. He is the author of *The Science Fiction of Phyllis Gotlieb,* and of articles on subjects ranging from Chaucer to comic books. He is also the coeditor of several collections of interviews with cartoonists and of books on Canadian comics, Canadian literature of the fantastic, *Twin Peaks,* and *Supernatural.*

Hayley Mitchell **Haugen** holds a Ph.D. in American literature from Ohio University and an MFA in poetry from the University of Washington. She is an associate professor of English at Ohio University Southern, where she teaches composition, American literature, and creative writing. Her work on King appears in *Stephen King's Contemporary Classics* and *The Modern Stephen King Canon.*

Rebecca **Janicker** is a senior lecturer in film and media studies at the University of Portsmouth. She received her Ph.D. in American studies from the University of Nottingham in 2014. She is the author of *The Literary Haunted House* (2015) and the editor of *Reading American Horror Story* (2017). Other publications focus on the fiction of Robert Bloch, Stephen King, Richard Matheson, and H.P. Lovecraft, as well as on horror in film, TV, and comics.

Erik **Junnola** grew up in Mississauga, Ontario, where he played sports throughout his youth. In grade nine, he attended an arts school where he discovered his love for acting. He moved to Florida in grade ten and joined the International Thespian Society, placing among top competitors. Moving back to Toronto a year later, he pursued an acting career, later to be picked up by an agency, leading him to book a role in *It: Chapter Two.*

Conny **Lippert** is an independent scholar who received a doctorate from the University of Bristol in 2014. Her thesis focused on topographies in Stephen King's and H.P. Lovecraft's Gothic works. She earned a master's degree from the University of Nottingham and a bachelor's degree from the University of Bayreuth. Her research interests include Gothic and horror fiction, popular literature and culture, and American literature.

André **Loiselle**, Ph.D., is the dean of humanities and teaches film at St. Thomas University in Fredericton, New Brunswick. His main areas of research are the horror film, Canadian and Québécois cinema, and theatricality in film. He has published more than forty refereed articles and chapters in anthologies, as well as a dozen books, including *The Canadian Horror Film* (2015, with Gina Freitag), *Stages of Reality* (2012, with Jeremy Maron), and *Cinema as History* (2007).

About the Contributors

June **Pulliam** teaches courses in horror fiction and film at Louisiana State University. She is also the author of *Monstrous Bodies*, as well as many articles on fantastic young adult fiction, Roald Dahl, and zombie studies. She has coauthored *The Encyclopedia of the Zombie*, *Richard Matheson's Monsters*, and *Ghosts in Popular Culture and Legend*.

Ron **Riekki**, Ph.D., coedited *The Many Lives of The Evil Dead* (2019) and four other anthologies. His books include *U.P.*, *Posttraumatic*, and *My Ancestors Are Reindeer Herders and I Am Melting in Extinction*. He acted in the film *Short Straw* (directed by Steve Balderson, Dikenga Films) and played the title role in the horror film *Flesher* (directed by John Johnson, Eternal Ground Films).

Brian W. **Smith** is an award-winning horror scriptwriter. His scripts have placed at Shriekfest, Screamfest, and the GenreBlast Film Festival. He is a programming judge and head of the screenplay competition at the New York City Horror Film Festival. He has also screened festival films for Tribeca Film Festival, Big Apple Film Festival, and SXSW.

Gregory **Stevenson** is a professor of the New Testament at Rochester University in Rochester Hills, Michigan. He received his Ph.D. from Emory University in 1999. In addition to authoring two books on the book of Revelation, he is the author of *Televised Morality* and also the editor of *Theology and the Marvel Universe*.

Katherine A. **Troyer** is the assistant director of the Collaborative for Learning and Teaching at Trinity University, a position that allows her to teach and assist faculty with their teaching. She studies both horror and pedagogy, and her publications focus on the intersections between cultural studies, genre studies, and humanist geography. She received her Ph.D. in humanities from the University of Louisville.

Kevin J. **Wetmore**, Jr., is the author and/or editor of more than two dozen books including *Post-9/11 Horror in American Cinema*, *The Streaming of* Hill House, the Bram Stoker Award–nominated *Uncovering Stranger Things*, as well as more than four dozen book chapters on everything from Godzilla to Jesuit horror. He teaches at Loyola Marymount University and also works as an actor and director in Los Angeles.

Index

abandonment 11
Abbott, Stacey 151
ABC 84, 86–87, 90–92, 102, 104–106, 151, 153, 183
abuse 16, 21, 50, 59, 98, 138, 142, 145, 149–150, 154, 156, 162, 166
acid 27, 64–65, 141
actor 90–91, 93, 109, 112, 123, 181–184, 188–191, 195
adaptation 6, 42, 71, 75, 84, 86, 90, 101–103, 105, 147, 151–153, 155–156, 166, 178, 181–183
adult 9–10, 12–13, 15–16, 20–26, 28–30, 32, 36–42, 50–54, 58–59, 62–67, 72, 74–78, 82, 85–91, 94, 97–98, 100–101, 105–107, 120–121, 127–128, 130, 139, 142, 144–147, 150, 152–157, 159, 163–167, 174–175, 177–179, 193, 195
African American 46, 71–82, 86, 88, 157, 193
AIDS 160
alcoholism 98
Alegre, Sara Martín 16, 150
Anderson, Harry 90
Anderson, James Arthur 12
Anderson, Linda 6, 37, 51–52, 54, 145, 162
Annabelle 188
anxiety 11–12, 37–38, 44, 48, 98–99, 101, 106, 125, 127, 130–131, 136, 141, 155, 185
apocalypse 28, 57–58, 60, 66, 171, 173–174
arthritis 65
asexual 86
assault 76, 191
authoritarian 170–172

baby boomers 75, 160
Bakhtin, Mikhail 6, 33–39, 42, 126
Balderson, Steve 195
balloon 35, 110, 115–116, 153, 184
Bangor 46, 191
bathroom 47, 91–92, 137–141, 144, 151, 153, 156–157
Beliveau, Ralph 134–146, 193
Bellis, Richard 84
Ben Hanscom 5, 14, 18, 20, 23–25, 27, 30, 32, 38–40, 48, 54, 60–61, 64, 81–82, 88–91, 115–116, 134, 139, 144, 153, 156–157, 162, 165–166, 169–171, 173–179, 185
Beverly Marsh 5, 10, 18, 20, 23–25, 28, 30, 32, 38–40, 45, 48, 50–54, 59, 61, 88–92, 97, 115, 117, 123–124, 127, 130, 134–146, 150–151, 153, 156–157, 162–163, 174–179, 185–186
biblical 57–58, 61–62
Bill Denbrough 9–19, 22–28, 36–41, 51–53, 59–62, 65–66, 78, 84–85, 88–91, 93, 117, 125, 127, 134, 139–141, 143–144, 149–150, 152–153, 155–157, 162, 166, 169–179, 183, 185–186
Bissell, Tom 4
Black Panther 75
blade 48, 92
blind 59, 64–65, 77, 142
blood 23, 25, 41, 53, 58, 85–86, 92–93, 117, 128, 131, 134, 137–140, 144, 151–153, 156, 162, 170, 178, 184
boat 20, 59, 91, 114, 155, 160, 183–184
Bob Gray 24, 51, 145, 178
Bolf-Beliveau, Laura 134–146, 193
Bottin, Rob 181
Bow, Clara 44, 47
Bowers, Henry 11, 15, 23, 30, 38–39, 48, 50, 52, 59, 71, 73, 77–78, 80, 87, 91, 163, 170–174, 185
Bradbury, Ray 120, 123, 127, 130–131
Bradley, Laura 84
Bradley Gang 25, 46, 160
bridge 20, 30, 53, 129, 145–146, 189, 191
Brock, Jason V. 95–108, 193
Browning, Mark 154
Browning, Tod 123
bully 2, 11, 14, 46, 71, 76–78, 87, 97–98, 115, 142, 163, 170–172, 185
Bundy, Ted 161, 164, 166
Bunyan, Paul 25, 161–162
Burnett, Carol 181
Burnett, Charles 80
Burnett, Frances Hodgson 20
Bush, George H.W. 76

197

Index

carnival 32–42, 96, 120–128, 130–132
Carpenter, John 2, 102, 183
Carrie 19, 100–101, 151
Carroll, Lewis 4, 30
Carroll, Noël 121, 123, 131
Chayefsky, Paddy 104
Chicago 193
childhood 1–2, 9–10, 12–13, 15–19, 21–22, 24–25, 27–29, 33, 38, 40–41, 50–52, 59, 62, 64–67, 78, 85, 87–89, 94, 97–98, 101, 106, 111, 128, 130, 144–145, 147, 149–153, 156, 159–160, 162, 166–167, 174, 179
Christian 58, 128
Chung-hoon, Chung 4, 113, 154
Cinderella 21
cinematography 110, 113, 154, 189
Civil Rights 72–75
cloud 50, 138
Cloud Atlas 188
clown 13, 18, 22, 24, 26, 32, 34–35, 49, 51, 56, 58–59, 74, 84–85, 90, 98, 109–112, 115–117, 121, 122–124, 126–127, 130, 138–139, 152, 155–156, 160–163, 172, 174–175, 178, 181, 183–186, 188
Collings, Michael 21, 30, 46
comedy 78, 87–88, 103, 181, 184, 191
community 10, 12, 41, 62, 78, 193
Connecticut 146
conquer 12, 16, 61, 131, 171, 174
conservative 103
Corwin, Norman 104
cosmology 60, 63, 95, 97
costume 93, 109–112, 116–118, 162, 164, 184, 190
Craven, Wes 182
creature 23, 27, 51, 53, 62, 85–86, 88, 93–94, 98, 114, 120–121, 124, 126–128, 131, 138, 153, 156, 161, 163–165, 174, 178, 183
Creed, Barbara 36–37, 85, 140
cripple 65
critic 2–4, 21–22, 29–30, 38, 46, 51, 75, 82, 90, 98, 103, 121, 141, 145, 173
crypt 124
Curry, Tim 32, 78, 84, 91, 94, 115, 121, 162, 164, 181–184, 186
dance 24, 32, 47, 58, 90, 98, 121, 127, 162, 172, 178, 183, 185–186
danger 16, 23, 26–27, 30, 35, 38–39, 45, 50, 53, 59, 89–91, 98, 111–113, 126, 130–131, 136, 139, 141, 153, 162–163, 166–167, 185

Danse Macabre 42, 122–123, 130–131, 148
Dante 96, 129
Darabont, Frank 4
dark 10, 29, 35–36, 42, 57–58, 66, 96, 98, 105, 109–110, 114–117, 120–121, 124–125, 127–131, 150–151, 154–155, 176
The Dead Zone 100, 107
death 9–10, 12, 14, 20–21, 30, 33, 36–37, 39–40, 42, 47, 53, 61, 77, 81–82, 85–87, 89–90, 126–127, 136, 152, 157, 162, 164, 174, 183
deity 60, 97, 128
demon 16, 56, 58–60, 63, 124, 127, 182
De Palma, Brian 151
Derry 9, 12–13, 16, 18, 24–25, 30, 32–33, 35–36, 38, 40–42, 47–49, 58–62, 71–82, 84–85, 87–92, 96, 98–99, 107, 120, 122, 125, 127–131, 136–137, 140–142, 145–155, 159, 162–163, 165–166, 169–174, 178–179, 183, 185, 189
desire 15, 17–18, 25–29, 45, 48, 50, 52–53, 91, 100, 110–111, 113, 135–136, 142, 155, 176–177, 179
Desjardins, Mary 44
despair 20, 56, 175
devil 58–59
Disney 21
disturb 3, 32, 39, 42, 50, 52, 86, 90, 92, 109–110, 112, 117, 123, 143, 149, 155, 175
dog 10, 23, 56, 73
D'Onofrio, Vincent 184
Dostoevsky 33–34, 37
Dracula 1, 88, 121, 178
drain 24, 32, 53, 92–93, 125, 137–141, 145, 153, 156, 162, 183–184
drool 184–185
drug 15, 98
Duma Key 127

Eddie Kaspbrak 5, 10, 14–15, 23–28, 30, 38–40, 49–50, 53, 59, 61–65, 80, 85–88, 90, 92, 116–117, 130, 134, 139–141, 143–144, 149–150, 152–153, 155, 157, 162–163, 169, 171, 174, 177, 185
effeminate 47, 86
Egypt 57
Elm Street 21, 86, 182
empathy 24, 172–173, 176
enchant 6, 56, 63–66
Englund, Robert 182
Enlightenment 63–64, 148
erasure 75, 81–82, 88
ethnicity 5, 73, 75, 78
evil 1, 2, 6, 25, 46, 56–67, 75, 81, 85, 97–98, 102, 107, 120–121, 123–124, 162–163, 166, 182–184, 195
The Exorcist 188
The Eyes of the Dragon 19

Fade to Black 90
fair 140, 189–191
fairy 15
fairytale 19–23, 30, 66, 89, 129, 131
faith 6, 17, 22–23, 27, 30, 56
fantasy 20, 23, 66, 86, 89–90, 103, 135, 178
father 11, 15, 18–19, 21, 25, 28, 30, 35, 39, 42, 50–52, 54, 59, 61–62, 73–74, 77–79, 81, 89, 91–92, 97–101, 106, 117, 127, 130, 134–145, 150, 153, 156, 162, 172, 174, 178, 182, 185
Faulkner, William 97, 157

FCC 90
fear 2–3, 12–13, 15, 17, 22, 24, 26–27, 32–34, 36, 42, 46, 48, 52, 61–62, 67, 78, 87, 89, 97–98, 105, 110–111, 113–114, 120–121, 124–125, 127, 129–130, 139, 147–149, 155, 159–167, 174–175, 178, 183–184, 186
female 37, 45–46, 48–54, 85, 97, 123, 127–128, 137, 143, 145–146, 162–163, 176, 182
Fifty Shades of Grey 103
Firestarter 19
flashback 77–78, 87, 94, 150, 152–155, 157
The Fog 183
fool 35, 123–124, 130, 138
Foote, Horton 104
Fortunato 124
Frankenstein 1, 125, 176, 178, 194
freak 11, 131
Freaks 123
Fredericton 194
Freud, Sigmund 49, 111, 121, 125, 127, 130, 148
friendship 1–2, 29, 38, 41, 62, 66, 86–88, 97, 120, 169
fright 16, 21, 23, 36, 53, 67, 84–85, 87, 93–94, 98, 114, 116–117, 123, 129, 147, 159, 183
Frost, Rebecca 159–168, 193
Fudd, Elmer 14
funeral 152
Furter, Dr. Frank N. 181

Gacy, John Wayne 161, 183
gay 33, 47, 86–87, 160, 191
gender 46–47, 49–50, 82, 86, 88–89, 121, 128, 130, 137, 145, 162
genitals 53
genocide 64
George Denbrough 9–16, 20, 24, 26, 35, 47, 60–61, 85, 89–91, 114–116, 141, 150, 152–153, 155–156, 160, 162, 172, 175, 183–185
Geraldo 81
Gerald's Game 4, 101
ghost 14–16, 20, 22, 40, 124, 195
Gilmore, David 122–123
Gingerbread Man 20–21
God 5, 36, 57–58, 60–62, 66, 128, 150
Godzilla 195
Goehring, Cory R. 3, 18–31, 193
Gompf, Michelle Leigh 6, 109–119, 194
gospel 66, 79
Gothic 22, 97, 120, 122–128, 131, 147–155, 157, 164, 193–194
grace 181
Grace, Dominick 5–6, 44–55, 194
grave 20, 37
gray 112, 114
Greek 33, 126–127
The Green Mile 1, 75
grey 88, 117
grief 20, 128, 150
grotesque 32, 36–38, 47, 127, 178

guilt 44, 61, 72, 81, 98, 163
Gurdon, Meghan Cox 29

Hades 128
Halloween 98, 104
Halloween 86, 183
The Handmaid's Tale 110–111, 118
Hannibal 109–111, 118, 161, 194
Hansel and Gretel 20–21, 25
Hansen, Regina 22, 75
Harry Potter 20, 29
Hartman, Geoffrey 10
Haugen, Hayley Mitchell 9–17, 194
haunt 10, 13, 16, 36, 39, 56, 97, 107, 112, 124–125, 128, 147–155, 182, 194
headless 115, 162, 166, 185
heart 12, 17, 22, 28, 33, 57, 59, 73, 85, 89, 93, 104, 138–139, 149, 166, 175, 190
Hercules 129
hetero 46–47, 86, 88–89, 176
hill 89, 91, 138, 195
Hill, Joe 19, 100
homoerotic 86–87
homophobia 33, 48, 87, 149
homosexual 46–49, 53, 86–87, 160, 176
hope 3, 5, 56, 62, 67, 84, 99, 102, 106–107, 145, 156, 191
Hopkins, Anthony 167
Howard, Charlie 191
hubris 130
Humphrey, Chris 121
Huston, John 181
Hutcheon, Linda 34

illusion 22–23, 76
imagination 2, 4, 9, 15–16, 21–27, 30, 38, 62–67, 99, 142–143, 149, 159, 163, 171, 178–179
indigenous 5, 72
Insidious 188
intertextuality 73, 125
Iowa 193
It Came from Beneath the Sea 45
It Came from Outer Space 45
It Conquered the World 45

Janicker, Rebecca 147–158, 194
Jewish 97, 177
Johnson, John 195
journey 2, 120–121, 128–130, 173
Jowett, Lorna 151
judge 4, 21, 56, 90, 195
Junnola, Erik 5, 188–191-194

katabasis 128–129
Keesey, Douglas 46
Killer of Sheep 80
King, Donald 100
King, Dr. Martin Luther 75
King, Ruth 100
King, Tabitha 100

kiss 47–48, 87, 89, 140, 176–177
KKK 74
Kristeva, Julia 85, 136–138
Krueger, Freddy 182
Kubrick, Stanley 4, 151

lair 17, 30, 40, 45, 126, 141, 143, 186
Largo 188
laugh 26, 30, 32–33, 35, 39, 93, 109, 123–124, 127, 130–131, 150, 167, 174, 182, 191
The Lawnmower Man 4
leader 14–15, 39, 143, 169–173, 175–180
Leonetti, John 189
leper 49, 116, 162, 165–166, 178
Lewis, C.S. 20, 45, 66
library 20, 32, 81, 144–146, 165, 178, 185
liminal 32, 40, 124–129
The Lion, the Witch, and the Wardrobe 20
Lippert, Conny 120–133, 194
Loewen, James 72, 74
Loiselle, André 169–180, 194
London 194
The Lord of the Rings 29, 54, 103
Los Angeles 80, 104, 195
Losers 2, 6, 10–12, 14–16, 18, 20–28, 33, 35–42, 45–46, 48, 50, 52, 54, 60–62, 64–66, 71–74, 77–78, 80–82, 87, 90, 92–93, 97–98, 106, 110, 118, 120, 124, 126–127, 129–130, 134, 136, 139–145, 147–150, 152, 154–157, 159–167, 169–180, 183, 186, 191
Louisiana 195
Louisville 195
Lovecraft, H.P. 98–100, 121, 155, 194
Lumet, Sidney 104
lynching 72

macroverse 5, 178–179
mad 15, 30, 37, 40, 42, 177
maggots 47
magic 6, 19–20, 22, 27, 33, 38–39, 41–42, 56–57, 61–67, 75, 88, 131, 141, 177
Magistrale, Tony 5–6, 11–12, 16–17, 45–46, 48, 50, 52, 54, 93, 129, 147, 150–151, 162
Maine 32, 58, 73–75, 96, 98, 100, 107, 129, 191
Malcolm X 75
male 45, 47–53, 74–75, 85, 91, 137, 139
Maseur, Richard 90
McDonald, Ronald 164
media 92, 96, 101–104, 121–123, 137, 147, 157, 165, 167, 181, 193–194
menstrual 92, 128, 134, 140
mercy 26
Michigan 193, 195
Mike Hanlon 5, 13–14, 20, 22–23, 27–28, 30, 35–36, 38–42, 53, 59–62, 64–65, 71–82, 86, 88, 90, 117, 125, 130, 149–150, 152, 154, 156–157, 160, 162, 171–172, 174–175, 177–178, 85
Miller, Arthur 4

Miller, Chuck 3, 5
miniseries 4, 71–73, 75–78, 80–82, 84, 86, 89–90, 94, 102, 105–106, 114–115, 147, 151–157, 159–163, 165–166, 177, 181, 183
minorities 71–74, 79, 88
Misery 4, 101
Mississauga 194
monster 5, 12, 16, 20, 25, 32–35, 37, 39–40, 44–46, 50, 52–54, 59, 65–66, 84–90, 92–94, 97–98, 106, 120–125, 127–132, 143, 145, 147, 154, 156, 159, 162–167, 169–170, 173–174, 177–179, 183–184, 193–195
Montresor 124
mother 10–11, 14–15, 19, 25, 30, 37, 49–52, 54, 57, 62, 87, 90, 98, 100–101, 106, 127–128, 130, 135, 138, 140, 142, 145, 150, 152, 157, 162, 183, 185
mummy 98, 121, 138, 153, 161–162, 165, 178
murder 11, 22–23, 33, 35, 46–48, 59, 87, 90, 110, 129, 136, 141, 143, 145, 160, 164, 172, 182, 184–185, 191
Muschietti, Andrés 84, 91, 111, 113, 154, 169, 176, 181
muscles 65
Mynhardt, Joe 1–3
mystery 17, 41, 63–66, 77, 181
myth 58–59, 75, 99, 106, 121, 123–124, 126–127, 129–131, 135, 145, 159, 161, 166, 176, 178

The Napkins 19
narrator 12, 20, 22, 84, 88
Nazi 47, 74
Neibolt 23, 26, 30, 49, 64, 141, 149, 153, 155, 185
The Neverending Story 24
New Brunswick 194
New York 56, 195
The New Yorker 111
nightmare 16, 32, 98, 111, 149, 151, 153, 184
A Nightmare on Elm Street 86, 182
1958 14, 35, 37–38, 40–41, 85, 88, 98, 144, 146, 149, 153, 157, 173, 177, 179
1985 40–41, 85, 98, 157, 179, 181
1986 32, 84–90, 92–93, 96, 101, 103, 120, 134, 147, 166
1987 21, 44, 101, 182
1990 71, 73, 75–76, 84–94, 102–103, 105, 112, 114, 121, 129, 147, 151, 161, 167, 169, 177, 181, 183, 185
Nixon, Richard 73

Obama, Barack 79, 82
Oboler, Arch 104
Ohio 194
Oklahoma 193
Ontario 194
ontology 57
oppression 25, 72, 74, 78–79, 172
Orpheus 129
O'Toole, Annette 90

Pan, Peter 20–21, 29
Parks, Rosa 75
patriarchy 86, 89, 134–135, 138, 142, 145–146
penis 5, 47, 51–52, 144
Pennywise 1, 5, 10, 13, 16, 22, 24, 30, 32–33, 35, 39–41, 49, 58–62, 64–65, 72, 78, 80, 84, 87, 90–91, 93–94, 96–99, 107, 109–118, 121, 124–125, 127–129, 131, 134–135, 137–142, 145, 149, 151–154, 156, 160, 162–164, 172–176, 178, 181–186, 188
Perrault, Charles 21
Persephone 127–129
Pet Sematary 4, 22, 107, 124
Peter Gordon 48
The Phantom of the Big Tent 92
pharmacist 25, 134, 185
Pittsburgh 193
Poe, Edgar Allan 4, 123–124
Poetics 33–34, 37
poetry 20, 89, 91, 139–140, 194
poison 27, 37, 73, 149
Port Hope 190
Portland 13, 100
Portsmouth 194
postmodern 22, 64
prayer 61
predator 25, 49–50, 91, 143, 183–185
psychoanalysis 125, 137
psychology 9–10, 16, 37, 49, 59, 61, 99, 121, 136, 138, 142, 179
Pulliam, June 84–94, 195

quest 20, 128, 142, 154

Rabelais 34–36, 126
race 2, 72–73, 75–76
racism 59, 64, 73, 75, 160
rationalism 22, 63–65
Reagan, Ronald 73, 76
redemption 56, 180
re-enchantment 63–66
Reid, Tim 76, 90
Reiner, Rob 4
repression 88, 97, 111, 122, 148, 150, 152–153, 155, 176–177
revelation 5–6, 25, 37, 45, 49, 51, 57, 59, 62–64, 127, 145, 154, 195
Richie Tozier 10, 26–27, 38, 90
ridicule 35
Riekki, Ron 3–6, 188–191, 195
riot 80
Ritter, John 90
Rochester Hills 195
The Rocky Horror Picture Show 181, 183
Romantic era 19, 21–22, 193
Rome 57
Rose, Jacqueline 29
Rose, Reginald 104

sacred 34, 42, 136
sacrifice 25, 36, 88, 120, 128, 143, 160
Satan 58
scare 23, 26, 30, 32, 36, 39, 41, 84, 87, 91, 109–110, 138, 153–154, 161–162, 171, 183–186, 188–189, 191
scars 22, 97
Scott, Ridley 181
scream 10, 15, 26, 39, 90–92, 124, 139, 152, 171, 183
Scuzzah 5, 191
secret 26, 50, 71–72, 76, 78–81, 87, 89, 142, 145, 151, 179
The Secret Garden 20
Secret Window 4
serial killer 57, 159–167, 183, 193
Serling, Rod 104
seven 11, 18–19, 24, 29, 38, 57, 60, 62
sewer 1, 10, 15–16, 24, 28, 48, 53–54, 76, 87, 91–92, 96, 114–115, 120, 124, 127, 129–130, 137, 140–143, 145, 155, 162–163, 175–177, 179, 183–184, 186
sex 3, 5, 10, 18, 25, 28–29, 39, 44–54, 56, 87, 90–91, 97, 110, 121, 123–124, 127, 135, 142–145, 160, 176–177, 181
sexism 2
Shakespeare, William 4, 34
The Shawshank Redemption 1, 4
The Shining 4, 19, 35, 73, 151, 157
sink 92, 138, 141, 153, 156
Skarsgård, Bill 4, 32, 121, 164, 173, 181–182, 184–186
slasher 182
Smith, Anna Deavere 4
Smith, Brian W. 181–187, 195
Smith, Johnny 100
Smith, Peter K. 11
Something Wicked This Way Comes 106, 120, 130
soul 58, 80, 136, 182
spell 61, 176
spider 15, 37, 42, 54, 84–85, 92–93, 126–127, 138, 145, 162, 178–179
spooky 149, 153
The Stand 56, 104, 129
Stand By Me 4
standards-and-practices 87, 90–92, 152
Stanley Uris 5, 10, 24, 36, 38, 90, 92, 150, 175, 177
Stevenson, Gregory 6, 56–68, 195
Stevenson, Robert Louis 20
stomach 48, 91, 123, 138
Stranger Things 102
strangers 35, 91, 115, 167, 183–184
strength 11–12, 16, 38, 40, 61, 124, 128, 141, 170, 175, 177, 186
stutter 9–17, 25, 39, 61, 170, 172–175
sublime 26
subterranean 92, 96, 120, 122, 124–128
suicide 9, 36, 92, 98, 154, 177

superstitious 81, 148
surviving 85

taboo 50, 123, 152
The Talisman 14, 16, 19, 62, 129, 177
teenager 29, 57, 81, 87, 120, 154, 161, 166, 182
television 14, 75, 81, 86–87, 90, 92–93, 103–105, 147, 151–152, 169, 172, 182, 193
terror 3, 10, 14, 22, 26, 30, 36, 42, 45, 49, 90, 93, 124, 145, 153, 155–156, 170, 183
terrorism 64
theology 6, 57–58, 60–64, 66, 195
Thomas, Richard 78, 90, 194
Thompson, Hunter S. 4
"The Three Billy Goats Gruff" 20–21, 30, 125, 129, 146
thriller 191
The Time Machine 125
Tolkien, J.R.R. 54, 66
The Tommyknockers 124, 129
torment 11, 182, 185
transvestite 181
Transylvania 181
trauma 9–12, 14, 16–17, 52, 88, 92, 97, 148–149, 151, 153, 195
trick 13–14, 41, 54, 59, 109, 117, 122–123, 126–128, 131, 164, 178, 186
troll 20, 30, 129, 146
Troyer, Katherine A. 6, 32–43, 83, 195
turtle 6, 24, 39, 42, 56, 58, 60–62, 65, 96, 179
2017 4, 22, 71, 75, 79–82, 84, 91–92, 102–103, 105, 109–110, 114–115, 121, 134–135, 138–139, 141, 144, 147, 154–155, 159, 161–162, 167, 169, 172–173, 175, 177, 181–183, 185, 193–194
2019 22, 83, 87–88, 102, 154, 165–166, 193, 195

uncanny 100, 109–111, 113–117, 123, 125, 148, 150–151, 153, 178
underground 30, 53, 74, 92, 120, 125–129, 141, 143–145, 186

Underwood, Larry 129
Underwood, Tim 5
underworld 54, 126–129

vagina 47, 49, 140
vampire 26, 56, 85, 142
venereal disease 44
victim 16, 22, 25, 38, 46, 48–49, 53–54, 59, 75, 79–80, 85, 92, 98, 110, 118, 121–122, 131, 160, 163–164, 171, 178, 182, 184, 193
Vietnam 5, 75
villain 14, 87, 109–110, 148, 182, 184–185
violent 9, 21, 48–49, 51, 71, 75, 80, 110, 127, 149, 153, 166, 170

Wallace, Tommy Lee 84, 86–87, 90, 183
war 58, 73–75, 77, 105, 160
Washington 194
Watts 80
Welles, Orson 104
Wells, H.G. 125
Werewolf 26, 53, 64, 121, 138, 141, 161, 164–166, 178
West Virginia 194
Wetmore, Kevin J. 6, 71–83, 195
Wolfe, Thomas 4
Wonderland 20–21
writing 1, 3, 5, 9, 11–14, 19, 21, 29, 37, 56, 60, 74, 81, 89, 96, 100–101, 103, 105, 122, 144, 151, 163, 193–194

yellow 53, 112, 117, 140, 184
Yellow Submarine 181
youth 3, 11, 22, 39–40, 97–98, 106, 112–113, 182, 194

Zinn, Howard 74
zombies 85, 165, 195

www.ingramcontent.com/pod-product-compliance
Ingram Content Group UK Ltd.
Pitfield, Milton Keynes, MK11 3LW, UK
UKHW042006140426
5217IPUK00015B/1013